THE
GERMAN SETTLEMENT
OF THE
TEXAS HILL COUNTRY

Mockingbird Books
18 Toepperwein Road
Boerne, Texas 78006
www.mockingbirdbooks.com

© 2007 by Mockingbird Books.
All rights reserved. First edition 2007.
15 14 13 12 11 10 09 08   2 3 4 5 6 7 8

ISBN 978-1-932801-09-5

Cover image copyright © 2007 by Hill Country Images and Kathy Weigand Photography

The German Settlement of the Texas Hill Country

Jefferson Morgenthaler

Mockingbird Books
Boerne, Texas

For Sweet Ann

Table of Contents

1: Germans 1

2: Adelsverein 7

3: Solms Departs 35

4: Fredericksburg 53

5: Darmstadters 73

6: Beyond Colonization 87

7: Boerne, Comfort and Comanches 107

8: Conflict 127

9: Violence 145

10: Illusions 163

Thoughts and Thanks 169

Bibliography 171

Index 179

Introduction

The Texas Hill Country is the sweet spot of Texas. Rolling hills covered with oak and cedar enclose flat, green bottoms coursed by prolific spring-fed creeks and rivers. Deer, wild turkey and fox inhabit the forests and venture into the fields at dusk. Four distinct but moderate seasons reinforce the cycles of life.

Geographically, the Hill Country is the rippling eastern portion of the Edwards Plateau. It is bordered to the west by less convoluted stretches of the plateau, to the south by the Balcones Escarpment, and to the north by rolling plains and prairies that extend to the base of the Llano Estacado. The Colorado River, curving from the west to the south and draining to the Gulf, is a reasonable but inexact definition of the eastern boundary. The Hill Country is not especially high: its maximum elevation is around fifteen hundred feet above the sea and much of it lies below one thousand feet.

Like the remainder of the Edwards Plateau, the Hill Country has a thin layer of soil over Comanchean limestone. This same limestone underpins the High Plains of Texas; despite the ripples in the Hill Country, the plateau is considered the southernmost unit of the Great Plains. Cotton and other crops have been raised in the Hill Country, but the scant local soil lends itself more to grazing. Cattle do well where soils are deepest and forage is greatest. Sheep are the livestock of choice as soils and flora thin; goats are the best alternative as hillsides become rockier and grasses turn into browse.

It may be limestone that most characterizes the Hill Country. Subsurface aquifers flow through limestone, making the waters exceptionally hard. Houses are built of limestone blocks. Long limestone fences divide fields. They've been quarrying limestone out of the face of the Balcones Escarpment for more than a century and, while the resulting scars are far from attractive, they've barely made a dent in the supply of stone.

Limestone makes the spring-fed creeks and rivers of the Hill Country run clear and cool. The most beautiful streams—the Guadalupe River and Cibolo Creek, for example—are lined with towering cypress trees that thrust immense roots into the cool current.

During the decades of Spanish Texas, Mexican Texas and the Republic of Texas, the Hill Country was unsettled; it was too remote, and too thoroughly in control of Lipan Apaches, and later Peneteka Comanches. The Spanish attempted to establish the Presidio de San Luis de las Amarillas and the Mission Santa Cruz de San Saba (near today's Menard) in 1757, but the mission was abandoned within two years and the presidio within fifteen. Between that time and the mid-nineteenth century, only bold explorers and military expeditions penetrated north of the Balcones Escarpment.

The first significant influx of settlers into the Hill Country began in 1845, when German immigrants founded the town of New Braunfels, then moved north to establish Fredericksburg. These immigrants arrived under the auspices of a quasi-charitable organization known as the *Adelsverein*.

Even today it is not uncommon to come across someone in the Hill Country whose ancestors arrived in Texas aboard ships chartered in Germany by the Adelsverein. The impact of organized German colonization has lingered in the Hill Country for more than 150 years.

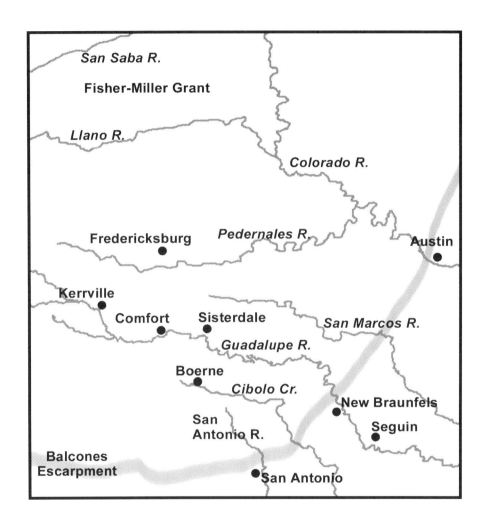

The Texas Hill Country

Chapter One
Germans

The German power structure reacted badly to the French Revolution of 1789, which took place in the midst of a war between France and the German states. The reaction was in part a rejection of natural law and the social contract as advocated by Locke and Rousseau, but it was even more a rejection of Napoleon I and his expansionist ambitions.

Napoleon battled and insinuated himself into a disintegrating Holy Roman Empire, bringing with him an end to feudalism, greater freedom of worship and a less absolute approach to government. Confronted by the common French enemy, Austria, Prussia and some smaller German states experienced resurgent nationalism and embraced enlightened despotism.

The architect and figurehead for German resistance to change was Klemens von Metternich, a nobleman who would become a prince. Metternich served as foreign minister for Holy Roman Emperor Francis beginning in 1809 and gained recognition for delicate maneuvering between the twin threats of France and Russia during the reign of Napoleon I. At first, Metternich sought to avoid direct conflict with France. Over time, that policy changed. His successful negotiation of a Quadruple Alliance between Prussia, Austria, Russia and England led to the downfall of France.

After the defeat of Napoleon I, the major European powers held the Congress of Vienna in 1814 and 1815 to redraw the political map of Europe. One consequence of the Congress was that nearly three hundred states of the former Holy Roman Empire were consolidated into thirty-nine new states under a loose confederation dominated by Prussia and Austria. Most of the states of the German Confederation were kingdoms, principalities or grand duchies, governed by royalty with or without a people's assembly.

Metternich emerged from the Congress of Vienna as Europe's most influential statesman. As concerned as he was about the balance of power among European states, he also kept a wary eye on the changing demographics of Europe.

Demographic change in Europe was no small matter. As the Industrial Revolution progressed, the old order of craftsmen's guilds disintegrated before the efficiency of mechanized factories. Fewer workers could produce more goods. Craftsmen in the protectionist guilds became unemployed.

Abolition of the feudal agricultural order had an equally dire impact. Farming tiny tracts, serfs and their descendants came under pressure from early agribusiness. As their population grew—and it grew more quickly as industry, agriculture and society evolved—the former feudal underclasses found that their lands would no longer support their families. German laws of primogeniture left all but the eldest sons landless, without means of support.

Metternich knew that the first revolution in France had been led by the bourgeois middle class, who wanted the right to own their own land and to compete in business without feudal restrictions. It was a revolution for liberty. The second phase, beginning in 1792, was an uprising of the working proletariat. It sought equality in a classless society. As he surveyed the political landscape in the 1820s and 1830s, Metternich saw that the German Confederation was experiencing a rise in the bourgeoisie and a frustration of the proletariat and peasantry. He sensed what was to come.

The 1830s marked the beginning of a period of great intellectual curiosity in Germany. The French Revolution stirred up ideas about democratic government, social equality and economic justice, but there was an impetus to go further yet; within the universities thinkers began to explore even more radical social and political theories put forth by Frenchmen who had witnessed the revolution and found it flawed.

Metternich was a dedicated reactionary. He saw royalty as the ultimate expression of the state—the people embodied. Sovereignty did not come from the people; the people were an element of the sovereign. Left to its own devices, society would vacillate between chaos and stagnation; it was the responsibility of the sovereign to achieve an ongoing and productive balance. Revolution was unavoidable; continuing counter-revolution was essential.

Not only was Metternich the ultimate royalist conservative, he was opposed to the unification of the German states. Metternich was for Austria; Prussia was his dearest enemy. The dozens of smaller German principalities and cities were, if consolidated, a threat to Austria's eminence. His views were echoed in the palaces of many other principalities, where unification meant demotion.

Nonetheless, German nationalism grew in popularity in the universities. After the conclusion of the Congress of Vienna, students organized themselves into associations called *Burschenschaften* that were meant to be a model for a united German fatherland under constitutional principles. The student associations were generally liberal and freethinking, and fell at odds with the conservative diet (assembly) of the German Confederation. In 1819 the diet, prodded by Metternich, passed a series of repressive measures, including supervision of universities by government agents, dismissal of professors with dangerous opinions and a ban on all secret organizations—most especially the Burschenschaften.

The reactionary power structure led by Metternich took some comfort from events in France, where since 1824 Charles X had relentlessly pushed the nation toward a more conservative stance. But when the French monarch imposed four repressive ordinances in the summer of 1830—dissolving the Chamber of Deputies, censoring the press, disenfranchising the bourgeoisie and calling for new elections without bourgeois participation—revolution broke out again and Charles X was forced to abdicate.

In 1832, partly in reaction to the events in France and a liberal rally at Hambach Castle in Bavaria, and viewing a united German fatherland as a threat to their individual power bases, the states of the German Confederation imposed even more intellectually repressive measures. Freedom of the press and freedom of debate were reined in. Political associations and meetings were banned.

An abortive Frankfurt putsch in 1833 prompted more repression. One observer said, "When the storm had subsided and quiet again restored by the liberal use of bayonets and police, a detestable system of espionage became rampant in many of the German states and principalities. Hundreds of men in all walks of life were put under rigid police surveillance, while many were even imprisoned for expressing or merely holding different political views from those of their governments. The reactionary element was triumphant, while progressive, liberal-minded men were harassed everywhere."

As the 1830s turned to the 1840s, German political ferment intensified. The bourgeoisie and the proletariat grew more antagonistic. The nobles of the old order found themselves at odds with an increasingly ambitious middle class. The radical social ideas that had been swirling for thirty years grew more powerful. The question of German unification became more pressing. An exploited urban proletariat, a displaced rural peasantry and a rising middle class all challenged the long-established order of the nobles.

The dislocation, dissent and repression of the Metternich years prompted an exodus of Germans to the United States, where freedom, equality and opportunity beckoned. Some of those who fled Germany were proletarians, peasants or bourgeoisie seeking a new life. Some were nobles who found themselves on the wrong side of a political confrontation. Some were utopians who sought to implement their social blueprints in a new land. In many cases, Germans came to the United States under the auspices of "immigration societies" that were formed for idealistic or commercial motives.

Some German states imposed harsh strictures intended to stem the outflow of capital, skills and intellect. Others permitted their citizens to flee across the Atlantic, seeing emigration as a way to reduce population pressure, distribute economic opportunity among a smaller citizenry and open new markets abroad. In general, the German business community supported emigration, envisioning a flow of goods back and forth between the fatherland and its new communities in distant lands.

Texas, which was not yet part of the United States, had long loomed large in the imaginations of some Germans, and the interest was not unreciprocated. As early as 1812 Spain considered establishing German colonies in Texas to fend off any ambitions of Napoleonic France. The idea surfaced again in 1814, and by 1819 a trio of Swiss businessmen proposed establishment of a Swiss-German colony on the Trinity River.

In 1821, J. V. Hecke, a retired Prussian military officer, reported on his trip to Texas two years earlier. He had found the climate temperate and the soil fertile. According to Hecke, the cotton yield was eight hundred pounds per acre and all manner of tropical and European vegetables could be grown. To his mind, the logical next step was to simply acquire Texas for Prussia: "if there is a piece of land on the transatlantic continent favorable to a colonial possession for Prussia, it is the province of Texas, whose acquisition by purchase from Spain, to whom it has neither use or political advantage, might be very easily made.... In a short time it would become a flourishing colony, if Prussia would make use of the emigrants from Germany, who, having become beggars through the voyage, suffered wretchedly in the United States. Furnish them free transportation on Prussian ships; give them the land gratuitously or grant them support, if only by advanced payments; then they would have cultivated after five years, or at the most ten, fifty acres of fertile land."

In 1826 Mexico granted a colonization contract to Joseph Vehlein, who was to settle three hundred German Catholic families in Texas. That contract was never fulfilled. Vehlein obtained a second contract for settlement of one hundred families in Texas, and—along with Texas notables David Burnet and Lorenzo de Zavala—organized the Galveston Bay and Texas Land Company, but again the project failed to flourish. Baron Johann von Racknitz created a flurry of activity about German colonization on the Brazos and Colorado Rivers in the early 1830s, without result.

German interest in Texas surged again after its 1836 declaration of independence from Mexico. Here was an independent republic with a vast expanse of land and a need for settlers. Proposals for German colonies were made to Texas presidents Houston and Lamar in 1838 and 1839, but no agreements resulted. A more informal approach by the Germania Society of New York resulted in 130 settlers landing in Galveston. Some went to Houston; others, learning of a recent yellow fever outbreak, returned to New York. The Germania Society entirely failed to support its Texas settlers, who floundered and dispersed.

Germans came to Texas individually and in small groups on their own initiative, as they did elsewhere in North America. Most of these immigrants settled in the lower stretches of the Brazos, Colorado and Guadalupe Rivers.

When Sam Houston began his second presidency of the Republic of Texas in 1842, he sought to attract settlers by issuing colonization contracts to empresarios with European connections. He signed eleven colonization contracts in total, of which only two succeeded in bringing immigrants to Texas. One of those, the Fisher-Miller Grant, became the foundation of the largest organized immigration into Texas, drawing more than five thousand Germans under the auspices of a society of nobles known as the *Adelsverein*.

German settlement of the Hill Country didn't begin until 1845, and it peaked before 1850. Individual German settlers came to the Hill Country during and after those years, but the most notable elements of German emigrants in the Hill Country fall into one of three categories: colonists of the Adelsverein; utopian socialists of the Forty; and idealistic refugee Forty-Eighters. We will meet each in turn.

Chapter Two
Adelsverein

The Society for Preservation of German Immigrants in Texas (*Gesellschaft zum Schutz deutscher Einwanderer in Texas*) promoted German settlement in the Texas Hill Country. Based in the ancient walled city of Mainz, on the River Rhine, it gained legal existence from its protector, the Duke of Nassau. More than twenty other nobles comprised its membership. Not founded until 1844, this relative latecomer came to be known as the *Mainzer Adelsverein* or just the *Adelsverein*. A "verein" is an association or society. An "adelsverein" is an association of aristocrats, which perfectly described this organization of princes, dukes and counts.

The Adelsverein was in significant part an effort by German nobles to relieve growing economic and social pressure on the proletariat and peasantry. In this sense, it was charitable and idealistic, but its members also saw potential commercial benefit in the enterprise. Trade might flourish between Texas and Germany. Land in Texas might prove valuable. Since Texas was not yet one of the United States, there were opportunities for all sorts of political developments—perhaps even the formation of a German state in North America.

The Adelsverein announced that its purpose was "as much as possible to guide German emigration into one favorable channel, to support the emigrant on his long journey, and in his first struggles to assist him in getting a home." The verein claimed that "it wishes to regulate and guide emigration so that a chance may be afforded the Germans of finding a German home in America, and that by maintaining an unbroken connection between themselves and the old country, an industrial and commercial intercourse may arise, morally and materially beneficial to both."

Baron Ottomar von Behr, who was an early settler at the Hill Country village of Sisterdale, had a more cynical view of the verein's purpose. He said that it wished to form a quasi-feudal state that would encumber the settlers with debt, with the result that they would be treated as chattels, as in the old country. Louise Weber Ernst, credited as the first woman to head a German family in Texas, hosted the verein's advance team at her home in Industry and concluded that they meant to form Texas into a German colony and organize a monarchy there. Her husband, Johann Friedrich Ernst, chastised that the proximity of Texas to the United States made that unlikely.

The notion that the Adelsverein plotted to carve an independent German colony out of West Texas has proven persistent. It is unquestionable that the Adelsverein's first commissioner general, Prince Carl of Solms-Braunfels, had a vision of that sort. He wrote a letter to William Kennedy, the British consul at Galveston, proposing a joint German-English enterprise that would form a large, militarized colony, obviously meant to be an independent blocking force between the United States and Mexican California. He wrote a long letter to his cousin, Great Britain's Queen Victoria, recommending that the British and Germans seize territory west of the Guadalupe River and convert it into a new nation. There are other clues in Solms's writings that he was thinking along those lines, and that he was urging the British to participate. But there is no evidence that the British ever took him seriously, nor any evidence that his Adelsverein associates were involved in his schemes. Perhaps the Adelsverein had a secret agenda of that sort. Perhaps the British entertained his ideas for a while. Perhaps it was Texas statehood that blocked their plans. But there is no proof.

The Adelsverein was a reorganization of another immigration society formed two years earlier. That society had acquired a league of land on Cummins Creek, not far from Round Top. Count Joseph of Boos-Waldeck traveled from Germany and purchased the land on behalf of the society, naming it Nassau Farm to honor Duke Adolph of Nassau. Accompanying Boos-Waldeck was Prince Victor of Leiningen. Boos-Waldeck and Leiningen both concluded that large-scale colonization was impractical, but Leiningen, who returned to Germany before Boos-Waldeck, changed his views. Leiningen became convinced that large-scale colonization was the best approach. Boos-Waldeck, becoming more and more familiar with the realities of life in Texas, had serious doubts.

The society's business manager, Count Carl of Castell, wrote to Boos-Waldeck after hearing from Leiningen: "Germany should not allow its emigrants to disperse so widely, but instead should make a large acquisition of land in once place in America and colonize it." Henry Fisher, of whom we will hear much more, had obtained one of Sam Houston's land colonization contracts. In Castell's view, "Most advantageous would be to enter into contact with Henry Fisher, who, as Leiningen says, has declared he would gladly turn his land over to colonization for certain compensations."

Castell moved forward on a plan to obtain a sizeable subsidy for the colony from the German government. Boos-Waldeck had been emphasizing the importance of getting the plantation up and running before tackling a large colonization project, and at times Castell professed to agree, but he informed Boos-Waldeck in September 1843 that the society had purchased an interest in a colonization contract—not Henry Fisher's, but one owned by Alexander Bourgeois d'Orvanne. The verein's investment was conditioned on Bourgeois's obtaining an extension of his contract, for it was about to expire.

Sam Houston had issued the contract to Bourgeois and his partner Armand Ducos on June 3, 1842, giving them the rights to a large tract of land west of San Antonio on the Uvalde, Frio and Medina Rivers. French-born Bourgeois was a wealthy pretender and speculator who had lived for a time in New Orleans. He had awarded himself the aristocratic "d'Orvanne" and sometimes added the title "Chevalier." In the same month that his colonization contract issued, he had agreed to use his French contacts to arrange a one-million-dollar loan to the Republic of Texas. There may have been a connection between the two transactions.

To earn a land grant[1] under their contract with Texas, Bourgeois and Ducos had to settle twelve hundred families or single men on their tract within eighteen months. Searching for a way to accomplish that feat, and for the million dollar loan, Bourgeois sailed for Germany, where he soon learned of the Adelsverein and its aspirations. It was September 1843—less than three months before Bourgeois's contract was due to ex-

---

[1] The term "colonization contract" refers to the document and the legal relationship that the document creates. The term "land grant" is an accepted, if inaccurate, term for the land itself, or for the ultimate transfer of the land from Texas to a person. When the names of the empresarios are attached to the land or the contract, the customary result is a proper noun using the term "grant." Bourgeois signed a colonization contract in order to obtain land grants for himself and colonists within the Bourgeois-Ducos Grant.

pire—when the Adelsverein inked a preliminary arrangement with him. On October 1 he wrote Texas Secretary of State Anson Jones to let him know that he was associated with a society that planned to settle ten thousand families in Texas, and to ask for an extension of the contract. Two weeks later he wrote again with a similar message.

When Castell told Boos-Waldeck of the decision to colonize on a large scale, he tried to explain how the nobles meant to mitigate the financial risk: "Our intention, then, is to colonize a grant, but only with money from the governments, so that the profit will belong to *us*; if they do not contribute anything, then we will not colonize." He let Boos-Waldeck know that Leiningen was more aggressive; he was "not satisfied with the course of the business; he wants us to begin a small colony at our own expense in spite of your objections, only he is finding no support."

Castell continued, "if the colonization comes to pass, then some families will immediately depart yet this winter for preparation under the direction of Mr. Orvanne, whom we have engaged for this." In fact, Castell advised, the society had already taken six to eight impoverished families under its wing, and would be sending them to Nassau Farm even though Boos-Waldeck had made it clear that he was not yet ready for colonists.

Boos-Waldeck sent an exceedingly strong reply to Castell's September letter: "after the bitter experiences that so many people have had in London and New York, no one else need be drawn into the web of land speculators. You, my friend—I must express this to you plainly because your fervor and haste cause me dread and anxiety—are on the direct path to becoming the dupe of such people."

"Believe me," Boos-Waldeck warned, "none of the grants allotted by the government will get away from you, because none of the contractors will fulfill the obligations undertaken. Henry Fisher, who apparently still has the best-situated grant, is getting in touch with you because he would like to dispose of his grant for very limited compensation."

"I will repeat it to you again, *in spite of the million* from the government you will bitterly regret the colonization business, make many more dissatisfied people, and still not be able to pay for the transportation and establishment of three thousand families with this million. What's more, you will be cheated by the agents, and you yourself will embitter your life without benefit to you or the society; for many years will still pass before the terrain in those outlying grants acquires value."

Boos-Waldeck had a personal view of reality on the ground, but back in Germany Prince Victor of Leiningen continued to lobby the society, and won them over to large-scale colonization financed by the nobles themselves. Frustrated, Boos-Waldeck left the society, which then reorganized itself into the Adelsverein.

The reconstituted verein met in March 1844, elected Bourgeois to membership in the society and named him to the society's colonization commission. His fellow commissioner was Prince Carl of Solms-Braunfels. A month later Bourgeois was named director of colonization for the future Texas colony and Solms was given the title of commissioner general. The two men embarked for Texas.

Most Germans arriving in Texas told stories of their long, sixty-day voyages from Bremen to Galveston aboard cramped brigs. That was not the route taken by Solms, who preferred to see the sights as he traveled. Departing Germany on May 16, and accompanied by Bourgeois and their servants, he crossed the channel and was in Dover in a mere five hours. He visited London briefly, then caught a train to Liverpool, where he boarded a ship for North America. Taking a northern course, and seeing icebergs en route, he landed in Halifax, Nova Scotia, eleven days later. By June 1 he was strolling about Boston. The next day he traveled to New York, where he stayed at the Astor House, enjoying visits and dinners. June 4 he took the train to Philadelphia, lodging at the Mansion House, which he considered excellent.

Then by steamboat and train to Baltimore. A train to Harper's Ferry ("poor dinner," in his words), a coach to Uniontown and Brownsville, then a steamer trip on the Monongahela to Pittsburgh. After a tour of a glass factory and an iron smelter, he resumed his journey on the Monongahela ("rather poor accommodations and even worse company"). Downstream to the Ohio River, then to Cincinnati (staying at the Broadway Hotel) and Louisville (the Hotel Galthouse, "which is terrible"). After a coach ride around falls on the Ohio, he resumed his river journey down the Ohio to the Mississippi ("The food is horrible. The captain is a drunkard." Nights were of "heat, mosquitoes, roaches"). Life became more civilized in New Orleans, where he and Bourgeois met up with Armand Ducos. There were dinners, social visits, business meetings, a visit to the slave market, a tour of a plantation and moonlight carriage rides. Solms got to shoot alligators.

Then Solms's introduction to the West really began. He departed New Orleans for Galveston on a smaller ship that carried barrels of whiskey and beer on its deck. That is where Solms ended up sleeping—atop the barrels ("What a horrible night! The bugs and the heat!"). He reached Galveston on July first and holed up at the Tremont Hotel ("Chased roaches and in the morning, ants"). From there, he took a steamer up Buffalo Bayou to Houston ("Bad quarters at the Old Capitol and even worse supper and a dirty bed"). He relaxed on a horse ride, met with local functionaries and was honored with a twenty-one-cannon salute. Then he departed on horseback for Washington-on-the-Brazos to meet with Texas officials ("a night without comparison, mosquitoes, fleas, lice").

Solms was thirty-three years old. Though his family castle at Braunfels was grand, his principality was minor. Still, he held a lofty opinion of himself. Moritz Tiling, in his *German Element in Texas*, described Solms as "a true cavalier of the old regime. A gentleman by birth and breeding, he was of a genial, prepossessing disposition, kind and obliging, stately in appearance and demeanor, with every advantage for court life and the drawing room. Transferred to the prairies of Texas and the life of the frontiersman, he could not but fail with even the best of intentions."

Rosa Kleberg, an early German pioneer in Texas, remembers Solms visiting their home in Cat Spring: "Prince Solms-Braunfels came to our house one day and wanted me to make coffee for him. He was attended by a number of persons on horseback, and was dressed like a German officer. He impressed me as a conceited fool. He was unwilling to eat at the same table with other people—a manner of conduct which, I fancy, did not serve to raise him in the estimation of the American farmers."

Solms reached Washington-on-the-Brazos on July 7, 1844. The capital was little more than a collection of ramshackle cabins on a hill above the Brazos River. In July, legislators were nowhere to be found, for the congress met only in the cool months of December and January. The standing offices of the republic were minimal, almost entirely lacking in administrators or administrative buildings. It might be more accurate to call Washington a camp instead of a capital.

Solms's mission there was critical—Bourgeois's contract would expire unless extended by the Texas Congress—but his diary shows only mild concern: "I sent immediately a message by courier to Dr. Jones [Anson Jones, Texas Secretary of State] because the president [Sam Houston]

Prince Carl of Solms-Braunfels. Photo from the Sophienburg Museum & Archives, New Braunfels

was still on the Trinity River. Washington must be the most miserable and unhealthy place in Texas. Thorough [personal] clean-up which was much needed. Visit in Dr. Anson Jones's office. He is a polite man with good manners but has cat eyes. I don't trust him." Solms wined and dined with Jones, who "offers the most wonderful promises of congress. We have to wait for the president's letter concerning my business." After staying two nights, Solms and his entourage departed for Independence, Mount Vernon, Round Top and Nassau Farm.

The diary written by Bourgeois, who was with Solms at Washington, takes a much more businesslike tone, ticking off the documents delivered to Jones: a report on the million-dollar loan to the republic; a report on the colonization effort; a letter of introduction; a French translation of the Adelsverein's platform; and the verein's membership list. According to Bourgeois, "the Secretary of State regretted that our grant on the Medina River could not be renewed without the approval of Congress. He assured us, however, that he had no doubt that Congress would consent to the Society's wish."

The diaries of the two men display marked differences in personality. Bourgeois, the promoter, was ever optimistic but always obsessed with the business of getting his contract extended and his grant occupied. Solms, the touring prince, was more concerned with personalities, food, accommodations and grand schemes. Over time, a rift arose between the two men, one focused on inspecting the grant lands and beginning preparations for the colony, the other becoming acquainted with places and personalities in the manner of royalty on tour. Solms seemed removed, above the minutiae of colonization, more suited to parlor conversation than colonization.

In Germany, the ebullient Adelsverein placed an announcement in a Frankfurt newspaper observing that "many causes are working together to increase emigration: the displacement of manual labor by machinery, the great periodic depressions affecting commerce; the increasing poverty, caused by overpopulation and unemployment, the reported productivity of land in the new country, and the hope of improving one's condition across the seas."

It continued, "After a long and careful examination, the Society has decided that Texas is the land which will best suit the emigrant. The healthy climate, the fertility of the soil, the abundance of its products, and the ease of communication with Europe have drawn many German emigrants to Texas. But without aid and assistance these have become separated and have frequently failed. The Society has sent capable men to Texas to get first-hand information and, on the basis of their reports, has selected Texas as the field of its operations.

"In the western part of Texas, in its most healthy region, the Society has acquired a large unsettled tract of land on which it will promote the settlement of those Germans who want to leave their Fatherland."

The society promised "large and commodious" ships to make the voyage and inexpensive food during the journey. On arrival in Texas, colonists would be provided wagons to transport them and their belongings to the settlement, where they would find "warehouses filled with provisions, gardening and farming implements, and seeds and plants of all sorts," not to mention "all the necessary oxen, horses, cows, hogs and sheep" at below-market prices. In addition to transportation, the verein promised to build cabins for the colonists and to feed them until their first crop came in.

Two members of the society were already in Texas making arrangements, said the society, and the first group of 150 immigrant families would depart Bremen in September 1844. According to the society's estimates, unmarried men would need capital of three hundred gulden ($120) and families twice that. Half of that amount was allocated to the cost of the services that would be provided by the verein; the other half could be drawn upon for farm implements, extra rations and so forth. Colonists could also deposit additional funds with the verein, receiving in return an account book. According to the verein, doing so "offers the advantage that the cash cannot be lost during the journey and it will also eliminate high rates charged by money exchangers in America."

The verein's estimates of the amount of money required to run its operation—which flew in the face of the opinion of Count Boos-Waldeck—had come in part from conversations with Henry Fisher, who represented that six thousand colonists could be moved from the Texas Gulf Coast, settled at their final destination and fed until crops were harvested with just $80,000. Less than fifteen dollars per colonist, that number was absurd on its face. Alwin H. Soergel, an Adelsverein immigrant who eventually settled near Round Top, calculated in 1846 (shortly after his arrival, but too late to do any good) that a more realistic sum for settling six thousand people was in the neighborhood of one million dollars. Boos-Waldeck would have considered even that sum inadequate. The naïveté of the society's nobles was astounding. Either the verein was going to raise more capital or there were going to be serious problems in Texas.

Solms was disappointed by what he found at Nassau Farm. The farmhouse was unfinished and the cotton crop was pitiful. Breaking the sod of the Blackland Prairie and tilling its heavy soil had proven formidable. The overseer hired by Boos-Waldeck had turned out to be a drunk. Solms quickly concluded that the farm should be divided into eight parcels and sold. The prince spent a few days in July attending to business and finance when not hunting "chickens" (wild turkey). At nearby Industry he met Johann Friedrich Ernst and his wife Louise, German pioneers in Texas whose views of the Adelsverein have been mentioned above. He also encountered "[Ferdinand Jacob] Lindheimer who is a botanist from Frankfurt [and Louis Cachand] Ervendberg, a Protestant minister who in payment of one cow and a calf will baptize…. He is the teacher to the Ernst children, candidate and demagogue of the Frankfurt Revolution."

Ervendberg was a German Episcopal minister who had been in the United States since 1836 and in Texas since 1839. By all accounts he was not a particularly inspirational figure, and his sermons were hardly moving. His stint among the Adelsverein ended in 1855, when he left his wife and moved to Mexico with seventeen-year-old Franzisca Lange, an orphan under his care.

Lindheimer was not a typical botanist. He had come to the United States in 1834 as a political refugee. In 1836 he signed up with a group of Kentucky volunteers to join the Texas Revolution. From 1837 to 1843 he collected plant specimens in Missouri, then returned to Texas shortly before encountering Solms.

Interested in the grand designs painted by Solms and Bourgeois, Ervendberg and Lindheimer joined the entourage.

Solms and his posse rode to San Antonio, arriving on July 25, and met with Jack Hays and John James. Hays was then captain of a company of Texas Rangers charged with protecting everything beyond San Antonio, and he had already developed a reputation for daring and bravery. He had also spent years as a frontier surveyor; for a period he served simultaneously as a Ranger and the chief surveyor of then-vast Bexar County. Solms encountered Hays between his epic battle with Comanche Chief Yellow Wolf at Walker's Creek (near Sisterdale) and his trip to escort Henry Castro's French and German immigrants to their colony west of San Antonio.

John James, Hays's deputy surveyor, had sailed from England at the age of seventeen to join the Texas battle for independence, but did not arrive until the conflict was over. He found work in San Antonio with Ludovic Colquhoun—an anti-Houston Senator of the Republic—managing his land interests. After becoming Hays's deputy, James rose to the position of Bexar County's chief surveyor.

Solms described Hays as "an honorable and trustworthy man, and perhaps the only one from whom accurate information of the mountainous regions can be obtained." Solms looked to Hays for advice about the Bourgeois-Ducos Grant and about other lands that came to the verein's attention, and relied on Hays' rangers for protection at critical junctures (though Solms insisted on forming a militia among the colonists, because "the Company of Captain Hays is fully occupied in watching its own frontier").

Solms traveled to the Bourgeois-Ducos Grant that summer and was disappointed at what he found. Much of the good land within the grant's boundaries had already been located by other claimants. What remained for the German colonists were poor flatlands and hillsides. Nonetheless, he and Bourgeois set about negotiating with landowners between the San Antonio River and Cibolo Creek, along the route from the coast to the grant lands, with the intent of establishing a stopping place for colonists moving inland.

Inspecting the grant lands and negotiating with landowners generated friction between Bourgeois and Solms. Bourgeois thought that the "first and ill-planned trip gave the Commissioners no information about the worth of their land." He groused that "there are too many individuals in our party who are really unnecessary." On one expedition, the prince split the inspection team and both groups became lost. When they finally reunited, Bourgeois felt that "all that we accomplished was a leisurely ride but not much in regard to inspecting the land. As long as we continue in this manner, the Society's business is in poor hands. Instead of handling ourselves business-like and acting like local people, we move around like children. We travel about the way in which Europeans take their leisurely walks.... I imagine that all future trips will be similar and our trips will be a waste."

Bourgeois wrote that the prince "is too supercilious and has no experience with the avariciousness of the people that we have to deal with here." For his part, Solms found Bourgeois "arrogant just like a Frenchman, knows everything."

The truth was that Solms had decided that Bourgeois's tract was unsuitable for colonization. He had decided to cast Bourgeois adrift. "The Bourgeois grant in its present state is of no earthly use to us because the small amount of cultivable and unappropriated land could only be settled if there were an established base to protect it or to fall back upon." In his opinion, if Bourgeois were able to get a renewal of his land contract, it would only be because of the verein's involvement. Without the verein, felt Solms, Bourgeois had no influence.

Instead of helping Bourgeois get a renewal, Solms felt the better tack was for the verein to go to the republic and get its own colonization contract for land in a different location. Solms recommended "land on the Medina River toward the southwest in order to be closer to the Rio Grande River, and thus attract trade from Chihuahua." This despite his low opinion of colonization contracts generally: "What really are grants? All are alike; they are nothing but a farce, a bad joke. They are useful to have if one desires to defraud others. The government grants an enormous extent of remotely situated land in which the grantee receives, under the most stringent stipulations, much unfit and a little good land."

While things were going sour for Bourgeois and Solms in Texas, the Adelsverein was receiving another suitor in Germany. Henry Francis Fisher (an Anglicized version of his birth name, Heinrich Franz Fischer), along with Burchard Miller (Burkhart Mueller), had obtained one of Sam Houston's eleven colonization contracts just weeks after the Bourgeois-Ducos Grant was finalized. Fisher and Miller were insubstantial speculators and lacked any visible means of performing their contract with the Republic. This is not unheard of in the history of Texas colonization contracts.

The Fisher-Miller Grant was even larger than Bourgeois's—some three million acres. It covered everything between the Colorado River and the Llano River (thus embracing the north side of the Hill Country) and extended far west. Like the Bourgeois-Ducos Grant, it reached beyond the existing limits of Texas settlement, into arid regions where natives roamed at will. The Germans were to inhabit and defend the Texas frontier.

In large part because the Fisher-Miller Grant was so far into the wilds that no one was fully acquainted with its geography, the two ends of its western boundary did not meet. This absence of closure was not fatal.

Texas colonization contracts were not deeds; they did not convey the land within the grant. Instead, they identified an area and provided that if families and single men settled there, they would receive a specified amount of land (in the case of the Fisher-Miller Grant, 160 acres for each single male and 320 acres for each family). If the promoter was successful in settling a stated number of families, then he would receive a substantial land bonus and the colony would receive lands for schools and churches. If the promoter fell short of procuring the required number of homesteaders within the agreed period of time, the promoter's bonus would vanish and the contract would terminate, but the individual settlers would not lose their lands.

A colonization contract often embraced far more acreage than was necessary to satisfy its terms. In a contract for a tract the size of the Fisher-Miller Grant, the requisite number of families and single men (six hundred in this case) might settle within the grant, and the promoters might receive all of their bonus land, yet the majority of the land within the grant would still remain unoccupied and available for settlement by others.

In the case of the Bourgeois-Ducos Grant, much of the land included in the contract had already been claimed before the first German arrived. Because the Fisher-Miller Grant was much larger and decidedly more remote, prior settlement was unlikely to be a problem.

Issued on September 1, 1843, the Fisher-Miller Grant had two important deadlines. First, it required settlement of at least two hundred families on the grant by the end of the first year. Second, it required that six hundred families be settled and the grant be surveyed within three years. Fisher and Miller—and their San Saba Colonization Company—missed the initial deadline for settlement of their grant, but (unlike Bourgeois) made a timely application for an extension and received that benefit on January 9, 1844, giving them until March 1, 1845, to settle the first two hundred families and until September 1, 1847, to settle the full six hundred families and complete the survey.

When Fisher presented himself to the Adelsverein in Bremen, he had already confidently exercised a clause in his contract that allowed him to increase the required number of colonists from six hundred to six thousand, potentially multiplying his bonus lands tenfold in the process. Adding to his prestige, he had persuaded the Republic of Texas to designate him the Texas consul to Bremen. By June 26, 1844—while Bourgeois and Solms were in New Orleans, en route to Texas—Fisher became formally associated with the Adelsverein. He convinced Count Carl of Castell, Prince Victor of Leiningen and other influential members of the society that attempting to renew the Bourgeois-Ducos Grant was futile. The Adelsverein discharged Bourgeois in absentia, purchased an interest in the Fisher-Miller Grant and committed themselves to its settlement. Under the terms of their arrangement with the Germans, Fisher and Miller were entitled to one-third of the profits that the verein made from land sales or industrial establishments.

Henry Fisher had recruited some colonists of his own in Bremen, before reaching his arrangement with the Adelsverein. Those immigrants set sail in the spring and arrived in Galveston on the brig *Wesser* in July. When Fisher's recruits arrived, Solms was in San Antonio and was caught completely off-guard; he had no alternative but to tell the new arrivals to stay put in Galveston until further arrangements could be made. By August Solms had learned of the verein's change in plans and was trying to extricate himself from the arrangement with Bourgeois, who was understandably perturbed.

Solms spent August wrangling with Bourgeois, then returned to Nassau Farm, where he submitted a report to the verein and inquired whether Fisher's unexpected newcomers were to be treated in the same manner as Adelsverein recruits. According to Solms "half of them died immediately; the rest are scattered about this area."

After spending September in Nassau, Solms returned to the windswept sand spit that was Galveston. Arriving on October 12, he found lodging at the Tremont House, the most civilized quarters in the treeless town of scattered wooden buildings. Eight days later Henry Fisher arrived for his first meeting with Solms, who "talked with him, afterward went riding.... Dinner with Fischer, talked until 12 o'clock." It had been four months since Bourgeois had been discharged, yet only now could preparations for colonizing the Fisher-Miller Grant begin.

Solms and Fisher spent October and November making plans to accommodate the colonists. Solms had consulted with Jack Hays in August, learning that the Fisher-Miller Grant was "hilly, but still choice land with plenty of good soil, well forested and watered; and since large stretches of land are still unclaimed, it is the most superior of all the grants." But Hays also felt that the grant was too far from the coast—and too deep into Comanche territory—to be settled in one leap. Though Solms was naive enough and arrogant enough to proclaim that the Comanches "will either make peace terms and keep them, or I shall immediately strike them such a blow that they will be rendered harmless for a long time to come, if not forever," he was also realistic enough to accept that a preliminary settlement would have to be made between the coast and the grant—a staging area for the colonial push.

After considering several locations, Solms decided on the vicinity of Comal Springs, which he called *La Fontana*—the fountain. "This area offers excellent land. It is a beautiful tract with first-rate cedar and oak forests and water power. Its proximity to San Antonio and Seguin assures support and help in case of need. Situated at the foot of the hill country, it will be the headquarters for the colonization project, since it is equidistant from the coast and the upper portion of the verein's land."

La Fontana was a well known location near the point where the old Spanish Camino Real crossed the Guadalupe River. More than one Spanish expedition had passed through the area. In 1756 Franciscans established the Nuestra Señora de Guadalupe Mission in the vicinity, but abandoned it two years later rather than fortify it against what they felt was likely (but not yet actual) Comanche pressure. By the time Solms learned of the valley, it was already being called *Comal*, after the round, flat, earthenware griddle used to cook tortillas. Solms heard that "a Senator Smith" owned four leagues of land there, and felt that the land could be purchased. Senator Smith was John William Smith, the last messenger from the Alamo, first mayor of San Antonio and then a senator of the republic, who had a business acting as an intermediary between Spanish-speaking landowners and English-speaking (or in this case, German-speaking) speculators.

Having decided to procure land at La Fontana from Smith (albeit without purchasing the land or making any on-site preparations), Solms set about arranging for the colonists to come ashore. Like Fisher's recruits, the Adelsverein groups would land first in Galveston. Then they would transfer to ships suited to shallow water and sail southwest into one of the bays lower on the Gulf.

In late November, Solms took a small sailing ship from Galveston to Matagorda Bay and Lavaca Bay, surveying the coast for the best landing site. He may have found the land unpromising. On gray winter days, long, thin clouds hover over the bays and cold winds roil the dark waters. The land is flat, barely rising above the waves, peppered with estuaries where

The Fisher-Miller Grant

shrimp, turtles and crabs become meals for egrets, herons and whooping cranes.

"I was looking for a place where the best harbor could be built," wrote Solms, "and at the same time good healthful land and fresh water could be found. I was also searching for a place from which the route would be shortest for transporting the settlers inland over the bad routes on the low prairies. It is very hard to obtain this combination."

Solms decided that Indian Point—just outside Lavaca Bay on Matagorda Bay—offered the best combination of attributes. There the colonists could be outfitted for travel across the coastal lowlands and into the prairies that led to La Fontana, just short of the Balcones Escarpment. They could follow the east bank of the Guadalupe River from the coast, then cross the Guadalupe and easily travel up the drainage between that river, the San Antonio River and Cibolo Creek to La Fontana. Though San Antonio was only thirty-five miles to the southwest of La Fontana, there was no need to travel by way of that town—the German colonists were to arrive fully equipped and prepared to settle.

The choice of Indian Point as a landing was a good one. Deep water gathered close to shore without treacherous shoals. The point was composed of shell and gravel, making a reliable all-weather surface. Its location at the west end of Matagorda Bay reduced the number of rivers that would have to be crossed on the way to the interior.

Time was short. The colonists would be arriving soon; there was no time to make improvements at Indian Point. The Germans would have to improvise upon arrival. Solms sailed for Galveston to deal with Fisher's recruits and to meet the first ships bringing Adelsverein colonists. He planned to arrive in Galveston on November 28, but a storm delayed his arrival until December 2. Unbeknownst to him, the first immigrants had arrived at Galveston on November 23 in the brig *Johann Dethard*, and had sailed on December 1 for Port Lavaca, near Indian Point. ("Holstein had the people transshipped. How stupid! This in spite of my instructions!")

He tried to follow, but a new storm set in and he did not sail for Port Lavaca until December 9. In the meantime, the brig *Herrschel* had landed at Galveston on December 8. Then the *Ferdinand* dropped anchor on December 14, and the *Apollo* on December 20. All brigs transferred their passengers to coastal craft that sailed for Port Lavaca after a brief layover in Galveston. In all, more than 400 colonists were about to land on the cold, rainy, windswept shores of Lavaca Bay.

When Solms finally sailed from Galveston on December 9, on board was Alexander Somervell, the Texas brigadier general and onetime Secretary of War who two years earlier had led an ineffective punitive expedition into Mexico. Solms considered him a "drunken bore" and a "scoundrel." Also aboard were Texas legends Samuel and Mary Maverick, who then lived in Decros Point (on the Matagorda Peninsula at Pass Cavallo, the entrance to Matagorda Bay). Solms was gentler on the Mavericks, observing that "Col. Maverick & mistress are refined but he didn't give any horses and he is tough."

When Solms did reach Port Lavaca, he found the first group of colonists already ashore at a camp two miles distant. "A small group of live oak trees provides them protection against the storm and also a source of firewood. A fresh water brook is only one hundred steps from the camp.... I found all of [the colonists] in good health. All were satisfied with the treatment and the food except four; these, however, were soon quieted by the others."

Solms had his own complaints, most involving Henry Fisher: "of all the draft oxen, livestock, etc. to be obtained, Mr. Fisher has not secured one head. Wagons are being delivered very sparingly; instead of fifty, there are only fifteen so far. Thus, everything is moving very slowly; and, as a result, it will be more costly than if Mr. Fisher had hurried here and had attended to everything with zeal and energy."

Solms also found himself in conflict with Fisher over the appointment of verein agents in Galveston and over Fisher's claim to the Texas legislature that he had invested $60,000 of his own funds in the project. "Everyone knows, from the President of Texas down to the smallest negro boy," said the noble Solms, "that if Messrs. Fisher and Miller were put under a cotton press, not $1.00, much less $60,000, could be squeezed out of both of them." Solms feared that Fisher's hollow boasting before the congress would impair the verein's credibility.

More immediate concerns loomed, however. Most obvious was the need to provide housing and other basic amenities for the new arrivals. After that, the promised wharf, warehouse and other facilities needed to be built. But there were formalities to be attended to first, for while Solms had selected Indian Point as his landing, he had not yet purchased the land. The owner, Samuel Addison White, wasn't entirely sure what terms he required for selling, but he was amenable to letting the immigrants come ashore and camp there—the details could be worked out later.

Obviously it was chaos in the camp that Solms would soon name Carlshaven (after himself and other noble members of the verein with that prename) and that would within a few years become the bustling port of Indianola (only to be destroyed twice by hurricanes and abandoned). The Germans managed to pitch tents on Indian Point and set about trying to reassemble their lives. Solms came up with an oak tree to use for *Weinachtsfest*. He asked the Reverend Ervendberg, now part of the Adelsverein entourage, to hold services and celebrate the Eucharist for the restive immigrants. The botanist Lindheimer was there, too—he slept behind the camp's simple altar on the night after Christmas.

The expectant migrants facing Solms, Ervendberg and Lindheimer were the first of thousands of German colonists who would pass through Carlshaven under the auspices of the Adelsverein and otherwise. Between January and March, about half of the first arrivals moved inland toward the colony. Some elected to stay behind along Lavaca and Matagorda Bays. Others returned to Galveston. The balance followed the first group north in April.

The Adelsverein's on-site colonial council, composed of Solms, Nicolaus Zink, Jean von Coll and Dr. Theodore Koester, oversaw the trek inland. Zink was the verein's chief engineer, Coll was its accountant, and Koester was the group's physician. The minutes of the council's eight meetings held during Solms's tenure as general commissioner are revealing. There were no reports submitted on travel, construction or finances as one might expect. Instead, the business of the council seemed to be criticizing the performance of its operatives and deciding minor administrative issues. The first meeting, held in January 1845 just after landing at Carlshaven, dealt with appointment of camp police, establishment of a border patrol and articles of war (presumably for dealing with hostile natives), extended criticism of Henry Fisher for his inadequate provision of wagons and teams and broad condemnation for the way that the verein's agent in Bremen, Dr. B. Hill, had handled provisioning for the colonists' ships. One complaint asserted that "two women were sent over as cooks for the Commissioner. They were of loose morals and, if one judges them by their appearance and looks, probably got their jobs in return for services rendered."

Three days' events may provide a feeling for the dynamics and discipline of the colonial council. On Tuesday, they held their first meeting. On Wednesday, according to Solms, "Duel Between von Coll and Dr. Koester, plenty aggravation, plenty spectacle. Ate late. Seconds: Cloudt,

Zink, Luntzel, Wedemeyer." The duel was almost certainly of the type indulged in by German university students; a formal and ceremonial event with swords that risked little more than a manly scar. On Thursday the council held its second meeting; there is no hint of conflict in the minutes.

Zink managed the January procession inland. He was a thirty-three-year-old civil engineer who had spent time building railroads in Greece, probably as a first lieutenant in the Greek army. He later served in the Bavarian army before sailing for Texas with his wife, Louise von Kheusser. It must have been an interesting voyage, for Zink's party also included his mistress, Elizabeth Mangold.

One person who met Zink described him as "a rather peculiar person with coarse, marked features, bald head, and spectacles on his nose, dressed in wide linen trousers stuffed in his boots, and wearing a short gray jacket." Zink gathered fifteen wagons provided by Fisher, rented three more wagons from settlers in the vicinity of Lavaca Bay and oversaw the construction of fourteen two-wheeled ox-carts. The ragtag convoy hauled itself north on January 5.

Although they began moving out of Carlshaven with relative promptness, none of the Germans—not even Solms—was certain of their destination, for no final arrangements had been made for staying at La Fontana. Moreover, Solms had decided that going by way of Victoria, Gonzales and Seguin was a bad idea, even though it would have allowed them to follow established roads along the Guadalupe River. "Firstly," he said, "every town inhabited by wicked rabble of Texas is to be avoided for a number of reasons. Secondly, this route passes through a large number of often-flooded streams over which there are no bridges…. Thirdly, none of those towns are our destination."

Comparing the route by way of Gonzales to be "like a bow to the string which would be a route on the watershed between the Guadalupe river on the one side and the San Antonio, Coleto and Cibolo rivers on the other," Solms decided to cross the prairies on a straight line between Point A and Point B, without having perfect clarity about exactly where Point B might be.

Solms's decision to bypass existing settlements was due to more than a desire for travel efficiency. He fervently wanted to establish a piece of Germany in Texas, and saw the "Americans" in Texas as pollutants and complicators to be avoided. His desire for separation was unconcealed; according to New York newspapers of the time, "German colonists under

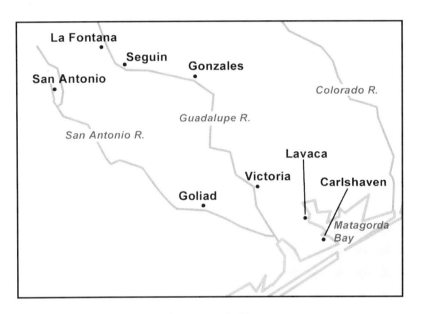

From the coast to La Fontana

Prince Solms have no more intercourse with the inhabitants than is absolutely necessary."

The Germans made camp first twelve miles from Carlshaven at a site on Chocolate Creek dubbed Agua Dulce, where Solms had established a headquarters of sorts. A company of twenty armed men assembled under the command of former Prussian army lieutenant Ludwig Bene, with the remaining men assigned to reserves. True to his style, Solms had the twenty troopers outfitted in long riding boots, gray blouses, black velvet collars decorated with brass buttons, broad-brimmed cocked hats trimmed with black feathers, and clanking sabers. It was a style not often seen in frontier Texas.

By early March the immigrants had progressed to a camp at McCoy's Creek, on the Guadalupe River, forty-two miles above Victoria. In sixty days, traveling in relays with the severely limited transportation, the group had traversed seventy-eight miles from Carlshaven. Solms had high praise for Zink, saying, "I must praise to the Verein the demonstrated enormous activity and tact of Engineer Zink, which no one can appreciate unless he is personally acquainted with conditions here in Texas." Unfortunately, this cordial relationship would soon fray under the strains of the frontier.

While waiting for the colonists to arrive, the colonial council held its fourth meeting, with Henry Fisher attending in his capacity as director of colonization. A squabble erupted over how Fisher had expected the verein to transport 350 people, baggage and farm implements for 150 miles with only eighteen wagons. Fisher replied that "he would have been able to do it, explaining that 'one only had to know how.'" While that dispute was still stewing, a disagreement arose over the relative authority of Solms as commissioner general and Fisher as director of colonization. Fisher asserted that one interpretation applied under his contract with the verein; Coll and Solms insisted that differing provisions of the verein's appointment of Solms prevailed. The minutes of the meeting state that "Because of [the] contrary vision regarding the execution of the colonization, a harmonious working relationship for the betterment of the whole was not only not possible, but a lack of same would cause the ruin of the undertaking." Fisher indicated that he would withdraw from the council if properly compensated, and the other members of the council leapt at the opportunity. A brief agreement was inked and a request was sent to Germany for funds to pay off Fisher.

That nasty bit of business concluded, Solms rode ahead of the colonists and detoured to San Antonio in company with botanist Lindheimer, two militiamen and others. On the way he stopped at the ranch of Jose Antonio Navarro, north of Seguin. He had met Navarro's brother Jose Luciano Navarro during the previous July while inspecting the area. Jose Antonio Navarro—a distinguished Tejano, former senator of the Republic of Texas and future senator of the State of Texas—had not been present in July; he had been in a Mexican prison after participating in the ill-fated Texan Santa Fe Expedition. The Navarro family dated back to the earliest days of Bexar, and they introduced Solms to another (and related) long-lineage Tejano, Juan Martin de Veramendi (the younger; his father, born in Bexar in 1778 and once Spanish Governor of Coahuila y Texas, had died in 1831). It turned out that the land at La Fontana was owned not by John Smith (who had died unexpectedly in January after a brief illness) but by Veramendi and his brother-in-law Raphael C. Garza. They had inherited eleven leagues of land surrounding La Fontana that the elder Veramendi had obtained under an 1825 Spanish land grant. Solms, who took great pride in his German nobility, was dealing with Tejano royalty, but he displayed his usual disdain, referring to the Veramendis as Mexicans and complaining of their "brash demands."

On March 15 Solms inked an agreement to purchase the Veramendi land, using in part the not entirely unimpeachable credit of the Adelsverein (the verein would ultimately fail to pay for the land in full, and epic litigation would ensue). Solms was proud of his acquisition. In his words, "on the right bank of the Comal Creek, which flows through it, lies a fertile prairie which reaches out to a ridge of hills. On its left bank there is richly wooded bottom land stretching to the cliffs, which are covered with cedar, oak and elm. These cliffs [the Balcones Escarpment], with the hills rising gradually back of them toward the north, resemble the Black Forest. Through the bottom land flows the Comal River, which, gushing out of the rock in seven large springs, shortly reaches a width of twenty paces and, becoming larger and larger, rushes along like a swift mountain stream. Its water is very deep and clear as crystal."

Having procured the La Fontana lands, Solms and his entourage rode to Seguin, where he was met by Zink and thirteen men from the verein's mounted company. The Germans crossed the Guadalupe River where it intersected the Camino Real. They rode on to La Fontana, with thirty-one immigrant wagons arriving a few days later.

There, on March 21, 1845, an estimated two hundred Germans established New Braunfels, named after Solms's estate in the village of Braunfels, along western Germany's Lahn River. The verein granted each family a half-acre in town and ten acres outside town. This was in a way generous, since it was in addition to the acreage to which they were entitled in the Fisher-Miller Grant, but the colonists were understandably eager for the verein to follow through on its promise of larger tracts of tillable land. When Jack Hays checked in on the colonists, though, he confirmed that the boundaries of the Fisher-Miller Grant were still some seventy rugged miles distant (in fact, they were more than eighty as the crow flies and many more by trail) and that very likely four to six more way stations of the type maintained at Agua Dulce and McCoy's Creek would be necessary before reaching the grant with settlers.

While they waited to advance north to their final destination, some colonists immediately set about planting crops, while others naively supposed that the verein would provide for their needs as promised. Most began building cabins and barns, though some single men continued to live in tents. Even the best of the buildings were rudimentary, though, for most of the colonists did not expect to linger at New Braunfels; their eyes were on the grant to the north. Nonetheless, over time, craftsmen and merchants set up their enterprises and some colonists built permanent homes in New Braunfels. (They did not realize it at the time, but New Braunfels would turn out to be the most hospitable and advantageous of all the verein's holdings.)

Nicolaus Zink began raising Adelsverein buildings—warehouses, storehouses, community buildings, fortified sanctuaries—but the work lagged because, he asserted, all hands were occupied meeting their own needs. Zink's first project was construction of a primitive stockade within which settlers could pitch tents. That camp, on the east side of Comal Creek, became known as *Zinkenburg*, in honor of Zink. Much more work remained for the civil engineer. It fell on his shoulders to survey the townsite and the farm lots, and he struggled to find materials and labor for building. A supply shed was so leaky that four wagonloads of corn spoiled, to the annoyance of the demanding Solms.

The colonial council met on April 7, April 11 and April 18. Although this was a critical period in the establishment of the colony, the matters considered by the council were entirely mundane: a colonist's credit was revoked at the warehouse; city lots were only for those who promised to build a house within three months; food rations for verein officials and functionaries were set; Dr. Koester should charge fifty cents for a house call; Zink was told to find a source for vinegar and oil. More importantly, the militia was instructed to organize an artillery, and the pharmacy would begin distributing medications for free.

Still there were no reports on the colony's finances, or on the details of its various projects, except when Solms complained that "Mr. Zink had not erected a government building or official residence." Solms apparently received some push-back from Zink, for the minutes of April 18 reflect an admonition "to work together for the success of the whole community, to keep private interests out of sight and also to keep an eye on the well-being of the community."

As was his nature, Solms was not overly worried about threatening natives: "there are signs of large and smaller camps of the Indians who, on account of the good hunting and excellent water, occasionally pitched their nomad tents here. However, as soon as civilization comes near, they withdraw because the sound of the ax in the woods is annoying to them. Should some go astray and wander this way, I believe that the clatter of the mills on the river and the noise of the forges would scare them off." Solms might reasonably expect behavior vaguely resembling this from the Tonkawas and Karankawas in the vicinity, or from the remnants of the Lipan Apache clans that once roamed the area, but it certainly did not describe the habits of the Comanches.

Despite Solms's expression of optimism, on April 28 he laid the cornerstone for a fortified headquarters on a hill known as the *Vereinsburg*. And laying the cornerstone was the end of it for Solms, for he departed soon thereafter, leaving only furrows in the dirt to signal where the walls should be. Solms dubbed his imaginary building the *Sophienburg* after Princess Sophie of Salm-Salm, with whom he was enamored and who would become his wife. To celebrate the Sophienburg's conception, he hoisted the Austrian flag on the site—for he was an officer in the Austrian military—and fired a cannon salute. Some of the colonists, embarrassed by their leader's German nationalism, later raised a makeshift Texas flag in the village commons.

It is difficult to make sense of the Sophienburg's location, more than a mile from the town's center, distant from the main thoroughfare of Seguin Street, high on a hill, far from water. When Comanches appeared, were colonists supposed to run up the hill and slam the doors of the

Sophienburg behind them? The key to Solms's vision lies in the laying of a cornerstone in a log-cabin town—suggesting that a grand and mighty reserve was in the offing—and in Solms's ancestral home. The castle Braunfels, which received its last major upgrade in the late nineteenth century, is a gigantic 184-room monument out of a fairy tale, with turrets and towers and crenellated parapets. It sits on a steep hill, high above the village of Braunfels. That must have been what Solms had in mind for the Sophienburg. But as ultimately constructed, it was a long, low, log blockhouse with little to distinguish it from any other frontier cabin. An early twentieth century photo shows it in sad disrepair, its shingled roof sagging badly. (Solms's diary suggests that the Sophienburg was built while he was present—in fact, the diary claims that it was built before the cornerstone was laid. This incarnation of the Sophienburg must have been a small hut of some sort.)

Down in New Braunfels, beneath the Sophienburg's site, Reverend Ervendberg established his ministry and began holding regular services in an oak grove at the base of the Vereinsburg. By August he and Herman Seele were conducting German-English classes at the same location. Ferdinand Lindheimer obtained a piece of land on the Comal River and built a home there, spending his time collecting plants and developing a botanical garden. New Braunfels's citizens began settling in and establishing the rhythms of their lives while still looking north, beyond the Llano, to their promised lands.

The decaying Sophienburg, circa 1885. Photograph from the Sophienburg Museum and Archives, New Braunfels.

Louis Ervendberg's German Protestant Church in New Braunfels. Photograph from the Sophienburg Museum and Archives, New Braunfels.

GERMAN HILL COUNTRY

Chapter Three
Solms Departs

In February 1845 the Adelsverein named Baron Otfried Hans von Meusebach to be commissioner general to replace Prince Carl of Solms-Braunfels. A contemporary described Meusebach as a substantial man, the best educated and most practical of all the verein members. His family motto, *Tenax Propositi*, was just what the colony needed: tenacity of purpose. He had spent four years at a mining and forestry academy in the Harz Mountains, followed by studies in law, government and finance at the University of Bonn. At age thirty-three, his reddish-gold hair and beard added to the distinction conveyed by his solid stature and commanding presence.

Though he had campaigned for the job of commissioner general, Meusebach began to wonder about the verein's finances even before leaving Germany. "I dare not conceal," he said, "the fact that the designated land appears worthless if the conditions do not justify a large working capital." When he quizzed Count Castell about the chances of the verein's funds being depleted, he was told, "the members will not allow that to happen; they will not leave it in the lurch." Unbeknownst to Meusebach, Castell was at the same time bemoaning the verein's situation in letters to Solms. He urged Solms to economize even on his travel back to Germany, because "we will otherwise be bankrupt before we earn a profit." Among the litany of problems relayed to Solms by Castell was the fact that the rejected and incensed Bourgeois d'Orvanne was in Paris on his way to Germany to sue the verein for $100,000 in damages.

Solms had received correspondence from the verein advising him of Meusebach's appointment. In late April a letter from Meusebach arrived. It was dated April 6 and mailed from New Orleans, so Solms expected his replacement to appear any day. He set May 15 as his departure date from New Braunfels.

The beleaguered prince must have been greatly relieved to have a date certain for leaving New Braunfels. He had done little but complain since his arrival. He had suffered fleas, ants, roaches, ticks, snakes, fevers, colic and strumpets. He had slept on ship decks and muddy ground, had been stranded in a land without culture or grace and had felt nothing but disdain for Americans, Texians and Tejanos. A memorandum to Queen Victoria that he wrote after returning to Germany is revealing: "The so-called American nation is composed of the worst element of all European nations, from the north to the south, from Sweden to Russia, down to Sicily, Spain and Portugal. Immigrants from all of these nations have passed on part of their makeup to their descendants, so that it can easily be said that the United States possesses the vices of all the European nations without having inherited any of their good qualities."

In another report on his trip to Texas, the prince opined that "no action is too vile for an American to perform, provided he thinks that he will profit thereby. In early times almost all the individuals who immigrated into Texas from the United States had been convicted of murder or theft, and to escape the law and prison, or often bankruptcy, they moved to Texas. It is a known fact that many of the offices and positions in the Republic of Texas were held by such men. Then who will expect any honesty or sincerity from such leaders?"

Solms had never been happy in Texas, and he had spent most of his stay looking longingly back at Germany and his beloved Sophie of Salm-Salm. He was not a man who had ever—for even a moment—thought of joining in the colonization of Texas. He considered no one among the colonists—no one in all of Texas, and possibly no one on the North American continent—his equal. He was in the miserable wilds of Texas to shepherd a few hundred colonists inland, and with that done he was leaving as soon as possible.

Meusebach took much the same route as Solms from Germany to Texas, landing at Halifax, proceeding to Boston and Pittsburgh, thence down the Ohio and the Mississippi to New Orleans. Setting sail from there, he reached Galveston, then took a schooner to Carlshaven, arriving on the evening of May 8, 1845. Shortly after reaching Texas, the Baron

John Meusebach, second Commissioner General of the Adelsverein. Photograph from the Sophienburg Museum and Archives, New Braunfels.

changed his name to John O. Meusebach. Texas was to be his new home and he wanted to fit in. Meusebach spent several days on the coast looking after business before embarking on the ride to New Braunfels.

On the 14th, before Meusebach arrived in New Braunfels, Solms delivered his farewell address to the colonists; he departed for the coast on the 15th as scheduled, taking with him his personal written evaluation of the local officials for submission to the Adelsverein. According to Solms, Zink "paid no attention to the job; neither reprimands nor scoldings had any effect. His private interest supersedes everything else. He has thousands of schemes in his head, none of which he has ever implemented." Not content with that scathing evaluation, Solms continued, "His character traits are falsehood, cowardice and uncouthness. He is subservient to his betters and excessively rough with his employees. He is unable to command trust and respect; hence, nobody wants to work for him. His lack of courage causes him to look at a mosquito as if it were an elephant and on wild pigs as if they were a tribe of Indians."

Solms was pleased with Coll, saying "Since he is an honest man, one can trust him completely. Von Coll always keeps the interest of the Verein in mind." He considered Dr. Koester, however, "a totally insignificant student who has neither knowledge nor experience as a Doctor nor does he have any common sense as a person. He looks at the whole enterprise as if it were a comic opera, which is to be used for the acquisition of as much money, provisions, wine and cognac as possible."

Solms was even critical of the colony's Reverend Ervendberg, asserting that "he doesn't preach very well and has made no special impressions on the community. The main drive of his character is greed."

Knowing that he would soon be departing for Germany, Solms encouraged his colonists—or at least selected colonists—to write letters that he might take back to Germany. These letters, addressed to relatives, ended up in the hands of the Adelsverein, which used them to promote their enterprise. Though candid about some of the hardships that the colonists faced, overall they are remarkably positive in their tone. Tellingly, though, several contain phrases along the lines of this from Peter Horne: "the time is too short for more special information as a messenger of the worthy Prince, who is leaving to take this letter and other association material, is waiting on me." There may have been some editorial pressure on the writers, who may have known that their letters would be shared with the verein. Nonetheless, they give a first-hand glimpse of life at the fledgling New Braunfels.

Nicholas and Anton Riedel reported that "We have not lacked any good here; we eat meat every day, as much as we want at 2½ cents per pound…. We have no black bread here; instead at every meal we make fresh cornbread from the so-called Welsh corn which we have planted in our gardens. The cornbread tastes very good. Every person has a pound of coffee a week."

Johann Hubert Lux, who appears to be one of Henry Fisher's early arrivals, had a more cautionary tale. "My wife and I battled the fever for four months. The cause was that we came to this land during the summer time and the lower coast of the land is feverish in the summer and unhealthy. We brought the fever from the low lands as all passengers who came in summer became ill. Those who came in the winter did not become ill. I therefore advise not to make the trip in summer but rather leave home in September."

Lux had another caution about the coast. "Whoever comes must not permit himself to be delayed in the lower coast land by Americans or stray Germans too lazy to work and involved in drinking alcoholic beverages or engaging in other debauchery. They must rather come up here at once as it is more healthy here than in the low coastal area."

Peter Horne had a better experience. "We are, however, very healthy and lively so it was not a wearisome trip. Instead, I can say, it was a pleasure trip for me. It went good for me because I was hired to help distribute the food. I had more work to do than others but I also received a salary which my fellow travelers did not get." Horne did have a few wants, however. He asked his brother-in-law in Germany to send thirty-two harrow spikes, two iron wedges, two pair of good plow irons with plowshares, two thousand spike nails, two thousand strong flooring nails, a dozen knives and forks, a half dozen pocket knives ("from knife-maker Hasselwein in Wiesbaden"), a dozen pipe stems, several pipe bowls, and "a wagon with the body made entirely of superior wood with long suitable arms and back made of birch. The arm not too short with a rotating shaft for horses and oxen. The iron axles should each weigh 60 pounds." He specified that the wagon should be built by blacksmith Peter Burod "so that it will be done well and can be tightened by screws later on." Horne's list continued on through a list of saws, blades, drills and other tools, then turned to two pair of striped summer trousers, a pair of boots and bolts of printed and calico fabric. His postscript added "a green and a white wide-brim hat from Heinzeberger in Ottstein."

Heinrich Schaefer was positively ecstatic over how his travels had gone: "By this you can see that all went well with us on a journey which ordinarily took three to four or at most five hours daily. I couldn't give enough praise for the fact that we and all the colonists have remained entirely well up to today and that the food has always tasted exceptionally well. I and mine are surely to be counted among the healthiest, for we haven't had a cold or any other thing the matter."

And he was pleased with Texas. "Briefly stated, Texas is a beautiful, healthy and exceptionally good land. It is really regrettable if emigrants go anywhere else…. The much discussed heat is not really so bad as is supposed." Of course, this evaluation was from a colonist who had arrived in December and was writing in May.

Some of the letters mention joining the verein's colonial plans at the last minute on the docks in Bremen. Schaefer tells us that the verein continued to recruit colonists after landing in Texas. "There are also many Germans from the United States in our colony. Also many Alsatians, who were formerly taken to San Antonio by a Frenchman named Castro, have come over to us; also many Germans of whom the Society did not know."

Oscar von Claren painted a picture of a colonist's day. "At first, in the morning, I arise at five o'clock, light a fire, dress, cook my tea, bake my bread and then I eat breakfast. After that I start my work, either in the woods or at the house. We work here only until eleven o'clock as then the heat is unbearable. At this time I cook my dinner and at three o'clock, when the heat subsides, I go to work again until it gets dark. Then I prepare my evening meal. This takes longer than we are used to because bread has to be baked for each meal as cornmeal bread tastes bad when it is not fresh. After I have finished my garden, chicken yard and other areas I will begin to build a house. It will be roomy and comfortable. I hope to complete it by fall, then furnish it to move in."

Christian Kaiser mentioned an aspect of his trip from the coast that contradicts Solms's declared intentions. He told his parents that he arrived at "Indian Point (a small town near the town of Lavaca) where we camped in tents. We celebrated here a real pleasant New Year and have thought about you very often. From here we were driven by oxen wagon through the towns of Victoria, Gonzales, Seguin and then across the Guadalupe River to here in the new colony of New Braunfels." Not only does this vary from Solms's plan to use only private camps at McCoy's Creek and Chocolate Creek as layovers, avoiding the "American" towns, Kaiser reports that "the land trip lasted very long as we had to lay over several weeks in four towns. The reason for this was not known by us." The reason was, of course, that Fisher had provided Zink with only eighteen wagons, and that layovers were necessary to shuttle relays of people inland. The realities on the ground in Texas had changed Solms's plans to keep his colonists entirely separate from the corrupting influence of prior settlers.

On April 13 Alois Russer wrote one of the last letters to be carried back to Germany. We know it is one of the last because in addition to being a surveyor helper he was a member of the colony's artillery company, writing that "I must now close as time is short because I must make a few cannon shots to honor the Prince as he prepares to ride away." He reported that "the area is pretty, the climate is healthy but very warm. My pleasure continues to increase as I am my own master here. I have no longer connections with Zink as I now work for myself."

Prince Solms might also have been thinking of freedom from Nicolaus Zink as he rode out of New Braunfels to Russer's cannonade. Thoroughly annoyed by his experience in Texas, Solms departed New Braunfels before Meusebach arrived, not bothering to preside over any welcoming ceremonies.

When Solms reached John G. King's boarding house west of Gonzales mid-morning on the next day, he learned that Meusebach had passed through the day before, headed for New Braunfels. He sent a messenger back toward New Braunfels and rode to Gonzales to wait. Meusebach accommodated the prince, riding back to Gonzales and talking business while accompanying Solms to Nassau, Houston and Galveston so that Solms's preferred travel schedule would not be upset. Solms sailed for New Orleans on June 4, leaving the verein's colonial ambitions in the hands of Meusebach.

Meusebach probably already had an inkling of the financial state of affairs that awaited him in New Braunfels. One informed account says that verein creditors prevented Solms from leaving Galveston until Meusebach paid their bills. Meusebach himself reports that he had to give $6,000 to Solms as he left Galveston, because more creditors would be waiting in New Orleans. Most of the $10,000 that the verein had provided Meusebach was now consumed. Meusebach gave Solms a letter to take back to the Adelsverein, asking for an additional $20,000.

Nonetheless, Solms's personal reports to the verein speak as if he had financial matters under control. He assured the verein's directors that he was attaching accountings of all expenditures, and said that D. H. Klaener, the verein's agent in Galveston, had assisted in keeping the books. "Since I am not familiar with commercial accounting, I could not do anything but promptly and with painstaking accuracy vouch for every item, and assemble and keep records of every transaction." Solms heaped criticism on Fisher, complaining that he had squandered $13,300. "I have as yet to see an accounting. That the account will balance there is no doubt; but how the accounting is made, that is the question on which the colonial council must pass judgment. In any case there is very little to show for it, not the quality nor the quantity that the directors commissioned Mr. Fisher to obtain." Despite Fisher's mismanagement and the difficulties that Solms had been obliged to navigate, he concluded in a February report to the verein (three months before his departure) that there was still about $7,000 in the colony's coffers.

And it was Coll—the verein's colonial accountant—whom Solms had found most capable, so there was every reason to think that the books would be in order, even if there wasn't much cash in the till. The state of the colonists themselves suggested sound management—those that came ashore under Solms's supervision had adequate (though hardly lavish) housing, plenty of food (often meat three times daily) and free medicine. Judging by the letters they gave Solms, they were a reasonably satisfied lot.

Looking back, however, it is clear that the colonists' good fortune was in no small part due to the prince's willingness to spend without watching the budget. Solms may in fact have tracked every penny of expenditures as he claimed. And he may have had a bit of cash left when he left New Braunfels. But the verein had authorized all of the members of the colonial council to acquire goods and services on credit; Solms had no records of what Zink, Coll, Koester and Fisher had spent. And so Meusebach encountered angry creditors wherever he went.

How had the accountant Coll let this situation arise? In the first place, Coll may not have been so much an accountant as he was a soldier: he had been a lieutenant in the army of the Duke of Nassau. And since his arrival in Texas, Solms had used him as much to train and drill the militia as he had to watch over finances. Coll seems to have been a loyal and steadfast worker, but his financial skills are unclear and his dedication to other tasks is manifest. He did what he was told to do by Solms, who knew nothing of accounting.

When Meusebach and Coll pulled the accounts of the colony together, they realized that it had incurred debts of almost $20,000. It was clear that even if the requested extra funds arrived from the verein, they would do little more than pay off the clamoring creditors. There would be no remaining money with which to operate.

Even if Solms had been given control over spending by the other members of the colonial council, it was clear that the verein had underfunded the venture from the start, naively relying on Henry Fisher's manipulative estimates of the amount of money required. Perhaps Solms or the others could have been more parsimonious, but there is no evidence of gross excess. And there is no evidence that Solms actively concealed the colony's financial state. The verein had not given him enough funds; his flaw was that he didn't foresee the problem and left it for Meusebach to resolve.

Meusebach spent the summer of 1845 bringing the colony's financial affairs back in order, seeing to the needs of New Braunfels and making plans to move north of the Llano River and fulfill the conditions of the Fisher-Miller Grant. In November he received word that an additional 4,304 immigrants were on their way from Germany. This immense influx of settlers was more than Meusebach expected and more than the already strained infrastructure of the colony could manage. Meusebach called it "a stupendous blunder." In connection with the departure of the second wave of colonists, the verein deposited $24,000 (less than six dollars per settler) in a New Orleans bank for Meusebach's use, but the verein's debts had already mounted to almost that sum. Meusebach estimated that his immediate requirements were another $35,000 to transport the new immigrants to New Braunfels, $45,000 to feed the colonists for three months, plus $15,000 to construct just the first two hundred houses. When the four thousand new colonists stepped onto the shore at Carlshaven, there would be little money to fund their needs.

As luck would have it, it was not four thousand new immigrants that appeared at Carlshaven from the autumn of 1845 to the spring of 1846. It was 5,247 men, women and children in thirty-six ships—enough to double the population of all West Texas. Not only had the Adelsverein failed to advance adequate sums to Meusebach for their care and transportation, it had failed to send the money—or even the account list for the money—that the colonists themselves had deposited with the verein in trust, to be withdrawn on demand in Texas. Some who had deposited thousands of dollars in Germany found themselves penniless in Carlshaven. Even Meusebach began to despair: "I regard this whole undertaking as a desperate one and its continuance as uncertain."

That winter was unusually wet and cold. Northers swept repeatedly across the low Gulf Coast, turning the land into mud and creeks into rivers. Though Meusebach had built some barracks at Carlshaven, and had erected tents to shelter more families, the accommodations were woefully inadequate. Families huddled in the cold, and built flimsy shelters of wood, grasses, sod and scraps. Influenza and fever raged through the camp, killing hundreds. Travel out of the camp was impossible; the coastal lowlands were impassable.

Meusebach was desperate for funds. The nobles of the verein were turning a deaf ear to his pleas. He tried to borrow using Nassau Farm as collateral, but could not. He attempted to raise funds in Houston and New Orleans, but failed. At Galveston he met with the Adelsverein's local agent, D. H. Klaener, who confided that he had already been obliged to mortgage his store and inventory to finance advances made for the verein's account. Meusebach decided to play hardball with the verein. In June, at Meusebach's urging, Klaener wrote a letter to the Mayor of Bremen outlining their circumstance. Klaener asked that the letter be published, and the mayor obliged. A furor arose, and the Adelsverein forwarded another $60,000 to Meusebach, though not without hard feelings. Because of the limits of trans-Atlantic commerce and some Adelsverein maneuvering, advice of the credit did not reach the verein's New Orleans bank until mid-August 1846 and was not communicated to New Braunfels until September.

Despite his as-yet-unresolved credit crisis, in March 1846 Meusebach persuaded famous Texas traders John and David Torrey to provide one hundred teams, wagons and teamsters for transporting the colonists to New Braunfels. These were not buckboard covered wagons, but twenty-four-foot-long, high-sided commercial wagons drawn by four to twelve mules or oxen. When they departed in March, it quickly became apparent that the prairies remained too soggy for heavy wagons. Axles broke, often within a few miles of the bay. Wagons bogged down in mud. Progress was foot-by-foot, with men heaving mightily at the rear of the wagons as draft animals struggled at the front. Disease from the coast traveled with the colonists, weakening them when they most needed their strength. Just as the weather appeared to clear and the trails began to dry, another wave of storms swept through in April, compounding the travelers' woes.

More than fifty years later Bernard Monken, then of Boerne, described his family's journey from the coast to New Braunfels with the Adelsverein colonists of 1845-1846. At the age of eleven, he had shipped from Germany in October 1845 with his parents, his brother Henry and his two sisters, Rose and Barbara, arriving in Galveston fifty-eight days later. The overloaded steamer that they boarded for the trip from Galveston to Carlshaven tried to navigate Pass Cavallo into Matagorda Bay in high winds. It grounded, sprung a leak and began to sink in the shallow waters. The passengers and their belongings were put ashore on Matagorda Island, a wind-swept sandbar of cactus, sea grasses and a few scattered houses that would turn into the town of Siluria, only to be abandoned after destruction by the same storms that ended the existence of Indianola. A passing schooner agreed to ferry the stranded passengers and freight to Carlshaven. It took three trips over two weeks.

There was a class system within the Adelsverein. The first-class passengers were first off Matagorda Island and received whatever accommodations were available at Carlshaven—likely for cash consideration. In Monken's words "no tents were intended for the peasants…. On account of the scarcity of building material a good many were compelled to dig sod and build sod houses, with whatever they could find for a covering, often entailing the severest hardships, as it all had to be brought together on our backs. Often after all this work was completed it began to pour down rain softening the sod so everything tumbled down again, making it, of course, look more like caves than living quarters."

When war broke out between the United States and Mexico in 1846, the army appropriated all of the Torrey's sound wagons and teams. Carlshaven was left with only a handful that were unfit for military service. With a war on, the army's voracious appetite soon led to shortages of ships, building materials, livestock and food. The colonists were effectively marooned at Carlshaven amid raging disease, rampant scarcity and soaring prices.

With transportation unavailable, winter passed into spring, and spring into summer. The sweltering Gulf Coast brought mosquitoes and misery. Every arriving ship carried disease from Galveston and New Orleans. Malaria, dysentery and fevers spread through camp, fueled by inadequate sanitation and contaminated water.

The Monkens were still stranded at Carlshaven. When an opportunity arose, they sent their daughter Rose ahead to New Braunfels with friends, hoping she could find employment there. Finally, tired of waiting, the Monken paterfamilias and a nephew from the Fietsam family decided to walk to New Braunfels to seek accommodations and transport. While their father was gone, the remaining Monkens were told that they would be going on the next wagon to depart. Sixteen people from three related families—the Monkens, the Fietsams and the Webers—and their belongings left Carlshaven on July 5 on a single wagon.

They made it to the colony's camp at Agua Dulce in one day, but the next day their overloaded wagon broke a wheel in the middle of an open prairie. There were no water sources in the vicinity, making it imperative that they keep moving. They procured a substitute wagon and a yoke of oxen from a nearby landowner, hoping to ride to the next watering place, where they could make arrangements for the repair of their broken wagon. Because the substitute was much smaller than their original vehicle, they were obliged to leave their baggage and belongings behind, on the prairie.

While at the watering hole on the verein's trail, their father crossed their path on his return from New Braunfels with a wagon. Now they had three wagons—one good, one broken, one borrowed. The elder Monken sent his good wagon to Indianola, and went with his family in the borrowed wagon to repair the broken wheel on their original wagon, leading young Bernard Monken to conclude that his father had "made his trip on foot to New Braunfels all in vain."

Once the wheel was repaired and the wagon re-loaded, the family headed toward Victoria, but soon the wagon's axle broke. After another repair, the Monkens, Fietsams and Webers pulled into Victoria—a trip of forty miles in fourteen days.

The Monkens' story makes it clear that the Adelsverein trail for the 1846 second wave of colonists went through Victoria, despite Solms's earlier reservations, for it was there that the verein required the Monkens to change wagon, team and teamster. All of the group were sickly and covered in mosquito bites from their journey. To lighten the load—and diminish the likelihood of further broken axles and wheels—the Weber family was left behind in Victoria to find other means of transportation. The Monkens and their kin, the Fietsams, once again headed north.

The two families made it to the town of Spring Creek, where their teamster inexplicably departed with the wagon and team. Meat and vegetables were not available; the family lived on corn meal left in their barrel. Soon Monken's mother died of a disease contracted on the coast, as did one of the five young Fietsam brothers. Bernard Monken, led by his grieving father and accompanied by his sickly brother Henry and his sister Barbara, carried on.

Another teamster took pity on the families and transported them as far as where Hochheim is today. Again they were stranded, despite the Adelsverein's promises to transport them to the colony lands. While there, three more of the Fietsam brothers died—including the one who had walked from Carlshaven to New Braunfels. Henry Monken and the last surviving Fietsam brother also took sick.

German colonists told stories of the trail from Carlshaven to New Braunfels that are hard to believe. People would be left by the road to die; following wagons would find the bodies and attempt a meager burial. Entire families would be lost during the journey of less than two hundred miles. Mounded graves and bleached bones lined the dismal trail north. Hundreds of souls were lost, almost entirely due to diseases contracted in the foul conditions at Carlshaven.

Experiencing just such a fate, the Monkens turned in desperation to a nearby merchant named Burkhart, offering to pay liberally for transport to New Braunfels. A local youth volunteered to serve as teamster and obtained two yoke of oxen from the Torreys, adding them to two of his own, and began the trek north. Burkhart kindly accompanied them on the first leg of the journey. The wagon bogged down crossing Peach Creek; Burkhart and the young drover went back to get more teams. It began to rain. The creek rose, threatening the Monkens' belongings. Providentially, two wagons appeared from the north. On one wagon—as if written in a Hollywood script—was Rose. Hearing stories in New Braunfels of the misery sweeping Carlshaven, she had hired a teamster and, along with another wagon heading south, had gone to find her family.

The southbound teamsters extricated the Monkens' wagon from Peach Creek, but not before also extricating a portion of the family's dwindling funds. One wagon continued south, while the family made arrangements with the teamster brought by Rose. Soon Burkhart reappeared with more oxen and offered to take the Monkens to New Braunfels himself, but the teamster who had hired the Torrey oxen refused to lend them to Burkhart, so the Monkens were obliged to cast their lot with the new teamster brought by Rose, despite Burkhart's warnings that the new teamster's two yokes of oxen were not enough to pull the load.

That teamster took the family two miles to a cotton gin owned by a family named Jones. Realizing that his teams were not up to the task at hand and, under the pretense of looking for more oxen, the teamster vanished, stranding the family yet again. They wrote to Burkhart for help, giving the note to a passing traveler. While they waited, young Henry Monken died of a fever brought from the coast, and a child of the Jones family took sick. Rose volunteered to ride to Gonzales for a doctor. On her way back, her horse reared and fell on her, the saddle pommel striking her in the chest. Seriously injured, she barely made it back to her family.

Burkhart sent a man—a Swiss named Kaeterly—with two yoke of oxen to take the Monkens to New Braunfels. Rose, the wounded angel of mercy, died during a brief layover in Seguin. It was September by the time the remaining Monkens—father, son Bernard and daughter Barbara—reached New Braunfels. Shortly after arriving, Fate put the finishing touch on their brutal journey: Barbara died of fever and was buried there.

Six Monkens had departed Carlshaven in July, after fifty-eight days at sea and more than six months of misery on the coast. It had taken them ninety days to travel to New Braunfels, in a tortuous journey that saw them repeatedly stranded by unscrupulous teamsters and beset by disease and death. Only two—Bernard Monken and his father—survived. All this under the promise of safe transportation, food, tools and shelter from the Adelsverein.

Dr. Ferdinand Roemer, a geologist who left us a remarkable travelogue of the Hill Country during its settlement, visited New Braunfels in April 1846, about the time that the first of Meusebach's five thousand new colonists began to arrive from the coast. He said that the results of Nicolaus Zink's surveying could not easily be discerned, "because the houses, instead of adjoining one another, appeared to be scattered at irregular distances over the entire plain. Only the principal street, the so-called Seguin Street, could be distinguished quite well, for although houses were not built on both sides, still the town lots, containing about one-half acre each, were enclosed by fences."

Roemer reported that "some houses were of logs, some were of studding framework filled in with brick, some were frame, while others were huts with walls made of cedar posts driven vertically into the ground like the posts of a stockade. The roofs, instead of being covered with the customary wooden shingles found throughout America, were covered with tent canvas or a couple of ox hides."

A German style of half-timbered construction that was used in New Braunfels, Fredericksburg and Comfort for permanent buildings is called *Fachwerk*. The buildings seen by Roemer were not that advanced. They lacked windows and doors, sometimes lacked even chinking between logs, had no fireplaces and often had dirt floors, reflecting the short-term mentality of the settlers, who aspired to large tracts of land to the north.

There were perhaps one hundred houses and huts in New Braunfels then, and Roemer observed that "several families were packed into one house, no matter how small it was. The interior of such a house, where men, women and children were cooped up with their unpacked chests and boxes, often looked like the steerage of an immigrant ship."

By the time Roemer arrived, the verein had built a small Evangelical church for the Reverend Ervendberg on Seguin Street. The church had openings for windows, but no windows proper. "Close by," according to Roemer, "stood a tiny house, the modest home of [Ervendberg], who does not perform his spiritual duties with the ease of most of his colleagues in Germany. He receives a very meager salary, which the Verein pays. He must preach on Sunday, teach school on week-days and furthermore cultivate his corn field and his garden in the sweat of his brow."

Though the hamlet clearly had strong religious underpinnings, Germans have traditions that extend beyond religion. The only building on the market square was the town's principal saloon, owned by Meusebach and Coll. "The taste for whiskey, which the German peasants and artisans unfortunately bring with them," opined Roemer, "is stimulated by the warm climate and further encouraged because the people are deprived of many delightful beverages of their native land, particularly good beer and light wine.... Unfortunately, most of the people are not aware of the fact that the indulgence in whiskey in the warm climate of Texas is more injurious than it would be in the cold, moist climate of Germany."

It might be more flattering to look at early New Braunfels from a different angle. It reportedly had a retail store, three groceries, a silversmith, a coppersmith, a saddler, six shoemakers, four cabinetmakers, a wagon maker, a locksmith, two tanneries, three cigar factories, a bakery and a house painter. That is a spotty and eclectic collection of disciplines (three cigar factories?), but enough to get a town moving in the right direction. On the other hand, the presence of three groceries is hard to reconcile with repeated pioneer accounts that the menu selection included little other than coffee, cornbread and meat (mostly pork and beef; occasionally turkey or venison), with fresh fruit and vegetables nowhere to be found.

That early reports of industry and commerce in New Braunfels may be more wishful than accurate is reinforced by Roemer, who found that most of the colonists—about eight hundred at that time, with more arriving from Carlshaven—were still drawing daily provisions from verein warehouses: "Daily great numbers of men, women and children, carrying sacks and other receptacles came to receive their ration or as it was commonly called in military parlance, 'grab.' The food distributed thus consisted regularly of corn, coffee, salt and pork; but in addition to this, small quantities of wheat flour, rice, sugar and dried fruits were also rationed out."

Although most of the verein's colonists came from Germany's underclasses, there were professionals and nobles among them. The town's doctor was also its pharmacist and its baker. There was a class of young, educated single men who fancied themselves true Texas frontiersmen. Over their traditional German cloth caps they wore Mexican sombreros, or fur-lined caps with a gray fox tail dangling from the back. Their coats were fringed yellow buckskin, or perhaps a blouse with sleeves slit almost to the shoulders—a style introduced by Solms himself. Long boots, almost to the knee, were frequently seen, not because of their practicality but because, in Roemer's words, "they met the requirements of the grotesque and romantic." On the heels of the boots were jangling Mexican spurs. Belts held a pistol and a stiletto or Bowie knife. Full beards were common, and in cold weather the men would throw a blanket or serape around their shoulders. As ludicrous as this outfit may sound, it was almost exactly—except for the fox-skin cap and the dandy blouses—the attire of Jack Hays's Texas Rangers, the most feared and respected fighting force in Texas.

New Braunfels was remote and crude, but it was not completely isolated. Ferdinand Roemer, militia commander Ludwig Bene and verein accountant Jean von Coll paid a visit to the Flores family ranch, just seventeen miles to the south on the Guadalupe. This was almost certainly a ranch belonging to the descendants of Juan Jose Flores de Abrego y Valdez, who began his cattle business on the lower Cibolo Creek around 1756—almost a century earlier. A palisade of mesquite posts surrounded the solid ranch house. Sheep and goats were penned in the compound. The patron was absent on business, but Señora Flores greeted the visitors and served them a meal of "chicken ragout, liberally seasoned with Spanish chili-pepper, baked eggs, cornbread and excellent coffee."

On that same trip, the Germans came across the less comfortable homesteads of two new American settler families that were still living in temporary huts. On another occasion, they encountered a Tonkawa deer-hunting camp, a freshly abandoned site where a group of Americans had been splitting cypress shingles for market, and two European gentlemen (and their two servants) "engaging in a pleasure tour of Texas." New Braunfels was a distant outpost of what might be called civilization, but it was not deep into unexplored wilderness. The push into the wilderness lay ahead.

Chapter Four
Fredericksburg

In August 1845, just months after arriving in New Braunfels, John (the former Baron von) Meusebach concluded that a second substantial settlement was necessary between New Braunfels and the Fisher-Miller Grant. This was consistent with a verein plan to provide way stations for immigrants traveling to the colony and was not inconsistent with the advice that Jack Hays had given to Prince Solms, though Hays had suggested several small camps.

Late that month Meusebach set forth into the wilderness and located a tract that he felt would be suitable as the final mustering point before the colony. North of the Pedernales River, about sixty miles northwest of New Braunfels, the site was blessed with stone and timber. All of the land along the Pedernales had already been claimed; Meusebach's plot—the future Fredericksburg—straddled two tributaries that he named Meusebach Creek after himself and Bene Creek after his militia leader. (The creeks are now called Baron Creek and Town Creek.)

The most expedient way to purchase uninhabited land in Texas was by buying land scrip that evidenced "headrights" and using the scrip certificates as tender to purchase the property from the republic (or later, the state). The Republic of Texas had adopted a practice of making headright land grants to citizens who met basic homesteading requirements. The most generous grants were "first class" rights for citizens as of March 4, 1836, giving heads of families one league and one labor of land (4,605.5 acres) and single men aged seventeen years or older one-third of a league (1,476.1 acres). The least generous were "fourth class" headrights for those who immigrated into Texas between January 1, 1840 and January 1, 1842. These settlers received 640 acres for heads of families and 320 acres for single men. Headright certificates for almost thirty-seven million acres of land were issued by the republic.

Even with land scrip in hand, no land could be secured until it was surveyed; this was often the largest obstacle to obtaining acreage in remote areas. Ferdinand Roemer tells us about the frontier surveyor: "Surveying in the uninhabited highlands of Texas is not the peaceful, dangerless occupation as in Germany, but is always connected with danger and great hardships and privations. Camping under the blue sky for months, often many days' journey removed from the homes of civilized people, the Texas surveyor finds his rifle just as necessary as his compass, on the one hand to supply meat for his needs, on the other to ward off attacks by hostile Indians. The latter, who regard the compass as the instrument or 'thing that steals the land,' know full well that the surveyor is only the forerunner of the white intruder who will drive them off the hunting grounds of their fathers. Therefore they pursue them with particular hatred. Although surveyors venture into such country only in companies of not less than six to twelve men, it nevertheless happens every year that such companies are attacked by Indians and all or some of the men are killed."

As dangerous as their job was, surveyors were also in a position to profit handsomely from their profession. While in the wilds surveying land for a client, they might easily spot another choice tract for themselves, or might accept a portion of their client's land as their fee. More than one frontier surveyor ended up a prosperous land speculator and developer.

Perhaps because of the prospects to be found in unsettled locales, surveyors tend to crop up in our story at moments of opportunity. Samuel Addison White, who held title to what would become Carlshaven and later Indianola, was a surveyor. Nicolaus Zink surveyed New Braunfels. Jack Hays was a Texas Ranger and a surveyor. His deputy surveyor, John James, still has a part to play in our tale. And we have more surveyors to meet.

In December 1845—the month in which Texas became one of the United States—Meusebach dispatched a well-equipped detachment of thirty-six men under the direction of militia leader Ludwig Bene, with orders to lay out a wagon road from New Braunfels to the new townsite near the Pedernales and to survey the site upon arrival. Meusebach would then buy ten thousand acres of headrights (using the Adelsverein credit that he was working so diligently to restore) and file the certificates to obtain the land.

The lead surveyor in the party sent by Meusebach was Johann Jacob Groos, who had arrived in Carlshaven the year before, aboard the *Herrschel*. Like Zink, he was a civil engineer. He and his wife Katherine Blieder Groos would settle in New Braunfels and raise five sons and two daughters. He served as surveyor of Comal County and during the Civil War was named a captain of the Texas State Troops. He became a Comal County Commissioner, New Braunfels alderman and mayor of New Braunfels, where he owned and operated the Guadalupe Hotel until 1873. For almost five years prior to his death in 1878 he was Commissioner of the Texas General Land Office. As we find him, though, he is a raw, adventurous twenty-three-year-old immigrant in the employ of the Adelsverein, venturing north in the cold of winter to locate the colonists' next stopping point.

When the trailbreaking and surveying party reached the site chosen by Meusebach, they planned first to construct a log shelter. As it turned out, though, their limited food supplies allowed them only time enough to survey boundaries—the minimum necessary to meet Meusebach's needs. When they departed toward the end of January, the cabin was still unfinished. They buried their tools and concealed the hole, then turned back toward New Braunfels.

Henry Fisher, still involved in the affairs of his colonization contract, recommended that a Dr. Freidrich A. Schubert (whose real name was Freidrich Armand Strubberg, whose doctorship was in doubt and who sometimes used the *nom de plume* Armand) be given charge of establishing and developing Fredericksburg, and of the program to expand north from there into the Fisher-Miller Grant.

In April, Meusebach went to Nassau Farm to meet Schubert. While there, he attended to the accounts of the verein and incessant demands from Count Castell for detailed reports and accountings, which Castell said were "more important than every operation you carry on where you are." Conditions at Carlshaven were still bad; Meusebach advanced his own monies to purchase medicines. Creditors hounded him at Nassau Farm for payment, but there were no funds available. Angry merchants were filing debt collection papers in court. By June, Meusebach advised Castell that "I can hold the situation at most four weeks longer. Unless money comes, all of us will have to flee as [verein bookkeeper Jean] von Coll in New Braunfels and [colonization contract originator Burchard] Miller in Indian Point mean to do."

This was a doubly difficult time for Meusebach and the verein. It was the spring when more than five thousand colonists lay stranded at Carlshaven, the spring when the Torrey brothers diverted their wagons from the verein to the United States Army. It became the summer when Meusebach persuaded D. H. Klaener to write the mayor of Bremen and tell of the verein's financial plight, the summer when the Monken family made their desperate and deadly trek from Carlshaven to New Braunfels.

As we know, Count Castell responded to Klaener's embarrassing plea by sending $60,000 to Texas. The money came in a note carried by Castell's special agent, Philip Cappes. There is an air of skullduggery about Cappes: his correspondence with Castell refers to the "complicated purpose of my coming." He seems to have been sent to gather dirt on Meusebach; Count Castell was making sure that there would be someone to blame for the colony's plight. Cappes spent time in Houston with Henry Fisher, who had his own reasons for favoring the demotion of Meusebach.

Cappes added to the pressure upon Meusebach to keep up with colonial paperwork. To his credit, he handled some of that workload himself, while sending page after page of reports on Meusebach—including the details of his eating habits—back to Castell in Germany. This was a time of intense interaction among Castell, Cappes, Fisher, Schubert and Meusebach—with Meusebach the odd man out.

While Meusebach and Schubert were still at Nassau Farm, on April 23, 1846, a party of 120 colonists assembled at the Sophienburg in New Braunfels. Their belongings were loaded on twenty Mexican-style two-wheeled carts drawn by yokes of oxen. These pioneers set forth to the future Fredericksburg, following the track laid by the surveying party. They were protected by eight of the verein's paramilitary soldiers under the leadership of the reliable Ludwig Bene. A company of Texas Rangers commanded by Major B. L. Beall was making preparations to join the expedition, but did not arrive in time.

From the colonists' perspective the new townsite was profoundly remote, but the trail from New Braunfels to Fredericksburg, as described by Alwin Soergel in 1847, is today no more than a pleasant drive in the Hill Country: "The road to Fredericksburg briefly follows the road to San Antonio; [after departing the San Antonio Road] it goes in a west-southwest direction until it crosses the Cibolo River. There it divides and turns to the northwest into the mountains and at the headwaters of Salado Creek [in today's Fair Oaks Ranch] it joins up with the Pindas [Pinta]

Trail—an old Indian trail. This trail winds through the mountains, up long and narrow valleys, through passes down to the headwaters of the Cibolo and runs north at a slight angle to the west. [The Pinta Trail and Soergel's route actually divert from northwest to due north on the north side of today's Boerne, somewhat below the headwaters of the Cibolo, and follow Farm-to-Market Road 1376.] It is beautiful countryside, idyllic, romantic, with a taste to each liking—but of little practical use. The valley of the Sabinas and the Guadalupe is broad, primeval and wooded; it extends before the traveler's eyes from west to east. Though beautiful and charming, it too offers little to the settler. The river is crossed by horse [just south of today's Sisterdale]. On the other side of Sister Creek a road follows the creek upriver. You ascend the Guadalupe Mountains [departing the Sister Creek drainage to reach Block Creek's drainage and climbing to today's Big Hill]. At the top is a plateau overgrown with shrub post oak and black Jack. The trail descends again to Grape Creek and a valley with fertile patches of land and timber growth. One more time uphill, one more time through a pass and them before you [on the ridge at the Cain City road] stretches the broad and wooded valley of the Pedernales, ringed on both sides by limestone mountains that are devoid of trees. Between them and the valley lie green and pleasantly shaped hills. There, six miles off [to the northwest], hidden in the trees, lies Fredericksburg."

Because spring rains had left the trail soggy and flooded in spots, it took the group sixteen days to travel the sixty miles. As they approached the Pedernales, a group of friendly Delaware Indians approached. Neither party spoke the other's language, reducing communication to signs. After a few minutes of amiable gesticulation, the Germans proceeded on.

A shot echoed through the woods. Someone called for help and a large knife. Panic surged through the colonists, only to be replaced by relief. The shout was from John Schmidt, a member of the militia, who had slain a large bear on the bank of the Pedernales. The wagons had no sooner forded the river than another shot resounded: trooper Conrad Merz had killed a panther.

The colonists reached their new home on the afternoon of May 8, 1846. They found nothing to welcome them except the shell of the surveyors' unfinished cabin. There, among giant live oak trees and heavy underbrush, they made camp and built a fire to roast their bear and panther. To the amusement—and not a little astonishment—of the colonists, a woman named Lochte ate the head of the bear and pronounced it delicious.

No sooner had the colonists arrived than a message arrived from Governor Pinckney Henderson, relayed via New Braunfels. "I am led to believe that the Mexican Government will add to its invasion of the soil of Texas an attempt at fomenting the hostility of the Indians on our frontier.... I would suggest the prudence of abstaining from a movement in that direction untill time schall prove that it can be made without a reckless exposure of human life. I do this… because circumstances may render it impossible to afford the military protection which was intended to be given to the expedition on the part of the state."

But the colonists were not to be deterred. They persevered in establishing their new town. Hermann Wilke was the surveyor of the expedition, and he proceeded to lay out the town of Fredericksburg, dividing it into half-acre town lots and ten-acre farms. The town lots were situated between the arms of Baron Creek and Town Creek, with through streets aligned northwest-to-southeast, paralleling the creeks. At the center of town was *Adolphsplatz*, a commons bisected by San Saba Street (today's Main Street).

It is worth noting that the founders of both New Braunfels and Fredericksburg chose to give principal streets names such as Seguin, Austin, San Saba, Comal and San Antonio. These mingled with Friedrich, Schubert, Ludwig, Castell and other German names, but in both towns the prime thoroughfare was given a Hispanic name: San Saba in Fredericksburg, Seguin in New Braunfels. These give lie to claims that the colonists envisioned an independent German republic. There is evidence, however, that some of these Spanish street names existed only on paper: what is today called Main Street in Fredericksburg was referred to in early correspondence not as San Saba Street, but *Haupt Strasse*—Main Street.

Freidrich Schubert accepted the responsibility for managing Fredericksburg. In June he led a second convoy of colonists from New Braunfels. By the time they arrived, the first wave had already constructed a blockhouse and a stockade. The future townsite was still heavily wooded, but clearing was in progress. Tall grasses were abundant, and the settlers used them to roof temporary huts.

The Germans planted a community garden and built a storehouse of sturdy logs. Petty politics bubbled among the local representatives of the verein in New Braunfels and Fredericksburg. Hard work and grumbling and whiskey and religion and the pioneering spirit mingled in a heady brew.

In late 1846 eighteen men—Schubert, a group of German colonists, a team of American surveyors and two Shawnee native guides—set forth northward on horseback accompanied by two wagons, one of which carried a small cannon. Politics and quarrelling carried into the woods, according to Julius Splittgerber's personal recollections: "one of the parasites who lived at the expense of the Society but contributed nothing in return (called by the colonists 'the Society's scamp'), a Captain Gunst from Carlisten in Spain, put some of the pack which he carried on his horse on the baggage wagon. Schubert saw this, and since he was not very fond of Gunst, told him: 'It is a sorry sheep that cannot carry its own wool.' Gunst was deeply offended, and, according to what I heard, challenged Schubert for a duel. I do not know whether the duel actually took place, but later in Fredericksburg Gunst lay sick in bed with a gunshot wound in his abdomen. Finally he committed suicide."

After a ride of several days, the group reached the Llano River—the southern boundary of the grant. The river at that point was swift and rocky, unsuitable for fording. Schubert sent the Shawnee guides to search for a better crossing. They returned to report that a large number of Kickapoos were camped on the opposite side of the river. Though Kickapoos were not known as hostile warriors, the explorers kept a nervous watch during the night; the next morning Schubert gave orders to return to Fredericksburg.

The expedition reached home on New Year's Day 1847 without having entered the Fisher-Miller Grant. Schubert wildly overestimated the number of hostile natives roaming between the Llano and the San Saba Rivers as between forty thousand and sixty thousand.

The first order of business upon their return to Fredericksburg was to have two duels (in addition to the rumored Schubert-Gunst shootout) to settle matters that had arisen during the trip. There was a fair mania for dueling then. The passion—fueled by exaggerated frontier notions of honor and manliness, not to mention the availability of strong drink—dated back to the early years of the republic, even though the practice had been outlawed in 1836. Dueling became such a nuisance that the official oath for taking a Texas government office during the nineteenth century included a representation that the official had never participated in a duel.

Dr. Schubert made a lasting impression on the young village of Fredericksburg. It was he who designed the *Vereins Kirche*, a church that was the first public building in town. Built in 1847, torn down in 1897 and reconstructed in 1937, this remarkable building was octagonal, a German Carolingan style that can be seen at Charlemagne's palace chapel in Aachen, and that has roots in early Byzantine churches. Nicknamed the Coffee Mill (*Kaffemuehle*) it was open to all denominations, though it nominally was the home of the Evangelical Protestant Congregation.

John Meusebach could not have been pleased with Dr. Schubert's timidity at the Llano, which had done nothing to advance the colony. Looking back, Meusebach commented that Schubert's report on the dangers that lay waiting above the Llano "could not be allowed to go abroad unrebuked. It would have created despondency amongst the emigrants and the company." Meusebach ended up concluding that Schubert was "a great humbug and adventurer…."

Meusebach had been in New Braunfels while Schubert was making his indecisive foray to the north, and learned of it only after the fact. Bitter northers swept in repeatedly, weakening colonists in both precarious Hill Country towns already beset by fevers brought daily from Carlshaven and beyond. The colonists were cold, sick, frustrated and restive, prone to vent their spleen upon the nearest representative of the verein.

Henry Fisher arrived from Houston at the invitation of Count Castell's special agent, Philip Cappes. Cappes soon departed New Braunfels on business, leaving Fisher to maneuver for position. On the morning of December 31, the day before Schubert returned to Fredericksburg, Meusebach was in his New Braunfels home having breakfast with Fisher when a commotion arose outside. More than one hundred angry colonists were assembled at Meusebach's door. Fisher went outside to see what they wanted (though, as later events reveal, he almost certainly knew). The men had been incited by posters that had appeared around town that morning. The posters called upon the citizenry to free themselves from the "tyranny" of Meusebach. They closed with the epithet "Curses upon Meusebach the slave driver."

A small group was given entry under Fisher's sponsorship; they made insistent demands of Meusebach, with Fisher acting as their lead negotiator. The crowd outside grew restless, and not having heard from their emissaries, forced their way inside under the rough leadership of one Rudolph Iwonski, shouting threats. The mob remained in the anteroom while Meusebach, Fisher and the mob's leaders huddled beyond.

After several hours of tense negotiations, the discussions yielded agreement on five points—points that fully revealed the hand of Henry Fisher in the incident and at the same time revealed the colonists' suspicions that favoritism was rampant in the verein's affairs:

1. All immigrants shall receive land in the grant without preference; Mr. Fisher shall look after the interests of the immigrants.
2. The survey of the lands shall be carried out without any preference; Mr. Fisher shall safeguard the interests of the colonists in seeing to an early survey.
3. The immigrants who did not receive town lots in New Braunfels, though they were in Prince Solms's original group, shall now receive those lots.
4. The disposition of the wooded area claimed by the colonists as a commons, the title of which is still held by the verein, shall be cleared by testimony of Prince Solms.
5. Mr. von Meusebach shall demand discharge from his present duties from the directors of the verein. He will continue to direct its affairs until the arrival of his successor.

Doubtless Meusebach was only too glad to offer his resignation, though he surely wished that it had been done in different circumstances. He had been overwhelmed by the demands of colonization. Understaffed, or perhaps reluctant to delegate, he had not developed a loyal administration to look after the crushing management burden. He found himself mired in paperwork and at the mercy of men such as Schubert, Cappes and Fisher. His situation was exacerbated immensely by the failure of the verein to provide adequate funds. But he also failed in management and diplomacy, for he let himself become the object of the colonists' ire, and he permitted interveners to incite his removal.

A dissenting group of New Braunfels residents—mostly Americans, not colonists—assembled the next day to deplore the actions taken by the mob. They denounced lawlessness and condemned violation of the sanctity of the home. But it mattered not.

Amazingly, Meusebach immediately set to work satisfying the demands of the angry colonists. He decided to push beyond the Llano on a surveying expedition, doing what Schubert had failed to do. Turning over the reins of the colonization to Cappes during his pending absence, he began making preparations. He had long been trying to convince John James to provide a crew to survey the grant, but up to this point James had refused to do so without a Comanche peace treaty.

Somehow, Meusebach managed to persuade James to provide a contingent of surveyors to join a company of mounted verein troopers led by Ludwig Bene on an expedition into the grant. Lorenzo de Rozas, one of the Tejanos in the group, had been kidnapped by Comanches as a child. Because of his familiarity with their language and the territory ahead, he served as the lead guide.

Most of the group left Fredericksburg as a unit, but Meusebach had some business to finish and lagged behind by a day. That turned out to be the day that Ferdinand Roemer arrived in Fredericksburg from San Antonio. He described the town of six hundred settlers as having been founded in a forest, and noted that not all the stumps had yet been removed from the streets. "The main street, however, did not consist of a continuous row of houses, but of about fifty houses and huts, spaced long distances apart on both sides of the street. Most of the houses were log houses for which the straight trunks of the oak trees growing round about furnished excellent building material.

"Most of the settlers, however, were not in possession of such homes, since they required so much labor, but they lived in huts, consisting of poles rammed into the ground. The crevices between the poles were filled with clay and moss, while the roof was covered with dry grass. Some even lived in linen tents which proved very inadequate during these winter months."

Roemer commented upon one culinary aspect of life in the Texas Hill Country, reporting that Shawnee natives would bring bear meat and bear fat to town for sale. "Not only was all the food cooked with bear oil during my stay in Fredericksburg, but the colonists also used it in their lamps instead of regular oil. Since it is easily digested, there was an advantage in using it in the preparation of foods instead of other fats. How plen-

Fredericksburg's *Kaffemuehle* church (the original structure) circa 1885. Photograph from the San Antonio Light Collection, UTSA Institute of Texan Cultures.

tiful bears were near Fredericksburg was attested to by the fact that each Indian often had sixty gallons of such fat for sale. I found bear meat very palatable, resembling pork."

Meat, corn and coffee remained the dietary staples, and Roemer reported their effect: "Dysentery and stomachache were still prevalent among the colonists. The latter, a loathsome and protracted disease, almost unknown in Texas and occurring seldom in New Braunfels, almost proved fatal, since it spread to the throat and lungs. Almost every day one or more deaths occurred. Medicine and medical attention were furnished without cost by the verein. It was a pitiful sight to see men, women and children gather daily with bottles before the room containing drugs, at a designated hour.… In consequence of the heavy demand, the supply of some of the medicine became exhausted, particularly citric acid which was used to combat stomachache."

The use of citric acid to combat "stomachache" and the nature of the diet that caused it suggests that the disease was scurvy, though the symptoms permit any number of other causes, including influenza or roundworms.

While Roemer was getting the lay of the land in Fredericksburg, Meusebach departed and caught up with his men on the trail to the Llano. The night that he rejoined the group, someone built a campfire carelessly and set fire to the grass. One traveler reported that they fought the fire vainly for thirty-six hours. "It destroyed the grass for miles around and threatened our provisions and baggage."

Meusebach's expedition reached and crossed the Llano without further incident. The first native that they encountered north of the river was a Shawnee. Meusebach invited him to join them at dinner, and learned that he was one of several hunting in the area. Recognizing their superior stalking skills, the former baron hired several of the natives to serve as hunters.

The Germans, Tejanos, Americans and Shawnees proceeded cautiously, always on the lookout for Comanches. At night the explorers would arrange their six or eight tents in a semi-circle and build a fire in front of each. They then pulled their wagons up to close the open side of the arrangement, and brought their horses inside the enclosure. Four-man watches stood guard all night.

"The Mexicans as a rule," reported one of the expedition's Germans, "slept near us, who, like all of their countrymen, were strongly devoted to the game of monte (a card game). Their lively manners stood in sharp contrast with the peaceful behavior of our Shawnies who lay speechless about the fire and smoked their sumac. The latter is a dried leaf of a common Texas shrub. Only at midnight did they let their melancholy songs resound. Another group included the Americans who grouped themselves with the Society troopers. It was a colorful assembly of people of different circumstances and different nationalities."

After Roemer had been in Fredericksburg for ten days and Meusebach and his men had been gone for that time, former Texas Army Major Robert Neighbors, an Indian Agent who had served with Jack Hays in the Texas Rangers, arrived in Fredericksburg from Austin with three companions. He bore yet another warning from the governor, advising Meusebach not to enter Comanche territory.

Neighbors knew what to do when he heard that Meusebach had already departed. His orders were to overtake the verein expedition and offer his services in negotiating with the Comanches. Neighbors was already personally acquainted with several of the Comanche chiefs and was intimately familiar with their customs. One of the men accompanying Neighbors was Jim Shaw, a six-foot-tall Delaware who could serve as interpreter. Shaw had originally been retained by Sam Houston in 1843 to assist in implementing the republic's peace policies. In 1845 he and Indian Agent Benjamin Sloat had conducted a meeting on the San Saba River (where Meusebach was headed) with the very Comanche chiefs that Meusebach would encounter soon. Shaw's manner of dress reflected his status as intermediary: he wore a military-style hat and a long cloth coat over a breechclout and deerskin leggings. The other two men with Neighbors were an Anglo and a Shawnee, each charged with driving two pack mules carrying the belongings of Neighbors and Shaw, including woolen blankets and cotton goods that could be traded.

Roemer decided to join Neighbors's mission. In his words, "my preparations were of the simplest kind and were completed within a few hours. I selected a large, fast mule which was also to carry my baggage. The latter was confined to my rifle, several pistols, several pounds of flour, ground coffee, sugar and salt, and a tin drinking vessel, holding about a quart, which was fastened to the saddle. This cup could be used for dipping water as well as for cooking coffee. I depended for a regular supply of meat upon the experience of my companions as hunters. Two woolen blankets, one under the saddle and the other on top of it, were to serve as a bed and cover during the night." And so Roemer set forth into Comanche country.

Without the heavy wagons that trailed Meusebach, Neighbors's team made better time than the verein's expedition. On February 8 they crossed the ground that the Germans had carelessly burned, finding that only a few cacti and yuccas had been spared. When they approached the Llano they noticed surveyors' marks chopped into the sides of trees.

After shooting a deer and a turkey and hooking several catfish, the group crossed the Llano, making every effort to catch Meusebach before he got himself into trouble. Rising on February 10 to a heavy frost and a chill north wind, they pushed north through more burned land to a broad meadow that they knew must be the valley of the San Saba River. In the distance they saw white tents—Meusebach's expedition. Though it must have felt like they were deep into Comanche territory, in truth they were only halfway into the Fisher-Miller Grant. A vast unknown still lay ahead.

The German contingent had been camped near the San Saba for several days. To the astonishment of Neighbors's small group, Meusebach had already encountered the Comanches and had made good progress toward friendly relations. In fact, a party of Comanches was camped nearby, on the other side of the river.

It unfolded that a few days earlier, while the expedition was riding through lands to the south, seven or eight Comanches had approached under a white flag. Meusebach sent Lorenzo de Rozas to greet them. The Comanches, led by Chief Ketemoczy, informed Rozas that they had been watching the expedition since it crossed the Llano, and that they were concerned about the Germans' intentions. Meusebach rode out to join the discussion and learned that the Comanches believed that his entourage was a war party. They demanded to know Meusebach's purpose.

Meusebach assured the Indians that his objectives were entirely peaceful; he had come to visit the Comanches and give them gifts. In return, he hoped that the Comanches would visit the Germans in one of the two towns that his people had built. Chief Ketemoczy took Meusebach at his word, and gave him the nickname "Red Sun" for his red beard. After ceremonies and negotiations, the Comanches accompanied Meusebach back to where his party had camped. The natives dined heartily and invited their visitors to come to the San Saba River, where several Comanche clans were ensconced.

On February 7 Meusebach and his men approached the San Saba. A white flag flew from a hill near the river. A Comanche village was at the base. The Comanches approached, riding in formation. In the center was a white flag; on the right wing were warriors divided into sections, each section headed by a chief; on the left were the native women and children, mounted on Indian ponies. A witness reported: "The entire spectacle presented a rich and colorful picture because the garb of the Comanches on festive occasions is indeed beautiful and in good taste. The neck and ears are decorated with pearls and shells and the arms with heavy brass rings. The long hair of the men is braided into long plaits which, when interlaced with buffalo hair, reach from head to foot and are decorated with many silver ornaments. For shoes they wear the so-called moccassins made from deer skins which, like the leggings—a kind of leg dress made of cloth or leather—are richly decorated with pearls. In addition they wrap a piece of red or blue cloth around their shoulders in a most charming manner which reminds one of the Roman toga. Their skin is painted in a most distinctive manner with a variety of colors, mostly red. Their principal weapons are the bow and arrow; however, most of them also use the long-barreled American rifle. Added to this equipment is a long spear decorated with feathers, the point of which is as effective as the best Toledo blade. The shield is made of buffalo hide."

As the two groups closed the gap between them, a wary Ketemoczy asked that only a few of the German party continue to advance. Meusebach, Rozas and a handful of others proceeded. Rozas told Meusebach that the Comanches would take it as a sign of friendship if they would fire their rifles into the air, emptying them. Meusebach, in a move that others later criticized as foolhardy, instructed his men to do so. Fortunately, Rozas was proven correct; the Comanches welcomed them into their camp for handshakes, welcomes and courtesies.

The Comanches invited the German group to spend the night in their village, but Meusebach demurred under the excuse of needing to find grazing for their horses. His men withdrew across the San Saba to the camp where Neighbors and Roemer would find them three days later. In the interim, the Comanches became frequent visitors and dinner guests, displaying a hearty appetite for Meusebach's hospitality.

Shortly after arriving, Neighbors conveyed Governor Henderson's warning to Meusebach. Neighbors and Meusebach had a brief discussion, then Meusebach announced that he would not turn back, and arranged a council with the Comanches for the next morning.

When they gathered, the peace pipe was passed around the circle twice. Then, with Jim Shaw serving as interpreter, they got down to business. The Meusebach-Neighbors party expressed their peaceful intent and again invited the Comanches to visit Fredericksburg and New Braunfels. Meusebach informed the assembled Comanche chiefs that he now planned to continue north to the site of the old Spanish mission and presidio at San Saba. Upon his return, he told his hosts, he desired a council with three principal Comanche Chiefs who were not present: Santa Anna, Buffalo Hump and Mope-tshoko-pe (Old Owl).

The Comanches intimated that they had been greatly alarmed when they saw so many people enter their lands without warning. They had been uncertain of Meusebach's intentions, but now were assured that the newcomers were friends. All was well.

That out of the way, Meusebach's men delivered gifts to the Comanches. Chiefs received red and blue wool blankets, copper wire for making bracelets, tobacco and cotton cloth. Warriors were given rations of tobacco and colored strips of cloth for making breechclouts.

Perhaps at the urging of Neighbors, Meusebach stressed to his new friends the importance of a council with the three high-ranking chiefs upon his return. The Comanches so promised, and Meusebach boldly—if not incredibly—proceeded deeper into Comanche territory.

It was more than the desire to explore the Fisher-Miller Grant that induced Meusebach to continue on to the old Spanish settlement at San Saba. There were persistent rumors of lost Spanish silver mines in the vicinity, and the presidio and mission had become surrounded in legend. If the mines existed, they might salvage the verein's finances, but Meusebach stated, "I do not really count the silver mines until we have them."

Meusebach and company proceeded north for two days, then were met by a messenger from either Santa Anna or Mope-tshoko-pe (accounts differ), who inquired into their intentions. Meusebach again expressed his peaceful purposes; the messenger collected a few gifts and departed.

The wagons were having great difficulty proceeding over the rocky, hilly ground and provisions were growing short. Still confident of the peaceful nature of the Comanches, Meusebach elected to send the two wagons and most of his entourage back to Fredericksburg. He proceeded north with only Neighbors, Shaw, Bene, Roemer, two Tejano muleteers, three Shawnee hunters, Neighbors's two hired hands and four German stalwarts by the names of Wilke, Plewe, von Wrede and Zeuner—a party of only sixteen, riding into country that few had dared enter since the Spanish withdrew under relentless Comanche attacks in 1772.

After eight days of travel along the upper Pinta Trail they reached the ruins of the San Luis de las Amarillas Presidio. The structure was 300 feet by 360 feet; its outer walls held fifty or more small rooms. Many walls remained, some more than twenty feet high. Three corners had projecting towers to allow lines of fire along the exterior walls; the fourth corner had a larger round turret. Near the main entrance, several prior visitors had inscribed their names: Padilla 1810; Cos 1829; Bowie "con su tropa" 1829; Moore 1840.

In 1810, Juan Antonio Padilla had been a Spanish cavalry officer based in San Antonio. Martin Perfecto Cos was a Mexican General who became famous for acting as President Santa Anna's Texas enforcer in 1835. Conventional wisdom has Jim Bowie (woodsman, speculator, poseur, Alamo hero and the son-in-law of Juan Martin de Veramendi) first entering Texas in 1830; the 1829 date provided by Roemer cannot be reconciled. John Henry Moore was a prominent pro-independence Texian, to the point that General Cos once had him arrested; it is said that he designed the "Come And Take It" flag at Gonzales; after Texas independence, he several times raised companies of volunteers to attack Comanches and other natives; he carved his name at San Saba during such a campaign.

Roemer, a geologist by training, spent some time searching for evidence of silver, or of smelting. He concluded that the local geology was not a likely host for precious metals. Worse, he made this assessment of the Fisher-Miller Grant as a whole: "After careful deliberations I must declare, although with reluctance, since so many exertions have been put forth, that the land in question on the right bank of the Colorado and the region north of the Llano is not the proper place for a settlement by the Germans, at least not at the present time." In his view, the soil was not as fertile as in the "lower accessible parts of Texas" and the distance from the inhabited areas of Texas was too great—as it had been from the start. Finally, he foresaw that "Comanche Indians will become (if not dangerous) at least very annoying to any settlement north of the Llano."

After exploring the region around the old presidio and mission, Roemer and the others ventured farther north on the Pinta Trail, remarking that "the path we followed was well traveled, for it was the war path of the Comanches into Mexico." Deciding that they had ventured far enough north, but without reaching the upper boundary of the grant, the group reversed course and headed downstream along the San Saba River, encountering a group of Kickapoos. Their Shawnee guides decided to take up company with the Kickapoos, because they had no desire to meet up with the Comanches, who would be perturbed by the large number of deerskins that the Shawnees had accumulated on their journey through Comanche lands.

Traveling on a ridge along the river several days later, Meusebach saw a Comanche village in the distance. It turned out to be the camp of Santa Anna, Buffalo Hump and Mope-tshoko-pe—the three chiefs with whom he wished to meet. Their enclave held more than a thousand natives. During the welcoming ceremonies, Santa Anna let it be known that he had just returned from a visit to Washington, D.C., where he had been suitably impressed with the strengths of the white man. In what might have been a moment of pointed native humor, the Comanches indicated that they were very short on food—so short that they didn't have enough for their Mexican slaves—and thought that it might be a good idea to slaughter and eat the expedition's horses. Not knowing quite what to make of the suggestion, everyone kept a close eye on their mounts.

The travelers made camp close to the Comanches. The next morning—March 1, 1847—they arose to find the three chiefs gathered around the campfire outside the Germans' tents, politely awaiting breakfast. After eating, all went to the Comanche camp to engage in greetings, trading and familiarization. Around noon all of the chiefs—fifteen or twenty in number—assembled in front of the expedition's tents. They built a council fire and spread buffalo skins in a circle around it. The chiefs and a group of distinguished warriors sat on one side; Meusebach, Neighbors, Shaw and several of the Germans sat on the other.

Roemer reports that the three principal chiefs "differed much in appearance. Mope-tshoko-pe (Old Owl), the political chief, was a small old man who in his dirty cotton jacket looked undistinguished and only his diplomatic crafty face marked him. The war chief, Santa Anna, presented an altogether different appearance. He was a powerfully built man with a benevolent and lively countenance. The third, Buffalo Hump, was the genuine, unadulterated picture of a North American Indian. Unlike the majority of his tribe, he scorned all European dress. The upper part of his body was naked. A buffalo hide was wound around his hips. Yellow copper rings decorated his arms and a string of beads his neck. With his long, straight black hair hanging down, he sat there with the earnest (to the European almost apathetic) expression of countenance of the North American savage."

The Comanche women and children, who had surrounded the group, withdrew to a respectful distance as a chief lit the peace pipe. The pipe circled the fire twice; all sat in silence. After the second circuit, Meusebach made a speech, using Jim Shaw as interpreter. "I have come a great distance to see you and to smoke the peace pipe with you. I hope you will listen to my words, for they are words of truth and spoken in sincerity to which we Germans are accustomed. The people of my fathers, which is a warlike people, brave, and, as you have seen, well-armed, sent me and I have come with some of my people from across the big water. We are united with the Americans; they are our brothers and all of us live under the same great Father, the President."

Meusebach continued in the stilted, oratorical manner that to this day characterizes polite contact between wary strangers of different cultures. He told the chiefs that his people planned to cross the Llano and establish permanent homes there. They would plant corn and raise cattle, and they would hunt deer and buffalo. But, he said, the Germans would not "drive you from the land of your fathers; my people will build their houses among you where the soil is suitable for planting corn and other things and we shall dwell together as one people of brothers. The amount of land which we shall need for ourselves is relatively small and much will be left for your permanent habitat.... When the buffalo moves to the north and the fleet-footed deer to the forest, when the grass dries or is destroyed by fire, when you are unable to kill game with your bows and arrows, when the north wind confines you to your tents and your horses get poor, then come to my people and barter for what you need. Now many of you have to go hungry for days; then you will always have plenty to eat, because our people will produce on the small areas much more than they need for their own meals."

Meusebach made three specific proposals to the Comanches: first, the Germans would be free to travel the Comanche lands without harm. In return, the Comanches could visit the German communities, so long as they "walked the white path" of peace; second, the Germans and Comanches would ally with each other in the event of attack or theft by third parties; third, surveyors would come to survey the land as far as the Concho river so that the Germans could know where to settle. Meusebach said that if these terms were agreeable, he would give the Comanches gifts worth three thousand dollars at a subsequent meeting to be held in Fredericksburg.

The chiefs conferred, then Mope-tshoko-pe spoke for them, saying that they needed more time to consider the proposition. They would reply in the morning.

The peace council reconvened around noon the next day. After the usual ceremonies and some protracted discussions among the Comanches, Mope-tshoko-pe spoke: "Before this I saw a black rim under the nail of my finger, but I notice that it is white today. My heart is glad to see the people who have come so far across the great water and have come to visit us.

"I have spoken to my people. I have counseled with the warriors and the old men. We shall leave the war path and walk the white path of peace with your people as my father proposed yesterday, and I shall do everything I can that we will always stay on the path after it is once agreed upon.

"But there is one thing which does not please my heart if you set your wigwams along the water you call Llano. My people here, we do not object to that, but I have not consulted all of my warriors. Many are following the buffalo and many other are on the red path to where the sun sets [on the war path to Mexico]." Mope-tshoko-pe proposed to defer a final reply until he could gather all the affected parties.

Satisfied, Meusebach made a brief acceptance speech. Mope-tshoko-pe announced that he would come to Fredericksburg after the second full moon to conclude the peace treaty. Santa Anna and Buffalo Hump added a few words of their own and then, after embraces all around, the two groups parted. Peace with the Comanches had been reached—for Mope-tshoko-pe would indeed ink the final peace treaty in Fredericksburg—and the verein's colonists were free to cross the Llano.

Chapter Five
Darmstadters

John Meusebach conducted the affairs of the Adelsverein under astounding pressure. Fisher's colonization contract, after its initial extension by the Republic of Texas, was due to expire on March 1, 1845, unless six thousand families settled on the grant by that time. On that date Prince Solms was still bringing the first contingent of colonists inland from Carlshaven. New Braunfels wasn't founded until three weeks after the deadline passed.

The Texian Congress, embroiled in debate over annexation to the United States, grew hostile to European interests, and passed a law in January 1844 that prohibited any further grants or extensions of colonization contracts. Nonetheless, Solms managed to extract a second extension from the Texas Congress on January 29, 1845, giving the verein an additional year to settle at least one-third of the agreed colonists—two thousand individuals or families—within the grant. In that act, the legislature waived the requirement that the colonists build cabins or cultivate a specific number of acres. They could earn their lands simply by residing upon and cultivating some portion of their claim for three years.

When Meusebach came ashore in April 1845, less than a year remained until the deadline. He dispatched surveyors to what would become Fredericksburg at the end of that year, but those lands were still far short of the grant's southern border. When March 1, 1846, arrived, Meusebach and his colonists were still in New Braunfels. They didn't advance even as far as Fredericksburg until after the two-thousand-family deadline had expired.

From that point on, Meusebach was playing a most uncertain game. He and Fisher must have believed that they could extract another extension from the congress. After all, they were proceeding diligently against great challenges. In fact, when they did finally enter the grant, it was against the explicit advice of Governor Henderson, who felt that the trip was inordinately dangerous. There is strong evidence that Fisher and Meusebach were in communication with the government, and that they believed that their rights would not be extinguished, but their legal situation was clear: Fisher's contract had expired.

And matters had taken an ugly turn in the summer of 1845 as the Constitutional Convention went about its business. The convention delegates were rightfully concerned about the amount of Texas public domain that had been tied up in land grants, colonization contracts, land scrip and other programs. A special committee was formed to consider the matter. It concluded that 236,803 square miles—more than 150 million acres—had been allocated in one way or another, leaving only 160,516 square miles of unappropriated public domain.

"These estimates, it is believed," concluded the committee report, "approximate very nearly to truth. There is left to Texas an unappropriated country not sufficiently large to subsist the various tribes of Indians now inhabiting the country.

"Texas will, doubtless, despoil the Indians of this country, whenever it shall be needed for the occupancy of civilized man.

"But upon a survey of the progress of settlement in the southern and western States of the American Union, this country cannot be reached in the next quarter of a century."

After doing some quick calculations, the committee concluded that the value of the land available for disposal by the nascent state was less than its debt. Texas was, in other words, bankrupt. This harsh economic reality prompted the committee to conclude that it was "the imperious duty of the Convention to reclaim from the unjust and fraudulent possession of the contractor, and unprincipled speculator, those large districts and tracts of country."

On August 28, 1845—while Meusebach was in the wilds, scouting for the site that would become Fredericksburg—the Constitutional Convention adopted an ordinance regarding colonization contracts. According to the ordinance, all of the colonization contracts had been unconstitutional from the beginning. It said that the contracts "would operate as a monopoly of upwards of seven millions of acres of the public domain of Texas, in the hands of a few individuals, when, in truth, the citizens, soldiers and creditors of the Republic of Texas had, by the laws and Constitution of said Republic, a clear and indisputable previously subsisting right to locate upon the public domain thus attempted to be assigned to said contractors."

The ordinance directed the attorney general of the new state of Texas, and the district attorneys of any district where colonies existed, to bring legal proceedings against all colony contractors (but not colonists) in an attempt to have the contracts declared unconstitutional. It further prohibited any further contract extensions.

For the ordinance to have the force of law, it had to be approved by the citizens during the process of ratification of the constitution. On October 13, 1845, the ordinance passed by a vote of 6,797 to 785. When the flag of the republic was lowered to make room for the flag of the United States above, Anson Jones, last president of the republic, gave a valedictory speech, noting in small part that under the newly passed laws, "I venture the belief that, without resort to taxation, the public domain, if properly husbanded and disposed of, will raise a fund sufficient to liquidate the entire national [Texas state] debt upon equitable principles, besides providing for the future support of the State government, a system of public schools, and other institutions for the intellectual, moral and religious improvement of the rising generation."

This seldom-mentioned ordinance that accompanied the new Texas Constitution was, of course, a breath-taking, eye-popping irony. It had only been a decade since Texas had proclaimed independence from Mexico in significant part because Mexico had changed the constitution and colonization laws of 1824. The 1835 Goliad Declaration of Independence thundered, "Our lands, peaceably and lawfully acquired, are solemnly pronounced the subject of indiscriminate forfeiture, and our estates of confiscation. The laws and guarantees under which we entered the country as colonists, tempted the unbroken silence, sought the dangers of the wilderness, braved the prowling Indian, erected our numerous improvements, and opened and subdued the earth to cultivation, are either abrogated or repealed, and now trampled under the hoofs of the usurper's cavalry."

It must be said that there are many distinctions to be drawn between Mexico's renunciation of colonization and that of Texas. Foremost among them is that Texas dispossessed only the contractors—the empresarios—and attempted to protect the vested rights of the colonists themselves (but did bar new settlers' claims). Still, the comparison is not entirely flattering to Texas, and the consternation of Meusebach and the verein must have been manifest and magnificent.

Yet Meusebach still plunged forward, establishing Fredericksburg in mid-1846 and exploring north of the Llano with surveyors in early 1847. His actions seem inexplicable in retrospect, especially considering the terrible epidemics of the winter of 1846-1847 and the apparent termination of further colonization.

But Meusebach did not stop. His expedition north of the Llano consumed more than two months. To the relief of the worried populace of Fredericksburg, Meusebach and his companions rode into the village on March 7, accompanied by Comanche Chief Santa Anna, his family and a small entourage. Soon the Germans were enjoying remarkably good relations with the Comanches. The final treaty was inked in May as intended, and a brisk trade in buffalo hides and deer skins developed. Comanches came and went in Fredericksburg without incident.

The winter rebellion hung heavy over Meusebach's head as he dutifully carried on through spring and into summer. Count Castell, Philip Cappes and Friedrich Schubert continued their machinations, maneuvering to put Cappes in Meusebach's place. But that was not to be.

In Germany, a group of idealistic young men had organized themselves as *Die Vierziger*—the Forty-ers, or just the Forty—in the first days of 1847. Most were students at the universities of Giessen and Heidelberg or at the industrial school in Darmstadt. They had become interested in the United States through the writings of Prince Solms and the stories brought to them by one of their number, Hermann Spiess, who had toured the United States beginning in 1845, visiting New Braunfels briefly in the spring of 1846. After his return to Germany, he—along with Ferdinand Herff and Gustav Schleicher—had assembled the cadre of bright young men that became the Forty. Taking to heart French social critic Charles Fourier's advocacy of community phalansteries to maximize cooperation and personal fulfillment in accord with each person's "natural talents, passions and inclinations," their plan was to establish a socialistic colony in Wisconsin.

In their dream of founding a utopian community, the Forty were also following tenets espoused by Etienne Cabet, author of *Voyage en Icarie*, who envisioned an all-encompassing elected government that would control business and society, with only the family remaining as an independent social unit. In 1848 Cabet and his fellow Icarians would found a short-lived utopian colony in Denton County, Texas, then retreat to New Orleans, only to venture forth again in a futile attempt to revive the abandoned town of Nauvoo, Illinois, as yet another utopian commune. Nauvoo had been abandoned because it was the town founded by Mormons who had sought refuge from persecution in Missouri. It was from Nauvoo that the Mormons fled to Utah.

When Count Castell learned of the intentions of Spiess's idealistic young German academics, he sent an envoy, offering to fund the group with $12,000 in cash, tools, livestock, wagons and provisions for one year. In return, the Forty were to abandon their Wisconsin plans and establish a settlement of two hundred families within the Fisher-Miller Grant. The Forty embraced their sponsor and a new effort to colonize the grant began.

Spiess and Herff preceded the others, landing in New York in April 1847 and continuing to Galveston and Carlshaven. There, Herff remained on the coast to make arrangements for the remaining members of the Forty (who had dwindled to thirty-three). Spiess continued on to New Braunfels. In his pocket he carried a letter from Count Castell on behalf of the verein, naming him as commissioner general to succeed Meusebach.

Meusebach formally resigned and transferred the office of commissioner general to Spiess on July 20, 1847. Eight days earlier he had tidied up one last matter, writing Schubert that "when an honorable man can no longer feel agreement with the principles of his superior, employment will cease.... Since that is the condition now, you are relieved of your position as of this day."

Schubert left New Braunfels for Nassau Farm, declaring his refusal to give up his position. He already held a lease on Nassau Farm (part of the arrangement under which he took leadership of Fredericksburg) and apparently intended to cement his control of that asset. Spiess was concerned, and undertook to force Schubert from Nassau. After negotiations broke down, a pre-dawn melee ensued in which two men were killed. Spiess and his men were charged with murder, tried and acquitted.

Thirty-one Germans described by New Braunfels merchant Viktor Bracht as "cultured, wealthy and respectable-looking young people from Darmstadt" came ashore at Galveston in the late spring of 1847, where Herff joined them. In Galveston they also added a new member—one Julie Herf (no relation to Herff), who possessed domestic abilities that the distinguished young men lacked, and who spoke fluent English. Among the others, only Herff had a passable grasp of the language. Their ranks included seven lawyers, two physicians, two architects, a musical instrument maker, a hotel keeper, a brewer and a theologian. More obviously practical vocations belonged to a miller, a blacksmith, a butcher and a handful of mechanics and carpenters.

But you never know what skills might come in handy. The Forty had arranged to take a reputable schooner from Galveston to Carlshaven, but the army commandeered the ship and they were obliged to board an older, disheveled craft. On the first night at sea, the captain and crew got drunk. In no mood to observe the niceties of seamanship, they lashed the ship's wheel to a sea chest, went below and left the schooner to fend for itself. The craft ran aground. Under the pretense of going for help, the crew attempted to abandon ship. They were stopped by Ferdinand Herff at gunpoint, but were not permitted to resume their duties. One of the Forty by the name of Kappelhoff was a ship's carpenter—a trade not in overwhelming demand on the Texas frontier—and was capable of making temporary repairs and sailing the ship to Carlshaven.

When these trailing members of the Forty came ashore in July, they were met by twenty-four wagons pulled by oxen, arranged by Meusebach. The Germans' baggage and freight turned out to be so immense, however, that they were compelled to purchase additional wagons and teams upon arrival. In addition to copious supplies brought from Darmstadt, the imaginative young men had purchased equipment and supplies in Hamburg and Galveston, including complete machinery for a mill, a kennel full of dogs and numerous barrels of whiskey. One young member of the party (fourteen at the time) later proclaimed, "We came prepared to conquer the world."

Burdened by their dogs, equipment, supplies, whiskey and dreams, the idealistic entourage took four weeks to reach New Braunfels. Louis Reinhardt, the young man who felt ready to conquer the world, characterized the journey as "relatively uneventful. We sang, drank and enjoyed ourselves the whole way as only the German student knows how to do. We lived like the gods on Olympus…."

The Darmstadters were surprised by what they encountered on the plains of Texas. "Instead of my expectation of pathless direction to be followed by compass," marveled Friedrich Schenck, "we found a road as well traveled and good as only occasionally an unpaved road is at home. Instead of uninhabited wilderness, we found friendly farms from six to ten miles apart, and instead of suspicious, dangerous people, we found friendlier persons than among us at home."

The Forty were delayed in New Braunfels while a few members recovered from disease and injury. This also gave them time to divert Spiess and Herff to procuring a farm—dubbed the Darmstadter Farm, naturally enough—on Comal Creek, less than three miles from New Braunfels. As Friedrich Schenck put it, they established the farm "so as not to waste this time idly, and in any case, should our Llano expedition fail in this year to establish a secure base." According to Schenck, "We quickly erected a neat log cabin and laid out a garden which is already providing admirable vegetables. We planted the grapevines we had brought along, and for the most part they are flourishing and greening happily in the beneficent sun of the southern heavens."

Once they were healthy and organized, the gentlemen of the Forty, under the direction of guide Emil Kriewitz, ventured forth to Fredericksburg and beyond, fulfilling their promise to the verein to enter the Fisher-Miller Grant before making permanent camp. Difficult trails and the delays inherent in driving a herd of cattle slowed the journey; they did not arrive until late September. They chose a spot on the north bank of the Llano where Elm Creek joins. In the shade of a gigantic live oak they circled their wagons, erected a large tent, positioned a cannon for defense and posted a guard. Then, formalities out of the way, they mixed up a punch and partied until the wee hours.

The Baron Emil von Kriewitz de Czepry, the Forty's guide, was an unusual character. He had been part of Meusebach's expedition that resulted in a Comanche peace in March 1847. Since that time Kriewitz had apparently been a sort of German Indian agent, living among the tribe. He had gone native, indistinguishable in appearance from a Comanche. Historian Moritz Tiling described Kriewitz as someone who was "very prudent and circumspect in his dealings with the different Indian tribes and secured the friendship of their chiefs for the German pioneers." But Louis Reinhardt remembered details that make it appear that Kriewitz may have been as much captive as agent. He said that Kriewitz was among the Comanches "according to the wish of the savages themselves. But the Indians did not trust him, looking upon him as a spy…." According to Reinhardt, when Meusebach, Spiess and Coll met with Comanche Chief Santa Anna in New Braunfels in the late summer of 1847 to confirm permission for German colonists to cross the Llano and settle, Kriewitz was present on the natives' side of the table and was unable to communicate directly with the Germans. He passed a note under the table, indicating that he would try to escape and report to New Braunfels. He did so a few days later. Santa Anna came looking for Kriewitz in New Braunfels, but he hid out for three days. It was only a short time later that he led the Forty to their new home, apparently risking dangerous personal entanglement with the Comanches.

The Forty—among the first colonists to attempt settlement above the Llano—built a temporary shelter of posts and beams covered with grass, measuring forty feet by twenty-two feet. It was furnished as a barracks, with rows of cots. Each colonist kept his duffel bags, firearms, toilet articles and a chair next to his cot. A lean-to on the side of the barracks served as Julie Herf's kitchen and dining quarters. Friedrich Schenck was proud of their accomplishments: "Our small company, after only a few weeks, has already accomplished more than the fifteen hundred emigrants in Fredericksburg have in a year's time. We have already such certain assurance of a rich harvest that several offers of credit have been given to us. That which hundreds of persons had previously not wanted to undertake, we few have done, and our example has taught the other emigrants that organized communal work produces faster results than divided effort."

Writing in November 1847, after only six weeks on the Llano, Schenck spoke glowingly of their life. "This land, upon which a few weeks ago only buffalo, lions, wolves and panthers confronted each other, is being transformed into a harmonious countryside. White tents and straw-roofed huts, the solid log cabin with warming fireplace and kitchen amply provided with venison and steaming pots, the vigorous songs of the hearty workers, the bawling of the herds, and the neighing of our horses, the wakeful barking of the dogs, and the crowing of the cocks calling to early work—they have all given the stranger a new home."

The two doctors among the Forty proved valuable, though one would surely have been enough. Dr. Ferdinand Herff became accustomed to dealing with the local natives, and eventually learned both the Comanche and Apache dialects. His reputation was made after only a few weeks at the colony, when a Comanche appeared with an advanced case of cataracts, asking to be healed. Herff had—amazingly—brought the most advanced ophthalmologic instruments with him from Germany, and had performed cataract surgery several times in Europe. But never without professional support and, needless to say, never in the wilderness.

Fearful that the Comanches would blame him if the native went untreated, Herff decided to risk an operation. Local anesthetics had not been discovered yet, so the doctor was obliged to use ether to incapacitate the patient. This created a problem since, according to Herff, "one of the outstanding essentials in a cataract extraction is adequate light. In those primitive days the only forms of artificial illumination were candlelight and kerosene lamps whose rays were intensified by magnifying lenses. But … the flammable nature of ether definitely contraindicated its use anywhere near a naked flame, so the only solution was to perform the surgery out of doors, aided by the sunlight."

Herff wasn't concerned about the risk of infection from working outside, because the causes of infection weren't understood at the time. He was, however, a clean and tidy man, and insisted on "a clear, entirely cloud-free, dustless, windless, insectless day. Surrounding the operating group stood a dozen of the Forty with palm leaf fans to keep the flies away."

Knowing that the eye is kept clean by a free flow of tears, it seemed logical to Herff to irrigate the eyes with water before surgery. Using his crude 160-power microscope, he had determined that the rainwater from their cistern, though mineral-free, was "infested with numerous small moving bodies which I called animalcules, [so] I decided to clear the substance by boiling it." This purified water was used to flush the eyes for surgery.

The crude, daring procedure was a success. The patient was ebullient, thanking the doctor effusively and promising to bring him a special present—a woman. Herff took a lot of ribbing from his compatriots over the promise, until the Comanche appeared three months later with a teenage Mexican girl. The native handed over his captive, grunted, walked away and was never seen again. Julie Herf took the "gift" under her wing; years later she became the wife of Hermann Spiess, organizer of the Forty and the last colonial commissioner of the Adelsverein.

By the end of the year, and still in a communal mindset, the pioneer Darmstadters had constructed a large adobe house that they covered with thousands of hickory shingles split on site. The structure was warmed by a fireplace twelve feet wide, and was capped by a decorative weathervane designed by one of the retinue's artists.

This was the first permanent structure in the Darmstadter Colony, which had for its motto "friendship, freedom and equality." The village was officially named "Bettina," after Bettina von Arnim, a popular German author and social activist of the 1830s. She had inflated what was apparently a casual relationship with Johann Wolfgang von Goethe into a book of somewhat fantasized intimate letters between them, provoking the ire of Goethe's wife. So it is not unfair to label her controversial.

Bettina was not much more enduring than the Icarian utopian colony founded by Etienne Cabet. Ferdinand Herff returned to Germany to marry, as did Friedrich Schenck; in their absence, the communal spirit waned. By the summer of 1848 it "broke into pieces like a bubble," in Reinhardt's words. The reasons were simple and predictable. "Since everybody was to work if he pleased and when he pleased, the result was that less and less work was done as time progressed. Most of the professional men wanted to do the directing and ordering, while the mechanics and laborers were to carry out their plans. Of course, the latter failed to see the justice of this ruling, and so no one did anything."

Gustav Schleicher, another of the Forty, puts it more succinctly than Reinhardt: "the bigger the men, the more they talked, the less they worked and the more they ate."

The Forty drifted their separate ways. Once cracks began appearing in Bettina, some backtracked to the Darmstadter Farm near New Braunfels, where they made yet another failed attempt at a utopian commune. Spiess continued with the work of the verein. Other members figured in the founding of Comfort and other Hill Country towns.

Perhaps because of his involvement with the Darmstadter Colony at Bettina, and despite the verein's financial troubles and the imbroglio at Nassau Farm, Hermann Spiess remained focused on settling the Fisher-Miller Grant for the verein. This would not be easy. Fredericksburg itself was beyond the effective limits of civilization in Texas, and its existence was tenuous; the fate of the Darmstadter Colony demonstrated the optimism of believing that Fredericksburg (or the more distant New Braunfels) could support more colonies even further beyond the Llano.

After an expedition to inspect the San Saba region in early 1847, New Braunfels merchant Viktor Bracht wrote Germany, saying, "The great distance from the sea would prevent me from establishing a permanent home beyond the Llano. I would rather own a single acre in the immediate vicinity of human culture and progressive civilization than to own a whole square mile in that uninhabited and almost inaccessible wilderness."

Even today it is apparent that the land at the Llano and beyond is entirely different from that in the Hill Country to the south. North of Fredericksburg there is a great savannah where Cherry Spring and Loyal

Valley were settled. Hills that seem more like buttes rim the valley. The vegetation turns more to cactus and mesquite. The Llano is a beautiful river, but it is quite different from the Guadalupe. No giant cypress trees line its banks. It flows across a plain, exposed to the sun, with willows, mesquite and grasses along the edge. There are oak and cedar, but they are scattered. Even more so than the rest of the Hill Country, the land near the Llano is for grazing, not farming, and life is not nearly so idyllic as along the spring-fed creeks in the wooded valleys to the south.

Nevertheless, from the time he first found a ford across the Llano, Meusebach had meant to establish a town there. To be called Castell, it was at Catfish Ford, where the Pinta Trail crossed the river. Spiess carried Meusebach's plans to fruition, directing Emil Kriewitz to again lead colonists into the wilderness. Castell still exists today, though it has relocated from the north side of the river to the south—outside the Fisher-Miller Grant. The original settlers—an uncertain number, probably around fifty but perhaps as many as two hundred at some point—were provided wagons, tools, tents and provisions from the dwindling resources of the verein. A plan for communal cooking and housekeeping fell apart quickly; by 1848 each family had a thatch-roofed log cabin and ten acres of land.

A traveler through the hamlet in 1850 found only nine families living among twenty-six cabins, but there are signs that Castell surged back again. In partnership with Emil Kriewitz, Franz Kettner opened a general store there in 1853. Kettner saw advantages in being on the frontier, where "grain and sweet potatoes are sold at very high prices. All the farmers around here are well-off and have enough money."

"My main occupation now," wrote Kettner to his family, "is the store, but for relaxation I go fishing. Our river, the Llano, is so very full of fish that you could not imagine it. Many times I have caught thirty to forty pounds of fish in two hours, so much that we cannot stand to look at, much less eat, any more fish for a week." An optimist, he noted that "the old Spanish silver mine has not been found yet, but soon will be."

Eventually, Indian troubles drove Kettner out of Castell. By 1855 he had sold his house on the Llano and was living in Fredericksburg. He served briefly as the Gillespie County Sheriff in 1858 and 1859, then—the dangers of the frontier having subsided somewhat—he returned to Castell. Remarkable Emil Kriewitz was still residing there, serving as Llano County Justice of the Peace and Castell postmaster before his death there at age eighty.

A few miles downstream of Castell, Emil Kriewitz planted the village of Leiningen. Little is known of Leiningen, except that it no longer exists. The same is true of Schoenburg and Meerholz—two other attempts to settle verein colonists along the north bank of the Llano. Meerholz never really took root at all, because the location lacked adequate timber for construction. Ironically, "Meerholz" is a German homonym for "more wood."

Though the peace treaty that John Meusebach reached with the Comanches is a historical landmark for German settlement of the Hill Country, Franz Kettner's experience is only part of abundant evidence that Comanche problems played a part in the demise of the settlements along the Llano. When John Bartlett rode to West Texas in 1850 in his capacity as Commissioner of the United States and Mexican Boundary Commission, he reported that Castell and the other Llano settlements were already in a precarious condition because of repeated Comanche attacks. Ferdinand Herff, while back in Germany in 1849, painted a rosier picture, referring to the towns as "originally destitute, now well-established settlements on the Llano." Herff was a booster of German settlement in Texas, so his prose was naturally optimistic, but even he allowed that the Llano villages (not his Bettina, certainly, but the other villages) had Indian problems: "When the Indians appeared to menace our settlements that lay beyond the military border, the majority sought aid with the minority, and our [Bettina] homes became for several nights the sanctuary for our six-times more numerous neighbors. Only our persuasion and support succeeded in keeping the colonists, so boastful before but so despairing during the danger, from moving back to the lower settlements behind the military frontier."

In the end, the clusters of settlers along the Llano proved too remote to succeed. The Fisher-Miller Grant was, as it always had been, beyond the limits of practical settlement. Whether it was due to Comanche pressure, crop failure, logistical difficulties or some other cause, the towns struggled, and then all but the durable Kriewitz's Castell vanished.

Together with the Darmstadter Colony at Bettina, these four pitiful, ephemeral hamlets were the verein's only official effort to settle within the Fisher-Miller Grant. Under the circumstances, it was audacious and inadequate. Four little clusters of cabins just a few hundred feet inside the boundary of the grant. A mockery of the verein's grand plans and promises. A futile colonial gasp of the dying verein.

In the last days of 1847, while the Nassau Farm murder charges were still pending, Spiess announced to the colonists that the verein would curtail its activities. The capitalization of the society was, as it always had been, absurdly inadequate. Surveying expenses had mounted to $80,000. The cost of founding and supporting New Braunfels and Fredericksburg was substantial. Repeated delays and difficulties had strained the treasury. The verein was incapacitated. Verein offices at Fredericksburg and Carlshaven were shuttered. Verein livestock and wagons were auctioned to raise money. Surveying of homesites and ten-acre farms for colonists continued in Fredericksburg and New Braunfels, but further efforts to expand into the Fisher-Miller Grant were abandoned. Bankruptcy loomed. Though it struggled to stay alive through the bankruptcy, in practical terms the verein had ceased to exist. The colonists were left to their own devices.

Conditions on the frontier remained daunting. Julius Splittgerber, a Fredericksburg resident, tells us about it: "The winter of 1847-48 was a time of great suffering for us. Sickness swept people away in great numbers, chiefly scurvy and its consequences, because the colonists' diet consisted chiefly of bread and meat and no vegetables. Without money, medicines were not to be had, and even with money they were difficult to obtain. Many of the colonists went to the Guadalupe to make and sell shingles. Others went to San Antonio and Austin to find work and earn some money to provide the necessities for their families. A cart drawn by oxen was busy all day carrying corpses to the burial ground and for a long time old Mr. Ludolph Meier was busy all day opening and closing graves."

Chapter Six
Beyond Colonization

The first Germans in the Texas Hill Country were economic refugees spawned by the German political and social unrest of the 1830s. The Adelsverein, reacting to circumstances in Europe, meant to export proles and peasants to a better life while implanting an improved political state (and a potential trading partner) in a new land; for at least some Adelsverein members, an unstated ambition was to carve a German colony out of the Republic of Texas.

The Forty followed. Though few in number, their impact was significant and they brought with them a more intense political and social philosophy. More than the Adelsverein's organizers, they valued individual freedom and had an idealistic view of the potential for a new society in a new land, viewing the world through the communal lenses of Saint-Simon, Fourier and Cabet. In contrast to how twentieth century communism evolved, however, these idealists saw society as capable of self-governance without central authority. Their communism was a benign, rational, free-will society of people contributing according to their abilities and interests. These were top-down utopian socialists of the French stripe, not bottom-up, revolutionary, class-struggle communists of the Karl Marx school.

In the Hill Country, the political and social experiments of the colonists and the communalists did not turn out well. The Adelsverein's naively conceived scheme collapsed under the economic realities of frontier settlement. The Forty's commune at Bettina foundered on the most basic elements of human nature. But these failures were not the end of German settlement in the Texas Hill Country. In a way, they were only the beginning, for once Germans were free of the expectation of free land within the Fisher-Miller Grant, once they were free of the notion that the Adelsverein would support them in some way, once they had only themselves to rely on (and once many of them realized that they were stuck in Texas without the means to return to Germany), their horizons expanded and they sought new ways to become successful settlers.

New Braunfels and Fredericksburg would endure and eventually flourish without the verein. Survivors of Bettina, Castell, Leiningen, Schoenburg and Meerholz would find better places in the Hill Country to take up residence. And there would be new arrivals: the Adelsverein issued its dying gasps just as an abortive 1848 Revolution began in Germany. When the revolt sputtered to an end, those who had advocated radical change found themselves subject to threats (and the reality) of imprisonment or death, and so another wave of German intellectuals found its way to Texas, chasing dreams of liberty, equality and an idyllic life.

Nicolaus Zink is a vivid example of how original German settlers dispersed from New Braunfels and Fredericksburg through the Hill Country, and how they were joined by the Forty-Eighters. Zink was the controversial engineer who organized the first wagon trains from Carlshaven to New Braunfels. He built the stockaded Zinkenburg in New Braunfels and surveyed the town, but fell into disfavor with Prince Solms. In the fall of 1847 a New Braunfels jury granted his wife (Louise, the first of three) a divorce because Zink "lived and lives in adultery and has abused and ill-treated and abandoned" her. Louise got the house, the furniture and five hundred dollars. Zink left town.

Between New Braunfels and Fredericksburg, along the Pinta Trail where it crossed the valley of the Guadalupe River, lay the beautiful dale of the twin Sister Creeks. Zink was enchanted with the location and decided to settle there, purchasing 1280 acres in September 1847 and immediately deeding the land over to his mistress, Elizabeth Mangold, who would become his second wife in January (and who would divorce him for abandonment in late 1865). The new Zink farm was in the sweet spot of the valley, straddling the Sister Creeks and abutting the Guadalupe. There, the Zinks established their homestead, building a large log cabin.

Ottomar von Behr became Zink's neighbor, purchasing 1129 acres just across the Guadalupe in February 1848. Behr had been friends in Germany with Bettina von Arnim, for whom the Darmstadter Colony was named. He was also close to Hermann Spiess, who spearheaded the Forty. Spiess and Behr had both been in Texas in 1846, and then had returned to Germany together before traveling back to Texas separately. Behr had penned a book titled *Good Advice for Emigrants to the United States with*

Special Reference to Texas, and it was being published in Leipzig at about the time that he settled into Sisterdale. In it, Behr described himself as a "practical farmer." Behr was thirty-three years old, and was accompanied in Sisterdale by his future wife Louisa, twenty-five; by the time of the 1850 census there were three children in the Behr household, and another would arrive soon.

    The third settler in Sisterdale was Frederick Holekamp, who purchased a little more than fifty-five acres from Zink in November 1848. Holekamp and his wife Bettie Wilhelmine were, like Zink, among the first Adelsverein colonists to come ashore at Carlshaven. They had established their initial home in New Braunfels, where the first of their seven children was born. They relocated to Fredericksburg before moving to Sisterdale. After only fourteen months they sold their Sisterdale farm to Ernst Kapp. They had similarly brief stays in San Antonio and New Braunfels before settling near Comfort in 1854.

    Zink likewise left Sisterdale early. Elizabeth and he sold their holdings to Edward Degener in November 1850 and returned to Fredericksburg to operate a grist mill on Baron Creek. Zink would end up in the Comfort area the year before the Holekamp family arrived there.

    Without meaning to slight the Zinks and Holekamps, it is fair to say that Sisterdale became much more interesting after their departure. Adding two Forty-Eighters—Edward Degener and Ernst Kapp—to the mix drastically changed the tiny cluster of farms. Behr, Degener and Kapp were all well-bred intellectuals, cut from much the same cloth as the members of the Forty. With their presence, and with the arrival of more Forty-Eighters, including August Siemering, Edgar von Westphalen, Julius Dresel and his brothers, Sisterdale became a center of freethinking and rose to the status of a Latin settlement.

    Freethinkers were committed to a secular, severely rational view of the world, unencumbered by traditional strictures, unfettered by past practice. Individuals sometimes thought of as freethinkers include Thomas Paine, Bertrand Russell, Isaac Asimov, Charles Darwin, Clarence Darrow and Albert Einstein, but there is no official certification of who is a freethinker and who is not; the label can be pinned on any dedicated rational thinker who is also an agnostic, atheist or religious skeptic. Today's secular humanists look very much like freethinkers. In the nineteenth century, freethinkers were likely to condemn hereditary monarchies and slavery and to advocate separation of church and state, Darwinian evolution, women's suffrage and the rights of the individual.

In 1853 the remarkable traveler, writer, journalist, naturalist, abolitionist and landscape architect Frederick Law Olmsted stayed in Sisterdale while journeying through Texas. Edward Degener hosted Olmsted in a cabin built six years earlier by Nicolaus Zink. Olmsted said that Degener had two sons named Hugo and Hilmar, and "regretted that he could not give them all the advantages of education that he had himself had. But he added that he would much rather educate them to be independent and self-reliant, able and willing to live by their own labor, than to have them ever feel themselves dependent on the favor of others. If he could secure them here minds free from prejudice which would entirely disregard the conclusions of others in their own study of right and truth, and spirits which would sustain their individual conclusions without a thought of the consequences, he should be only thankful to the circumstances that exiled him [from Germany]." That, in a nutshell, is freethinking. Sadly, in the case of Hugo and Hilmar Degener, freethinking would lead to tragedy. We will get to that in due time.

A cluster of freethinkers does not necessarily make a Latin settlement. Comfort, for example, was known as a center of freethinking, but was never a Latin settlement. Some people consider Bettina a Latin settlement, but the Forty were not considered a group of freethinkers. Latin settlements existed across the United States, wherever German immigrants were to be found. They were akin to intellectual vereins that formed themselves into communities. Groups of educated, affluent Germans—the type that might be found among the Forty or the Forty-Eighters or in leadership positions with the verein—would gather into small villages committed to intellectual freedom and excellence. Residents would spend hours in reading, study, discussion and argument—often in Latin, thus the name.

Moritz Tiling, in his book *The German Element in Texas*, describes how Sisterdale comported itself: "a library of the ancient and modern classics was to be found in almost every house and the latest products of literature were eagerly read and discussed at the weekly meetings of these gentlemen farmers at the school house. It sometimes occurred at these meetings that Comanches stood listening gravely at the open door, while one of the Latin farmers was lecturing on the socialistic theories of St. Simon or Fourier."

Ottomar von Behr seems to have been the intellectual anchor of Sisterdale, closely linked to Kapp and Degener. In addition to pondering the great questions of the universe, Behr raised sheep, maintained a lending library and served as justice of the peace. Olmsted was there when Behr interrupted his work on a meteorological table to tend to judicial duties: fixing the value of a dog that had been shot and making peace between the parties. Staying for dinner, Olmsted reported, "His house was the very picture of good-nature, science and the backwoods. Romances and philosophies were piled in heaps in a corner of the logs. A dozen guns and rifles and a Madonna in oil, after Murillo, filled a blank on the wall. Deerskins covered the bed, clothes hung about upon antlers, snakeskins were stretched to dry upon the bedstead, barometer, whisky, powderhorns, and specimens of Saxony wool occupied the table."

John Bartlett, the United States and Mexican Boundary Commissioner, visited Behr's farm on his way to the Rio Grande in 1850 and, "while we were listening to the conversation of our friends, a tame peccary [javelina] thrust his long nose against me to receive my caresses, much as a faithful dog would. But the propensities of the swinish family, to which the peccary is closely allied, were so strongly exhibited in this specimen, that I could only gratify his affection for me by rubbing his back with a stick, which seemed to afford him all the pleasure he desired."

Life in Sisterdale was eclectic: high intellectualism and Comanches; meteorological journals and snakeskins; Madonnas and javelinas. Olmsted reported an evening of "waltzing to the tones of a fine piano and music of the highest sort, classic and patriotic" at the Degener home, where he enjoyed a supper of wild turkey. His midday dinner at Behr's farm was Texan of cornbread and frijoles, with coffee served in tin cups, but the salt was Attic, and the talk was worthy of golden goblets."[1]

Ernst Kapp, who bought Holekamp's farm, certainly added to the mix at Sisterdale. While a professor of cultural geography in Westphalia, Kapp published a liberal treatise titled "The Despotic Constitution and the Free Constitution" that compared despotic governments to megamachines that absorbed citizens into their machinery. As his later writings revealed, Kapp thought that the contrast between natural organisms and machines

---

[1] "Attic salt," is an old expression meaning refined, artful wit.

translated to societies: despotism is mechanistic and contrived, freedom is organic and natural. For expressing ideas of this sort he was arrested and jailed in Germany. As soon as he was released, he fled to Texas, bringing his wife Ida and five children to Sisterdale in 1849. He was forty-one when he arrived and faced a complete mid-life makeover, becoming a farmer, sheep man and carpenter. Ida Kapp observed that he "has shown little desire for physical labor when given a job to do, although for his years he shows a remarkable skill and untiring eagerness in cultivating a small plot in our garden given him to till all by himself. However, he insists upon doing it his own way absolutely, which leads me to believe that republican principles, the love of freedom, have already taken root in him."

Kapp also operated a spa called Badenthal, where treatments consisted largely of sitting in the cool, healing waters of the Sister Creeks. Olmsted described him as "a professor who divides his time between his farm and his library. The delicious brook water has been turned to account by him for the cure of disease, and his house is thrown open to patients."

There is a lithograph of Kapp's Sisterdale spa drawn in 1855. Titled "Dr. Ernest Kapp's Water Cure," it shows a gentleman in a high hat and frock coat sitting in a chair, reading a newspaper. The chair has a large ruffle around it to conceal the parts of the reader that are resting in a tub of healing water. Another sketch shows a man sitting with his legs in the running water. There are drawings of an exercise yard, a shower bath, and a man being wrapped in wet sheets. Centered in the lithograph is a drawing of the spa's idyllic setting, with gracious oak trees and orderly rows of crops extending to Sister Creek.

It is possible that royalty may have sat in Kapp's hydrotherapy chair. Moritz Tiling, in describing life at Sisterdale, said that "their social life was most refined and reached its climax when Prince Paul of Wuerttemberg, brother of the reigning King, arrived at Sisterdale ... where he was highly pleased to find real drawing-room conversation on the borders of civilization."

August Siemering, who taught school at Sisterdale during its early years, described the Prince's visit. "Prince Paul of Wuerttemberg had an especially good time. In the cabin that night were Baron von Meusebach and his wife, the countess of Coreth, Herr von Roggenbuch and his wife, and also Herr von Stockmann from Schleswig. It was 'Your Royal Highness' and 'Your Ladyship' all evening. We dyed-in-the-wool republicans began to grow gray over it."

There was an indisputably awkward delicacy to Prince Paul's visit, given that German royalty had jailed many of the Forty-Eighters. As Siemering put it, "the old revolutionaries were in a fix as to how to address the prince, since they did not recognize any title or nobility. One suggested 'Mr. Wuerttemberg,' another 'Mr. Paul.' Eventually, they agreed to call him 'Prince' and this they did. Only the ladies continued to call him 'Your Royal Highness,' and they were always rewarded with a 'Madam.'"

The incongruity of royalty in Sisterdale highlights an important aspect of the republicanism embraced by some Forty-Eighters. These "dyed-in-the-wool republicans" were far from offended by Prince Paul's visit. They were flattered, even honored. These men may have rejected royalty, but they did not reject nobility or social status. Notice that unlike John Meusebach or Ferdinand Herff, Ottomar von Behr did not quickly drop the noble "von" from his name—and notice that August Siemering took the liberty of restoring the "von" to Meusebach. In 1850 it was still entirely possible, without a hint of hypocrisy, for a German nobleman to be against monarchy, in favor of a parliamentary republic and opposed to political participation by the bourgeoisie, proletariat or peasantry. The struggle in Germany in the 1830s and 1840s was to a large extent about whether the nobility—not the populace as a whole—would usurp governance from the crown.

Because of the nobility's rejection of the masses as their equals in any sense, one of the topics likely to be vigorously debated in the Sisterdale schoolhouse was whether the proletariat had any ability to govern themselves. Republicans might argue that the proletariat's condition must be improved through benevolent governance by the noble class. Some who took the French utopian socialist point of view might argue that if society were restructured into ideal communities, then each person could govern himself without central authority. But other utopian socialists—those of the Icarian stripe—would argue that central management of a utopian community by intellectuals and capitalists was essential to maintaining society's balance.

German parlor discussions revealed strong elements of paternalism and condescension. These were people who genuinely pitied the lower classes, and who wanted to improve the underclass condition, but who felt that the nobles' rationality, culture, education and breeding set them permanently apart from those who labored for their bread. A dyed-in-the-wool republican was not necessarily a dyed-in-the-wool egalitarian.

Ernst Kapp's Badenthal spa in Sisterdale. Photograph courtesy of the Boerne Area Historical Preservation Society.

The Forty's Dr. Ferdinand Herff, an honorable nobleman and distinguished Texan by any measure (and a frequent visitor to Sisterdale), had returned to Germany in 1848, believing that Bettina was on its way to success. Unaware of the disintegration of the commune in his absence, he said that it had set an example for the lower-class colonists at Castell and Leiningen. Writing on the topic of government-sponsored emigration of the German proletariat (of the type found among the verein's colonists) to Texas as a way to relieve social pressure in Germany, he said, "The one year which we spent on the Llano has proved to me again how easy it is to awaken the spirit of order and industry even among the most intractable and barbaric people if along with kindly instruction another cultural influence is exerted." He viewed the task before a manager of colonization as "the organization of ignorant and undisciplined masses," and advocated controlling the proletarian colonists by making their first year's access to the colony's food, tools and assistance not a right (as was the case with the Adelsverein) but a privilege doled out only to the industrious. "Some will criticize me and claim that the mere dependence on food and agricultural aid is not sufficient coercion to lead people to industry, discipline and the doing of work organized according to plan; but, in this respect, the many experiences made in Texas have proved sufficiently that a piece of bread, apparently tendered in conjunction with the alluring prospect of early independence, has the greatest effect on people of that kind. It is almost unbelievable what an influence, already shown on the ocean trip, a tasty morsel, a double portion, and the like, has with the steerage passengers; much greater will be the effect of an assured piece of bread for a whole year."

Herff, and the many other nobles who surely agreed with him, were not necessarily wrong on this point, but it does draw a marked contrast with the dreamy idealism that permeated other aspects of their thinking. These were men who stood on lofty heights to debate the best way to help the crude, unruly masses below.

In fairness, however, Herff came to the views quoted above only after witnessing reality on the ground in Texas. He knew something of what he wrote. The behavior of some Adelsverein colonists in Carlshaven, New Braunfels and Fredericksburg could not have been encouraging; tales of drunkenness, disruption and indolence remain to this day. Tighter discipline, closer management and a dose of tough love might have made a big difference in the verein.

Clearly, Herff's first year in Texas stripped him of some of the idealistic notions that originally drove the Forty, even if he did still believe that Bettina would succeed. While in Germany, he complained that the Darmstadt newspaper "has already more than once portrayed me as the preacher of a new Utopia, our society as a kind of partner to Cabet, and Texas as the happy Eldorado of the dreamers and visionaries…. I deem it to be necessary, considering the great fear which many a sincere old fellow undergoes at the mere mention of the words communist, Cabet, Phalanstere, and Icaria, here once more openly and directly to protest against our, or my, participation in such foolish institutions as Icaria and Phalanstere or such equally foolish personalities as Cabet and Fourier. Texas, Iowa or any other state of the Union can never be an Eldorado, an Icaria, for a man who has seen those lands and has become acquainted with their resources as well as the hard work connected with a colonization enterprise."

We can picture Herff, a utopian socialist reformed into an upper-class realist by harsh experience, gathering with elitist republicans and idealistic social utopians in the Sisterdale schoolhouse to debate the future of society in their new land. But what the discussion would have lacked was a Marxist, arguing the inevitability of class struggle, revolution and the rise of communism. As it turns out, though, Sisterdale would not have lacked that element at all, for Edgar von Westphalen might have finished his chores and walked over to join the discussion.

Westphalen and Karl Marx were school chums, having grown up next door to each other. He co-signed some of Marx's manifestoes. His father, the Baron Ludwig von Westphalen, was Marx's mentor, and—though not a communist himself—inspired Marx to explore the leftward margins of political thought. Marx's wife was Westphalen's sister Jenny, and they named their first-born after him. Edgar von Westphalen was not just a Marxist; he was a charter member of the club.

But Westphalen was not truly committed to either Sisterdale or communism. One of Marx's biographers describes Westphalen as "an amiable chump and dilettante with revolutionary inclinations." Another Marx biographer says, "He never became a very reliable supporter [of Marx]. He went overseas and experienced changing fortunes, returned and turned up here and there, a thoroughly wild character whenever he was heard of…."

If anyone in the Westphalen family was a notable political thinker and power player, it was not Edgar but his half-brother Ferdinand, who was a notoriously reactionary Prussian Minister of the Interior. It is said that the fruit never falls far from the tree, but in the Westphalen family some fruit fell off the left side of the tree, some off the right. Edgar von Westphalen would return to Prussia from Texas in 1865 after adding to the remarkable intellectual mix at Sisterdale and witnessing the unrest of the Civil War.

But not all was esoteric political diatribes, sitz baths, frock coats and nobility along the Sister Creeks. Vera Flach, who married a great-grandson of Ernst Kapp, wrote a wonderful book titled *A Yankee in German America*, in which she recounts her acculturation into a German Hill Country family and uncovers some of the Kapp family past. Her family collection includes the dismounted front door to Ernst Kapp's Sisterdale cabin, which was "studded with big iron nails about an inch apart, designed to discourage arrows." There was a long gallery along the front of the house, she reports, that "must have been dark inside, for the windows were very small, but large enough to poke a gun through them at a hostile Indian."

Julius Dresel was one Forty-Eighter and Sisterdale resident who quickly learned about the need for vigilance against Comanches. When he arrived in the dale on Christmas Eve 1848, he immediately visited von Behr. "Otmar's clothes looked neglected. His open forehead proclaimed the candidness of his soul; friendliness and kindness spoke out of his blunt features and the sound of his voice was heartening and sympathetic. He introduced me to the people of the house and to Luise, the housekeeper and governess of his children, later to be his wife, after which we asked and answered questions and talked endlessly of old and new times."

During the afternoon, "Behr's shepherd, a brave hunter from the Harz Mountains, went to the crossing with his rifle, hoping to shoot another turkey for the festival...." Later Dresel heard two shots and laughter, but as the daylight faded and a norther blew in, the shepherd did not return. "Early the next morning the whole settlement was asked to hunt and we found him, stabbed by spears and scalped on the spot where the devils had laughed because he was lame and could not run well."

They buried the shepherd under a pile of rocks. The funeral was pure Sisterdale: at graveside, Dresel met Ferdinand Lindheimer, the New Braunfels naturalist who had traveled with Prince Solms. Lindheimer "had been camping on Behr's farm with his wife, child and sister-in-law and living in a hut made of tree stems and twigs, the width of which was nine feet but which accommodated the whole family."

Dresel's diary tells of a disturbing evening soon after at Frederick Holekamp's farm: "conversation suddenly ceased. Everyone listened—a many-voiced, horrible, long-drawn-out howling sounded dismally through the quiet which had followed the norther. 'The wolves are pulling the shepherd from his grave,' said Holekamp, who understood the sounds of nature well. He then swallowed a drink of whiskey."

Dresel purchased 640 acres of farmland from John James, surveyor and land speculator, in December 1848. The land was on West Sister Creek, just upstream of Nicolaus Zink's farm. Dresel was soon joined by his brothers Emil and Rudolph. A fourth brother, Gustav, had been the verein's representative in Galveston, but caught yellow fever in the fall of 1848. Ferdinand Herff had rushed to Galveston to try to cure him, but he died just two months before his brother Julius came ashore.

Dresel was there when Sisterdale's name was chosen: "Behr and I visited the Kapps, who were already quite comfortable on the hill. After an interesting conversation with the professor about the influence of geographic location on the culture of people, and after Mrs. Kapp had read aloud several poems of Freiligrath's translation of Longfellow's *Hiawatha*, Behr brought the conversation to the naming of the settlement. He thought as long as we already had Bosom Hill, Sister Hills and Twin Sisters, we might as well continue with the feminine gender and call our settlement Sisterdale."

The unusual personalities that made Sisterdale a Latin settlement did not lend themselves to the hard life of farming and, while Sisterdale was intellectually active, it was too small and remote to satisfy ravenous academic curiosity. As Kapp, Degener and Behr anchored the community, others drifted away. Degener's farm suffered foreclosure, and Kapp bought it at auction. Behr returned to Germany for a brief visit, but he fell sick and died there in 1856. Kapp likewise returned to Germany in 1865, meaning to return, but took ill and never did. Though they died far away, both men left legacies—and descendants—in the Hill Country.

Another settler to live for a time near Sisterdale, then depart, was none other than John O. Meusebach. Though he is not usually considered a member of the Latin settlement, it was no coincidence that Meusebach was present when the locals entertained Prince von Wuerttemberg. After ending his relationship with the Adelsverein, Meusebach occupied a farm and an inn at Comanche Spring, outside today's Leon Springs, on the present Camp Bullis Military Reservation. Julius Dresel, who leased the farm and inn from Meusebach in the spring of 1849 (perhaps because Meusebach was traveling too much to attend to the business himself), reported that the place was "the favorite stopping place on the roads from New Braunfels and San Antonio to Fredericksburg." That status may have been in part due to Meusebach's reputation for mixing up a batch of "brandy and curacao, the mixture of which was well-liked for strengthening the heart muscles and was known as Meusebachlein."

In 1851 Meusebach returned to Germany to visit his family, returning with a new commitment to life in Texas. During his sojourn to his homeland he was elected to the Texas Senate, representing Bexar, Comal and Medina Counties. As he settled into permanent residence in Texas, his mind turned to marriage. His first betrothed, Elizabeth von Hardenburg, had died in Germany in 1847 while he was working in Texas for the Adelsverein. Now his eye fell upon seventeen-year-old Agnes von Coreth, daughter of Meusebach's New Braunfels compatriot, Count Ernst von Coreth. Coreth had brought his family to New Braunfels six years earlier. Meusebach had watched young Agnes as she matured.

They married in September of 1852, when Meusebach was forty. Though some accounts say that they settled at Comanche Spring, that is not entirely the case. Between 1849 and 1851 Meusebach had assembled eight hundred acres on the Pinta Trail, a few miles south of Sisterdale, at a spot on Sabinas Creek. In October 1853 he sold Comanche Spring. When Frederick Law Olmsted rode the trail from San Antonio to Sisterdale with Adolph Douai in early 1854, he reported coming over a steep ridge into the Guadalupe River valley and being met by two men in red shirts. One was the teacher at Sisterdale, probably August Siemering. The other was a German baron. In Olmsted's customary way, he does not give the baron's name, but there were only two German barons who ever frequented the Sisterdale area: Meusebach and von Behr. Some say that Edgar von Westphalen was a baron, but that is not clear (though his father Ludwig was a baron). Since Olmsted visited von Behr (whom he called "the judge") after leaving this first baron's farm, and since this baron had a wife and child, which von Westphalen did not, the baron in question is Meusebach.

Meusebach took Olmsted to his new cabin, where his wife and new baby were living in a lean-to until the cabin roof was finished. Olmsted said that the baby was just seven days old and noted that he was three times the size of a German baby of that age. Olmsted probably misunderstood, or perhaps there was a slip in translation: in January of 1854 the couple's first child, Ernst Otfried Meusebach, would have been seven *months* old.

Olmsted traveled to Sisterdale from San Antonio again in March of 1854. This time he took the route via Comanche Spring. He noted that the road was the "old, now disused Fredericksburg Road," and reported that Comanche Spring was in the ownership of "a German stock-farmer with a considerable settlement." Olmsted made no mention of a baron at Comanche Spring, because Meusebach was already living near Sisterdale. (The German stock-farmer was Henry Habermann, to whom Meusebach sold the farm a few months earlier.) Likely it was the opening of a better route to Sisterdale and Fredericksburg that prompted Meusebach to move; his inn at Comanche Spring would no longer have received many visitors, and he might have wanted to build a better house for his new family near his friends at Sisterdale.

While serving as a state senator, Meusebach introduced legislation to provide relief to the Adelsverein colonists who had come to Texas in good faith, only to see lands promised them disappear with the troubled colonization scheme. In 1854 Governor Elisha Pease appointed him commissioner to oversee the process of issuing land scrip to qualified colonists, effectively leaving Meusebach in charge of cleaning up the mess left by the verein. In keeping with the Texas tradition of generosity when it came to land grants, Meusebach's commission ultimately issued rights to over 1.7 million acres of land within the Fisher-Miller Grant.

Meusebach's activity in Texas politics drew him away from his Sisterdale farm and required more time in San Antonio, New Braunfels, Castroville and Austin. Life along the Pinta Trail must have been difficult for a young wife whose husband traveled widely. Meusebach sold his Sisterdale homestead in 1856 and moved to Fredericksburg, where he operated a mercantile business.

When he retired from public life in 1869 Meusebach and his family relocated to Loyal Valley (northwest of Fredericksburg but ironically still short of the Fisher-Miller Grant), where he operated a store and nursery and served as postmaster and justice of the peace. He died there in 1897.

Like Meusebach, most of the founders of Sisterdale soon departed for one reason or another. But unlike Comanche Spring, Sisterdale continues: though freethinkers are scarce, the community still has a few houses, a general store and a post office. Most Latin settlements cannot claim even that degree of survival.

Ferdinand Herff returned from Germany in January 1849 to discover that Bettina had vaporized. Upon arriving in New Braunfels, "to our surprise, we heard that our organization had fallen apart, and this much I could extract from the truths, the half-truths and the malicious stories about how and why this painful end of the organization took place. The story as to what happened is rather complicated and involved and even now I am not quite clear about the role played by Speis and Schleicher [Hermann Spiess and Gustav Schleicher]. All I could find out it that both acted dishonestly and revolting. Speis acted more as a fanatic, whereas Schleicher's motives are plain dishonest."

The Forty's purchase of Darmstadter Farm and the venture at Bettina had not been inexpensive. Even with the cash incentive provided by the Adelsverein, each member of the Forty had been obliged to make a significant investment. It seems that the business affairs of the Forty had been conducted with some similarity to those of the Adelsverein. When financial collapse loomed, Spiess and Schleicher looked out for themselves. As a result, felt Herff, "to receive any moneys it would be necessary to sell the [Darmstadter Farm] which made up our entire investment. This is not possible since as yet no buyer can be found. Speis and Schleicher did not cheat, at least in a legal sense, but those two, who had received the trust of all in every respect, put their own personal gain ahead of that of the organization. They used that trust to obtain moneys through advances and other means. And by such means made a valuable part of the organization's money their own. Those members, however, such as [Wilhelm] Friedrich, [Adam] Vogt, [Leopold] Schultz, etc., who worked hard and in every respect—maybe with some few exceptions—proved to be men of highest character, were left with empty hands." There are indications that the rift between Herff, Spiess and Schleicher eventually healed, but there is no doubt that the end of Bettina was traumatic.

And so Spiess and Schleicher went their own way (Spiess as a New Braunfels businessman, Schleicher as a prominent San Antonio politician, both as pro-Confederacy Germans during the Civil War) and Herff went his (as an eminent surgeon in San Antonio). The other Bettina survivors dispersed, some returning to Germany, others settling elsewhere in the Hill Country.

When lightning rod Nicolaus Zink—who left a trail of lawsuits and foreclosures through the Hill Country—tired of his grist mill in Fredericksburg, he moved to Cypress Creek (sometimes called Cypressville), a dispersed community of about fifty farms along Cypress Creek and the Guadalupe River, west of where Comfort is today. The Schladoer and Wiedenfeld families were the first settlers in Cypress Creek, arriving in 1852. Zink, along with the Boerners, Lindners and Saurs, arrived in 1853, and more followed. Though it never had a townsite, Cypress Creek established a cemetery, shooting club (*schuetzenverein*), militia and school. In the early years there were no churches in Cypress Creek—evidence of the secular freethinking philosophy of many of the first settlers. The farms of Cypress Creek community still exist, but Comfort has become the social and commercial center for the area.

Elsewhere, along South Grape Creek, which flows to the northeast and joins the Pedernales River east of Fredericksburg, paralleling a western branch of the Pinta Trail known as the San Saba Road, was a string of farms that might be thought of as a single community. Within the Grape Creek drainage were two early German social and commercial centers: Grapetown and Luckenbach. Two other erstwhile Grape Creek villages, Blumenthal to the north and Bankersmith to the south, grew slowly and were named after the turn of the century.

Surprisingly, Grapetown's first settler was not a German; he was John Hemphill, who purchased land there in 1848. Grapetown's glory days began in 1860, when Friedrich Wilhelm Doebbler opened a general store and inn. School began in Doebbler's home, and a cattle market developed. Residents in Grapetown and along Grape Creek in that year included families named Toepperwein, Weber, Frantzen, Schumann, Vater, Kleck, Land, Kusenberger, Beckmann, Pehl and Schmidtzinksy. The pinnacle of Grapetown's existence may have been in 1887, when its combined singing club (*gesangverein*) and schuetzenverein, known collectively as the *Eintracht* (Unity) hosted the first annual Gillespie County *Schuetzenfest*, at which 140 kegs of beer were consumed in four days. Grapetown got a boost in 1913 when the Fredericksburg and Northern Railway was built through town, but it declined in 1932 when the local highway was rerouted and faded to a shadow when the railroad ceased running in the 1940s.

Downstream (north) on South Grape Creek, closer to Fredericksburg, was Luckenbach, established by the Engel and Luckenbach families, and others in the 1840s and 1850s. Its name was bestowed by Sophie Engel; while engaged to Albert Luckenbach she became the first local postmaster, giving her naming rights. The town boasted a store, post office and saloon, and later added a dance hall, cotton gin and blacksmith shop. From a peak of perhaps four hundred residents around the turn of the century, it steadily declined to the handful who live there today.

Other small settlements in the German region of the Texas Hill Country that once were but are no more (though towns with their names may survive elsewhere in Texas) include Hortontown, Neighborsville, Comaltown, Yorks Creek, Schumannsville, Santa Clara, Mission Hill, Honey Creek, Waco Springs, Buffalo Springs, Cibolo, Live Oak and Grape Creek. Tiny villages (or road crossings) at Anhalt, Cherry Spring, Welfare, Waring, Center Point, Kendalia, Bergheim and Flugrath still cling to life in the German part of the Hill Country. The once endangered settlements of Spring Branch and Smithson Valley now find themselves becoming suburbs of San Antonio, sprouting high schools and shopping malls. Each of these German-originated towns has a story to tell. Some are farm communities; several sprung up as railroad whistle stops; some were just a good place to put a village.

Kerrville, which still thrives, is a German settlement that transformed itself into something else. Once an American shingle makers' camp, it grew up around a grist and lumber mill founded by Germans Christian Dietert and Balthasar Lich. It is named after James Kerr, a notable early Texian who never lived there. The town owes much of its early success to the enterprises of merchant, rancher and banker Charles Schreiner, who began his empire with the help of Comfort merchant August Faltin. Schreiner was French by birth, though of German stock. With impetus from Schreiner, Kerrville diversified beyond German traditions; he began trading cattle in Grapetown and San Antonio, and by the 1880s and 1890s Kerrville was an important cattle drive station at the junction of the Old Trail (through Castroville, Bandera and Camp Verde) and the Matamoros Trail (Brownsville, George West, San Antonio, Boerne and Comfort). In Kerrville those trails merged to become the Western Trail, also known as the Dodge City Trail or the Fort Griffin Trail. As early as 1879 the Western Trail replaced the Chisholm Trail as the major route to northern cattle markets. The cattle trade changed Kerrville forever; it is now the home of the Cowboy Artists of America Museum.

There are similarities between Kerrville and Bandera, which also began as an American shingle makers' camp and became first a lumber mill, then a cattle trail town (today it calls itself the Cowboy Capital of America). But Bandera's first residents were Upper Silesian sawmill workers recruited in 1855 from a Polish colony in Karnes County. Bandera was founded as a commercial venture by John James (the surveyor and land speculator whom we have met before), John Hunter Herndon (Kentuckian turned Texian, resident of Fort Bend and Brazoria Counties, once the wealthiest man in Texas) and Charles DeMontel (Prussian, real name Carl Scheidemontel, arrived in Texas in 1837, attended the founding of Castro's colony and once commanded a company of Texas Rangers). Despite DeMontel's involvement in the project, Bandera was not part of the German settlement of the Hill Country.

There are other interesting non-German settlements in the portion of the Hill Country that was settled primarily by Germans. The now-gone Curry's (or Currie's or Currey's) Creek settlement, along the watercourse of the same name in northeastern Kendall County, bore some similarity to German farm communities, but it was founded and largely populated by Anglos and lacked the typical German institutions. In 1848 a Mormon splinter group led by Lyman Wight settled at Zodiac Mill near Fredericksburg, then moved to Mormon Mill near Marble Falls, and then to Mormon Camp near Bandera before breaking up.

Charcoal City was an extended string of charcoal-burner camps along the Guadalupe River between Sisterdale and New Braunfels. Lasting from about 1880 to 1919, it had a post office in the Sueltenfuss home, called first the Guadalupe Post Office, then the Schiller Post Office. Though the area was first settled by Germans, and though the Germans first began burning cedar to make charcoal, commercial production and sale of charcoal (mostly to the San Antonio market) arose when Anglos and Tejanos were hired to clear land on a sharecrop basis—they could live on the land and make charcoal in return for clearing the land for the German farmers. Most residents of Charcoal City lived in tents. The camp—and its sub-camps, including String Down, Happy Valley, Richter's Flats, Engel's Crossing and Willke Bend—was not German; it was an overlay upon a German farming community.

We have yet to address Boerne and Comfort, two early post-Adelsverein German settlements. These two distinctly German towns are geographically close and similar in their origins, but have always been fundamentally different.

Chapter Seven
Boerne, Comfort and Comanches

Czech descendant Ludovic Colquhoun was born in Virginia; in 1837 he moved to San Antonio, where he became a successful lawyer and land speculator. He was a senator of the Republic of Texas, a member of the anti-Houston contingent and a part of the faction that favored war with Mexico. Colquhoun became entangled with Samuel Maverick in a dispute over a piece of property on Cibolo Creek. In 1842, while they were in court battling it out, Mexican General Adrian Woll raided San Antonio, taking everyone at the courthouse hostage. They were imprisoned in infamous Perote Prison and released in 1844 upon the intervention of the U. S. Ambassador to Mexico.

Colquhoun returned to his San Antonio land business. By 1845—when the second wave of Adelsverein colonists was still coming ashore at Carlshaven—he and his partner William H. Steele had gathered headright certificates for more than 170,000 acres of land. In that year the partnership dissolved, with the lion's share of the assets going to Colquhoun, and he used one of his certificates—purchased from Maria Ynacia Leal in 1837—to claim two-thirds of a league and two-thirds of a labor of land (more than three thousand acres) on Cibolo Creek, about thirty miles northwest of San Antonio. The land was assigned survey number 180 in Bexar section three.

Colquhoun was savvy. The land was wooded, gently rolling acreage along a particularly beautiful stretch of Cibolo Creek. The Pinta Trail approached from the southeast, ran through the tract to the Cibolo, followed that watercourse westerly upstream for a mile or more, then crossed the creek and jogged back to the northeast through the length of the tract. There was a flat stretch through the center of Colquhoun's land that would make excellent farms.

But it was 1845. There were few settlers in the Hill Country except at the German colony established by the dandified and beleaguered Prince Solms. Colquhoun's purchase was pure speculation. His fellow land speculator and Bexar County surveyor John James acquired the tract from Colquhoun almost immediately after Colquhoun secured a patent from the Republic of Texas. In all likelihood, this transaction was part of a larger arrangement in which James provided surveying services on a great many Colquhoun tracts (for a survey was necessary before a patent could issue) in exchange for a portion of the land surveyed. Given James's extensive travels in the Hill Country, it may be that he—more than Colquhoun—appreciated the strategic location of Survey 180, as evidenced by James's assembly of several more parcels of land in the vicinity.

In May 1850 James sold four hundred acres of land immediately west of Survey 180 to Wilhelm Friedrich for four hundred dollars. Two months later James sold 1330 acres in the southwest corner of Survey 180, adjacent to Friedrich's land, to Christian Hesse. Hesse's land sat where the town of Boerne is today. Friedrich and Hesse had both been part of the Bettina experiment. Soon four other members of the Forty (Christian Flach, Adam Vogt, Leopold Schultz and Phillip Zoeller) joined Friedrich in building a small compound on his property. Their habitations sat on a knoll about a half-mile from Cibolo Creek, near where the Pinta Trail crossed. Darmstadt medical student Friedrich Kramer arrived soon. Almost unbelievably, they were attempting to found another Latin settlement.

The group on Friedrich's farm called their humble camp "Tusculum," after Cicero's country home. We know few specifics about the Texas version of Tusculum except its location. Subsequent owners built new buildings and tore down old ones. A doctor named Crosky, who was also a surveyor and land trader, used a building there during the early twentieth century. A ten-foot-deep excavation by 1960s-era owner Hugh Schwope uncovered stone curbing that once rimmed a Tusculum spring.

Friedrich's ownership of Tusculum lasted eight months; Adam Vogt bought the land from him in January 1851 for sixteen hundred dollars. The fourfold increase in price from Friedrich to Vogt probably reflected the value of improvements made under Friedrich's ownership, and may have included some livestock.

Vogt may have accommodated the idealistic gathering of Darmstadters for a time after he bought the land, but no one claims that Tusculum survived for more than a year or two as a Latin settlement. There is some vagueness about exactly who was present at Tusculum: even though he was nearby, Hesse is not considered a member, because he had his own farm; Boerne businessman Rudolph Carstanjen and Fredericksburg fixture Jacob Kuechler are sometimes said to have been present, but supporting facts are scanty.

Other than their shared intellectual underpinnings, it isn't fair to compare Tusculum to Sisterdale. Tusculum was more of a small Bettina—affluent German idealists camping in the wilderness until reality set in. That element was present in Sisterdale, but there were also committed settlers who bought land, built cabins, plowed rocky ground and raised crops and livestock. And where Tusculum was a compact camp, Sisterdale was a collection of neighboring farms—some quite large—that relied upon each other for support, socialization and protection.

Across the Cibolo from Tusculum, Christian Hesse planned to farm—or possibly develop—his 1330 acres with his brother. His aim was frustrated when his sibling did not come to Texas. Around the time that Tusculum faded, Hesse decided to leave Texas (for Australia, the county records say, but this may be a mis-transcription of "Austria"). Some loose ends had to be cleared up first. He struck a deal in May 1852 recombining his choice tract with John James's land so that they each owned an undivided one-half interest in all of Survey 180. Then he reached an agreement with Gustav Theissen of San Antonio under which Hesse gave his half interest plus $1,140 to Theissen in return for Theissen agreeing to pay off several promissory notes that Hesse had outstanding. Because Hesse was leaving North America, he gave a power of attorney to his fellow member of the Forty, Ferdinand Herff, authorizing him to deliver a deed to Theissen once the loans were paid.

When Theissen bought into Survey 180 in May 1852 he and John James already had an agreement, reached the month before, to divide and sell the land. In July James filed a survey plat laying out Boerne's town lots and outlots (oversized tracts on the periphery of town meant for a farm, not a residence). Circumstances had changed since Ludovic Colquhoun first patented the land. The U. S. Army had built Fort Martin Scott outside of Fredericksburg, securing the road from San Antonio north and opening what would become the Upper Military Road to Fort McKavett, Fort Lancaster, distant Fort Fillmore and El Paso. The road through Boerne was San Antonio's access route to Fredericksburg, New Braunfels, Sisterdale, the fledgling town at Kerrville (then Brownsborough) and all of

West Texas. Boerne was a day's ride north from San Antonio—a stream-crossing where stables, inns, stores and taverns were sure to sprout.

James and Theissen took the initiative to develop Boerne, but it would be a mistake to think of them as the only people who understood the area's potential. Adam Vogt had already settled into some of James's other land. After selling his interest in Tusculum to Vogt, Wilhelm Friedrich stayed in the vicinity and bought more land, including a forty-four-acre outlot in the southwest corner of the Boerne survey. Boerne's Friedrich Creek ran across Friedrich's farm, thus its name. During the Civil War Friedrich was employed by the Confederacy to build and operate a gunpowder plant in San Antonio; he died when it exploded.

John N. Simon Menger, who had just opened a soap and candle factory in San Antonio—its first manufacturing plant—invested in 1280 acres just across Cibolo Creek to the south of town, and sold that tract to Joseph Bergmann in 1853. Bergmann sold off some of the acreage along what became South Main Street and farmed the remainder for many years; he and his wife Teresa raised six children there.

Ferdinand Herff—doctor and member of the Forty—was already investing in the area, purchasing a choice 320 acres on the Cibolo in 1852 and 640 acres just south of the Tusculum site in 1854 (he would split that acreage with Wilhelm Friedrich in 1856). Herff remained a resident of San Antonio, but the Boerne area became his private retreat and a place where he invested heavily, purchasing ten thousand Hill Country acres over time and involving himself in several local businesses.

Boerne was not an instant success, taking more than a decade to show staying power. Early purchasers of town lots from James and Theissen included Johann Burke (1852) and Mathias Baumann (1853). Burke sold his two Boerne lots to Julius Fabra four months after buying them. Fabra farmed and freighted locally. Later generations of the Fabra family were known for their Boerne butcher shop and smokehouse. Mathias Baumann opened a blacksmith shop near where Boerne's Main Street crossed the Cibolo. It was the first business in town.

Early purchasers of Boerne outlots were Patterson D. Saner and August Trefflich, who took title to their land in 1854. Saner had spent his early Hill Country years at the Bandera shingle camp. After arriving in Boerne, he farmed, freighted and involved himself in community affairs, serving over the years as constable, judge, justice of the peace and postmaster.

Trefflich bought his lot for sixty dollars, sold it in 1855 to Andreas Blum for $175, and Blum sold it to William Vogt (no relation to Adam Vogt) in 1856 for two hundred dollars. Vogt and his wife Ernestine had come ashore at Indianola in 1852, and lived in Seguin until buying their Boerne tract from Blum. In 1859 they purchased forty more acres on the edge of Boerne, where they built a one-room log cabin. Then they built another one-room cabin, and then a third. The three sat side-by-side, each with its own entrance but under a common roof, making it an unusual double-dogtrot design that still stands on Boerne's Plant Street.

William Dietert was an important early arrival in Boerne. Hugo Clauss, who was in Boerne almost from the beginning, tells us what change Dietert wrought: "We had to pulverize corn with a hand axe. One could not mill the corn in our coffee grinders because the corn was too hard for that. Then an American joined the settlement and brought with him a metal corngrinder. Now we had corn meal, though it wouldn't be called that today.

"Soon a miller [William Dietert] arrived and built the first flour mill and sawmill on the Cibolo. You could exchange your corn for fine corn flour. What progress for the young settlement, since we now had decent cornbread." Building Dietert's mill involved constructing a dam across the Cibolo for water power, backing the creek up into an attractive mill pond in the center of town.

Clauss also tells us about the (possibly greater) importance of August Staffel, who arrived around 1853. Staffel began Boerne's first store, but it wasn't much. According to Clauss, Staffel had worked as a survey chain man for John James, and as payment for his services took a few town lots, "upon which he built a hut covered with long reeds." Soon Staffel was running a store from his shanty. Clauss says, "Naturally Sundays everybody gathered at August Staffel's, where people hatched plans for the future and told hunting and Indian stories."

"During our meetings we had only Schnapps. The German national drink—beer—was missed very much, as you can imagine. Friend Staffel brewed something out of corn and sugar, etc., which he called beer. For lack of anything better we drank that and smoked a cigar imported by a Mr. Rexroth from Bremen, who had given it to August because it was extremely cheap, or rather August had to take it to satisfy a debt."

The beer drought did not last forever. In 1855 William Menger opened the Western Brewery on Alamo Square in San Antonio. Clauss reported that "although most of us had some doubt that beer could be brewed in Texas, it was welcome news that the brewery was operational and the beer on the market. Friend Staffel brought the first little keg from San Antonio, for testing, he said.

"On Sunday the keg was ceremoniously put on the table, adorned with oak leaves and flowers and tapped. We stood around the small barrel and held a glass of beer after years of deprivation; we sang German songs and danced around the barrel until the litmus test was emptied.

"With this first barrel, we also laid the foundation for the Boerne Gesangverein [singing club], which still exists today."

Clauss was writing in 1882; the Gesangverein—formally organized by Karl Dienger in 1860—endured until 1976. There is an 1860 picture of its twelve members in formal attire. They include such familiar names as Anton Bergmann (son of farmer Joseph Bergmann), William Vogt, William Dietert and his brother Henry Dietert. Also present is Herman Toepperwein, son of Lucian Toepperwein, who settled along Grape Creek; several of the Toepperweins moved to Boerne. Oddly absent is August Staffel, but there is stout, solid Hugo Clauss with a bushy beard and a receding hairline. (Karl Dienger was also the impetus behind formation of the Boerne Village Band, in which the family of Sisterdale's Ottomar von Behr participated.)

The keg of beer that August Staffel imported from San Antonio grew into a Boerne institution—Staffel's Tavern. Clauss said that in early years "every stranger under the straw roof of the Mexican jacal was greeted and strengthened, since in this little store one could get a drink of firewater, the only one between San Antonio and Fredericksburg." Later, when the tavern had added solid walls and a floor, people said that they could set their clocks to noon when Adam Vogt headed to Staffel's to spend the afternoon reading and talking with friends.

The Gesangverein became more than a singing club; it became a gene pool. Anton Bergmann had four sisters. Rosa married William Dietert. Amalie married Henry Dietert. Johanna married Herman Toepperwein's brother Ferdinand. Adelbertha married outside the circle, but her daughter Kathinka married Paul Toepperwein, the brother of Herman and Ferdinand. Why didn't Herman Toepperwein marry a Bergmann? Because he married Jacob Luckenbach's daughter Amalie, from the Grape Creek community. Boerne Gesangverein member and cartwright Henry Wendler married Amalie's sister Pauline Luckenbach. One of their sons,

Henry J. Wendler, married their niece and his cousin Adele Luckenbach. Another son, Adolph Wendler, married Paul Toepperwein's daughter, Wally Bertha Toepperwein, making their children Bergmann-Luckenbach-Toepperwein-Wendlers.

That brief example of local breeding habits, which omits such important intermingled Boerne gene stock as Dieterts, Fabras, Stendebachs, Holekamps and Theisses, only scratches the surface of the tight-knit German community. It leaves out Boerne names that came from Sisterdale, such as the Behrs, and those that struggled to reach Meusebach's New Braunfels before coming to Boerne, such as the Monkens. Even Luckenbach paterfamilias Jacob Luckenbach eventually retired to Boerne, where he lived out his days.

As intricate and interrelated as Boerne's founding family trees are, they are no more so than those that can be found in Fredericksburg, New Braunfels, Comfort or in the tiny villages that still linger at places like Luckenbach, Waring and Center Point. The towns of the German Hill Country remained small, tightly knit and German-speaking for generations after their founding, making them somewhat closed societies.

One point worth noting about Boerne is that it became a German town simply because it was in a predominantly German region. It was not a planned community like Fredericksburg or New Braunfels. It was not a land-grant necessity like Leiningen, Meerholz, Schoenburg or Castell. It was not something that grew out of the social and economic needs of neighboring farms, as did Grapetown or Luckenbach. And it was not a socialist experiment like Bettina or Tusculum: the Boerne townsite was in the hands of land investors long before Tusculum germinated, and Tusculum did not relocate to Boerne—it vaporized. Boerne was a straight-up commercial development driven by Anglo surveyor and land speculator John James.

Which leaves the question of how Boerne got such a fine German name, instead of being called Jamestown or Cibolo Crossing. The answer isn't entirely clear. Ludwig von Boerne never visited the United States. Born Lob Baruch in 1786, he was a German Jew (later baptized as a Lutheran) and a radical Frankfurt political essayist during the early phases of nineteenth-century political discontent in Germany. He was cynical: "The secret of power is the knowledge that others are more cowardly than you are." He was allegorical: "In a rolling ship, he falls who stands still, not he who moves." And he was romantic: "Nothing is permanent but change,

nothing is constant but death. Every pulsation of the heart inflicts a wound, and life would be an endless bleeding, were it not for Poetry. She secures to us what Nature would deny; a golden age without rust, a spring which never fades, cloudless prosperity and eternal youth." He was popular with the Forty-Eighters and remains a respected German literary figure to this day.
We don't know enough about Boerne promoter Gustav Theissen to judge whether he was a fan of Ludwig von Boerne. He appears to be the "Mr. T" mentioned by Olmsted as having the uppermost Sisterdale farm on the Guadalupe. Olmsted says that Theissen had been a member of the Frankfurt parliament. We know that he and Joseph Deutz opened a hardware store on the northwest corner of San Antonio's main plaza in 1856. He was a freighter; his wagons worked the Chihuahua Trail from Indianola through San Antonio to Ciudad Chihuahua. He was an organizer of the German social club and theater in San Antonio called the Casino Club, and was one of the founders of San Antonio's German-English School. He appears to have left Texas for New York during the run-up to the Civil War. It was probably he who chose the name Boerne, perhaps in consultation with the members of the Forty lingering at Tusculum. Hugo Clauss said that was the case. In all likelihood, giving the town a German name was considered a good marketing move, considering the ethnicity of most potential buyers in the area.

It needs to be said about Boerne, and about the Hill Country generally, that not all German immigrants were thrilled by what they found.

Storekeeper and tavern owner August Staffel was accompanied to Texas by his brother Heino and Heino's wife Adeline, who tried Boerne but ended up settling in Leon Springs to the south. Adeline referred to her new home as "detestable Texas." The Staffels arrived in 1852 and did not have a good trip from Indianola (as Carlshaven was already being called) to New Braunfels. After chronicling the thunderstorms, broken axles and cold weather, she reported that "we seldom saw a pretty view, an attractive house or a green meadow. Everything remained barren and dreary until we reached New Braunfels, which lies at the foot of some hills, with a clear stream flowing below. We did not like New Braunfels at all, and remained there only two days until a teamster took us to San Antonio."

William Vogt and Herman Toepperwein observe the fiftieth anniversary of the Boerne Gesangverein. Photograph courtesy of the Boerne Area Historical Preservation Society.

Looking to get a business going, "Heino immediately had a desire to start a garden and seed business, and soon he located a garden by the river which rented for one-third of its crop, seed included. Soon the garden flourished so that it attracted everyone's attention. After the first four weeks, however, a drought set in which lasted two months so that most of the garden was ruined despite diligent work. Now Heino is sick [with a fever], and farewell to garden and income." The Staffels were neither the first nor the last to learn that the local climate is much more forgiving of grazing than of farming.

Adeline Staffel sounded almost optimistic when she reported that "a new town [Boerne] is to be founded between San Antonio and Fredericksburg, and everyone believes that it will be a good investment to purchase land there. Our situation has a been such so far that we have saved no money, but we have no fear and need have none as ways and means can always be found for willingly working hands to learn a living." But then she allowed that "the certainty that one can establish an existence here is the only thing I like about this country. Otherwise Texas is a very miserable country, a vast prairie-like desert with only a few oases which one could call attractive.... The country, almost to Fredericksburg, where it is mountainous, is very unhealthy and no German coming here remains free of malaria fever.... Many Germans would move to Fredericksburg on account of its healthier climate, but the Indians that live there murder and plunder and nobody dares travel without adequate escort. Almost every week one hears about travelers being cruelly murdered there."

Adeline Staffel was not exactly a Texas booster, but her concern about hostile natives was not entirely misplaced. Mary Ann Schertz Becker, a Boerne innkeeper who claimed to be the first "white" child born in Boerne, used to tell tales of early days in the area. Her paternal grandparents were Castro colonists; her maternal grandparents also came to Texas with the Castro colonists, but her grandfather died of cholera in Indianola and her grandmother moved to San Antonio with her mother in tow. When her mother, Segunda Ruede, married John Schertz, they moved to their farm three miles outside Boerne, where Mary was born in 1854. In the florid words of a 1932 edition of the *San Antonio Express*, "Living in constant dread of the marauding bands of Indians which roamed the country, and menaced by other dangers common to the wilderness into which they had come to establish new homes, these pioneers set an example for undaunted courage. Their resolute fortitude and indomitable will has found few equals in history."

According to that same article, "When the Schertz family moved to Kendall County the hill country was filled with roving bands of hostile redskins who were a constant menace to the settlers. They made frequent raids on the sparsely settled communities, running off stock and often murdering or scalping some settler caught off his guard. When a family retired at night they had no assurance that they would not be butchered before the morning dawned."

Probing a bit deeper, it occurs that the only actual encounter with natives that Mary Becker had was once in her childhood, while she was scooping a bucket of water from Cibolo Creek. In the nearby brush she saw "an Indian buck gazing intently at her" and ran home. On another occasion her father thought he heard natives outside their cabin, so he fired his rifle through a window in the direction of the noise. Investigating later, he discovered that he had shot one of his horses. A few nights later natives were trying to steal horses from their corral but, the story goes, Fritz Wendler was on guard in the adjacent hayloft. Wendler was so agitated by the raiders' appearance that he fell out of the hayloft. The ensuing commotion scared the natives away.

Not all encounters between Germans and (usually) Comanches were so benign. In 1855 Jesse Lawhon and a ranch hand were looking for some oxen on Curry's Creek near Boerne and Sisterdale when they were ambushed by natives. The ranch hand dashed for home and made it safely, but Lawhon endured a cat-and-mouse chase through thickets and down a steep cliff before being shot dead. Mysteriously, the ranch hand reported that one of the attackers "was a white man and the other four Indians, naked and armed with guns. The white man was dressed in dark clothes with a white hat."

It is impossible to tell whether Boerne was more peaceful in the 1850s than in the next two decades, but most local tales of conflict with natives occur in the 1860s and 1870s. This difference could stem from any of three reasons: fewer stories remain from the earliest years, when people were more intent on pioneering than on recording their lives or printing newspapers; as more settlers entered the Hill Country, the natives felt more pressure and reacted more violently; and when Union troops withdrew from Texas during the Civil War, West Texas natives resurged and all of Texas experienced renewed resistance.

In January 1862 a thick fog settled over Boerne. A man named Reinhardt, who sold firewood to local residents, asked teenager August Theis to help with chopping, splitting and loading, but his father felt the weather was too favorable for a Comanche raid and kept his son home. Reinhardt went to the woods surrounding Boerne and began his work. Henry King received two loads of firewood from Reinhardt that day, but an expected third load never arrived. That night Reinhardt's wife came to King's house, crying—Reinhardt had not come home.

At four o'clock in the morning, a messenger arrived from George Kendall, after whom Kendall County is named, "saying his head shepherd had been chased to the house by Indians the evening before, and a number of his sheep flocks had come home without their shepherds. He asked that we raise a party and help him make search for the missing men. Soon after day break fifteen men were in the saddle and moved out of the town toward Kendall Ranch."

At the top of the first hill above town, just east of where the Kendall County Courthouse is today, they found Reinhardt's wagon and, a distance away, his body. King said, "It appeared that he was being chased by the Indians, his horses at a full run probably, when the left fore-wheel struck a stump on the roadside, breaking off the spindle and of course bringing the wagon to a stop. Then seizing his axe, his only weapon, with the idea of defending himself, he had run about fifty yards toward the town, when he was overtaken and killed. But for the fatal stump he might have escaped. He was almost home!"

Continuing on toward the Kendall ranch, "within a few hundred yards of the premises another ghostly spectacle had been discovered. Under the branches of an old oak lay the butchered body of a German lad of about sixteen years who had been in charge of a lamb flock which was herded close to the house. By him also lay the body of a dog, one of the scotch shepherd dogs of the ranch. The faithful creature had evidently been killed while attempting to protect the young shepherd and his flock."

Reaching the Kendall property, the men from Boerne learned that the head shepherd had run to the ranch house the evening before, shouting a warning of Indians. George Kendall was in the field; his wife sent the head shepherd and a helper out to look for the three flocks that were tended by hands named Schlosser, Fechler and Baptiste. Then she gathered all of her children, with her mother and Schlosser's wife, into one room in the Kendall house. Putting on her husband's overcoat and hat, she took a double-barreled shotgun and paced the front gallery, keeping guard. George Kendall returned that night and, learning of the circumstance, sent to Boerne for help.

The young man found dead under the oak tree was Fechler. Following the attackers' trail, they found the body of Baptiste face-down in a creek, four arrows in his back and his dog, Pink, standing guard. They looked all day for Schlosser, without success. Three weeks later they found his mutilated body.

It turned out that the raiders had begun their rampage on Wasp Creek, seven miles northeast of Boerne, where they intercepted a farmer Louis Donop, who was riding to the creek to carry a day's rations to a man who was making shingles for him in the cypress bottoms along the creek. Donop was riding a farm horse, not nearly as fleet as the attackers' mounts, and they quickly caught him and ended his life. In one day on the outskirts of Boerne the natives—reportedly twenty-five or thirty men—had slain five settlers.

In October 1864, natives again raided Donop's widow's farm, killing and wounding horses. Three miles downstream on the Guadalupe, they stole four horses from a Mr. Helligman. In July 1868, five Indians attacked eighteen-year-old Herman Stieler two miles from Comfort. He managed to defend himself with rifle and pistol, but lost the contents of his wagon to the raiders. In the spring of 1870 natives rode up to the home of John Stendebach while he was absent, terrifying his wife and children. Luckily, according to the *Boerne Star*, "all the Indians wanted was food. They grabbed the still hot boiled ham from the table and while one Indian held it in both hands, the others bit out huge chunks and chewed. They scooped up the beans and cornbread with their hands and disappeared almost as fast as they had entered. About fifteen minutes later a band of Rangers rode up, asking if any Indians had been seen. Upon relating her story, Mrs. Stendebach was told that the Indians had just murdered a family a few miles away and the Rangers were hot on their trail."

That same spring, schoolboys Willie and Herman Lehmann were captured by Apaches on Beaver Creek near Loyal Valley, where John Meusebach had retired the year before. The Lehmann boys had never been to school and spoke only German. Willie escaped, but eleven-year-old Herman lived among the Apaches and Comanches for nine years. He adapted readily to his new life, showing great reluctance when he was forcibly reunited with his family. A year after the Lehmann kidnappings, Clint and

Jeff Smith were kidnapped by Comanches while herding sheep on their parents' farm on Little Joshua Creek near Boerne. John Sansom's company of Texas Rangers, assisted by local militia and a citizens' posse, pursued the kidnappers, but failed to catch them. The boys spent five years with the Comanches before being returned to their families. Herman Lehmann, Clint Smith and Jeff Smith became local celebrities, touring parades, rodeos and Wild West shows in their Indian costumes.

Though these are only a few of the violent incidents that occurred in the Hill Country, it probably was a stretch for the *San Antonio Express* to claim that "the hill country was filled with roving bands of hostile redskins who were a constant menace to the settlers." Life was hard for the early settlers, and dangerous in many ways. But it is likely that Anglo attacks on Germans took more lives than did Indian raids. One town that bore a disproportionate burden of that dark passage in Hill Country history is Comfort.

No one knows why they named it Comfort. Local historian Guido Ranseleben speculated that the German equivalent, *Behaglichkeit*, would have been too difficult to pronounce, but that is the sort of answer that leaves one still scratching their head. Presumably the name is meant to suggest a pleasant and beautiful place to live, which aptly describes the town.

Franziska Wiedenfeld and her brother Theodore had landed in Texas in the company of their parents, Adelsverein colonists, in June 1845, during the disastrous second phase of arrivals. Franziska was twelve when she made the voyage from Germany; a few years later, in her early teens, she married Heinrich Schladoer in New Braunfels. Theodore married Magdalena Joseph in November 1851. His seventeen-year-old bride had come to Texas with an uncle and aunt, who came ashore at Indianola in December 1846; they were not Adelsverein colonists. The following year the two related young couples migrated to a spot near where Pfeiffer's Creek enters the Guadalupe.

Though they were nearer Pfeiffer's Creek, the informal community of farms that grew up around the Schladoers and Wiedenfelds was named for the larger Cypress Creek. This community is where Nicolaus Zink came in 1853 with his second of three wives. The Zinks were preceded by two non-German families, the McFadins and the Dentons, who settled along Cherry Creek, about five miles from the future site of Comfort. In the same year that Zink arrived, Magdalena Joseph Wiedenfeld's adoptive parents, the Saurs, settled in Cypress Creek.

The Wiedenfelds and Schladoers were cattle ranchers, which meant that they were in need of large tracts of land. They had their eye on several thousand acres along the Guadalupe River and Cypress Creek, but were unsure of its ownership. Theodore Wiedenfeld asked a relative named "Rossi" (likely Alexander Rossy) in New Braunfels to help determine the owner. Rossi had to travel to San Antonio to complete the task, because Cypress Creek was then still in Bexar County, but he reported back that the land was owned by one John F. C. Vles of New Orleans.

Vles was a cotton trader and speculator, and had never seen the land he owned. When he received an inquiry from Wiedenfeld about purchasing the acreage, he dispatched one of his employees to Texas to inspect his investment and report back about its value. The employee was twenty-two-year-old Ernst Hermann Altgelt, the son of a German government official. Altgelt set sail for Indianola, where he and other passengers hired a teamster to take them to New Braunfels. He didn't get far, falling ill with yellow fever—most likely brought from New Orleans—in Gonzales. After recuperating under the care of a blacksmith and his wife, Altgelt continued to New Braunfels and determined enough about the location of the land to go in search of it.

After looking over the tract and visiting with the local settlers, Altgelt concluded that Vles's land was an excellent location for a townsite. He wrote Vles, recommending that the land be surveyed into lots and blocks. Altgelt was so taken with the prospects for the region that he wrote to his father in Germany, asking for enough money to buy one thousand acres for himself from Heinrich Schladoer.

Armed with instructions and authority from Vles, and having received the requested funds from his father, Altgelt returned to the future site of Comfort in the summer of 1854 accompanied by surveyor Friedrich Grothaus and several other Germans who would be among the first settlers within the city limits: Fritz Goldbeck, Freidrich Brunko, Louis von Breitenbauch and Anton Beyer. Grothaus divided the townsite into three hundred lots, thirty of which were quickly sold. In its November 3, 1854, issue the *Neu-Braunfelser Zeitung* reported that "as we understand, the plan is for Comfort to become a little town. The Germans like to live together in small towns where, besides the advantages of town life, such as sociableness, proximity to medical help, and schools, the pleasures and independence of rural life may be enjoyed. May Comfort be for its settlers what its name implies, a comfortable place to live."

Though the settlers along Cypress Creek raised cattle and crops, many of the first citizens of Comfort made their money by splitting shingles or freighting for the Fredericksburg and San Antonio markets. As early resident Ferdinand Lohmann put it, "as long as shingle making and driving freight was still lucrative, nobody paid much attention to farming. Corn was just about the only crop."

Soon Altgelt—who had concluded his land purchase from Schladoer and intended to remain in Comfort—recommended to Vles that he invest in a sawmill and, as was typical once water power was harnessed, that the mechanism also be put to work for a grist mill and a flour mill. Under the direction of Christian Dietert, who had built the mill at Kerrville, the first local mill was erected and named "Perseverance Mill." The name turned out to be ironic. A flood soon wiped out the dam. After Altgelt re-built the dam, a drought set in and the mill was abandoned.

Ferdinand Lohmann wrote that "the clothes of the settlers were as simple and plain as their habitations and lifestyle. The usual outfit was a blue, checkered, Hickory shirt and pants made out of blue or brown Kentucky denim. A pair of heavy shoes completed the outfit. Nobody wore socks or underwear…. Also, many wore homemade hats, which were woven out of the hard, pointy leaves of the yucca plant…. The women wore slouch hats that had been strengthened with small pieces of shingles, sun bonnets and simple linen dresses. During work they also wore a sturdy dress made out of Kentucky denim. Sometimes someone only owned one outfit. He or she would bathe in the sun while washing and drying it by the river or creek."

Theodor Goldbeck (Fritz's brother) built a cabin in 1854 and opened a mercantile business there. In 1856 he sold it to new Prussian arrival August Faltin, whose store became a Comfort institution. Soon Comfort had a shooting club, a vocal quartet and a small school. Some buildings exhibited the German half-timbered style called *Fachwerk* that was also common in Fredericksburg and New Braunfels. The village even had a fledgling newspaper called *The Beggar's Bag*. But it had no church; Comfort was long known as a settlement of freethinkers and it was not until 1892 that someone possessed the temerity to erect a church.

In Comfort, freethinking meant much more than secularism. The town managed itself cooperatively and its residents steadfastly resisted forming a formal government. One of its historic buildings is named Bolshevik Hall. To this day, Comfort remains unincorporated—technically not a municipality, but just a gathering of citizens. It has no mayor, no council, no city hall, no police force, and no local sales taxes, and Comfort likes it that way.

Comfort organized itself for defense against Indians, though the local native population—mostly Delawares—were generally peaceful. The Germans procured a small cannon from New Braunfels, and it was agreed that a cannon shot would be a call to arms. It was fired only once, on a hot second of July. The locals dropped their tools, grabbed their weapons and rushed to Goldbeck's store, where it turned out that the emergency was not of the military sort. The brothers Goldbeck had stocked a supply of beer from Menger's brewery in San Antonio, only to discover that most of their customers were planning on going to Fredericksburg to celebrate the Fourth of July. The beer would spoil quickly in the warm weather, and there was a serious risk of good beer going to waste. After a few moments of consternation and some discussion of cannon-firing ethics, the good Germans of Comfort set about addressing the crisis.

A mutual love of brewed beverages, freethinking ways and communal governance did not necessarily imply harmony in Comfort. "It is a well-known fact," one settler observed, "that if lawyers move into town, the population as a whole is going to file more lawsuits, even if they coexisted peacefully until that point." When the citizens of Comfort began to get a reputation as litigious, they blamed it on "Buchanan, the lawyer and peace killer. In the end his instigations were so obvious that he was asked to leave the area."

The contentiousness was obvious to more than the locals. When Hermann Seele visited Comfort in the autumn of 1860, he reported that "Comfort, the town that I found so prettily situated, had been enlarged and its external appearance improved. I liked the town just as much as before, but I could not say as much of many of the residents.… Where had the happy, always cheerful optimism—in spite of the often very hard times—of the first settlers vanished? What had become of the harmonious, easy-going neighborliness and the good humor of this inoffensive group of people? Dissension, vindictiveness, petty envy, discord and contentiousness seemed to dominate all with whom I spoke. This one had been filed on or was the defendant in a suit; another had the intention to sue; while still another was afraid of being taken to court. The large number of civil and criminal cases entered on the dockets of the district court and the justice of the peace in such a young and sparsely settled county gave witness to the prevalence of this unholy mania for litigation."

It may have been more than the presence of a lawyer in Comfort that upset the town's equilibrium. When Kerr County was organized in 1856, a contest arose between Comfort and Kerrville (then Brownsborough) for the status of county seat. Kerrville aligned itself with citizens from Center Point (then Zanzenburg) and, according to Dr. J. Clark Ridley, appointed by the Texas legislature to oversee county organization, Kerrville won the election. It turned out that Ridley had thrown out all the votes for Comfort because it was close to the Kerr County line, and the act authorizing the county required its seat to be near its center. Comfort—believing that it had gotten more votes—felt cheated.

Four years later, Indian attacks around Kerrville were impeding its growth, so the county citizens voted to remove the county seat to Comfort, thereby enraging the good citizens of Kerrville. By the time that Hermann Seele visited Comfort, he was witnessing the aftermath of a rancorous, politicized battle for control of the county.

Comfort's discomfort with its place in the county pecking order would not improve. In December 1859 ninety-five citizens of Kerr, Blanco and Bexar counties drew up a petition for the creation of a new county to include parts of the existing three. The petitioners complained that the territory where they lived was too distant from the county seats at Kerrville, Blanco and San Antonio, and that they needed a center of government somewhere in their vicinity—the lands surrounding Sisterdale, Boerne and Comfort. The first signature on the petition was that of George Wilkins Kendall, after whom the county would be named. Other familiar names appear on the petition: Wendler, Degener, Vogt, Fabra, Staffel, Herff, Theis, Bergmann, Dienger, Stendebach, Dresel, Rhodius, Zink and more.

The Texas legislature created Kendall County on January 10, and appointed Adam Vogt, member of the Forty and Tusculum veteran, commissioner to oversee the organization of the county government. The voters elected Vogt to be county judge and former Texas Ranger John Sansom as sheriff. To the consternation of Comfort, only Boerne and Sisterdale were far enough from the county's perimeter to qualify as county seat. In the ensuing election, Boerne prevailed over Sisterdale; Comfort was once again denied a chance at the advantages afforded the center of government.

Why was the county named after George Wilkins Kendall, a recent non-German arrival? His signature at the top of the petition hints at the important role he played in getting the legislature to create the new county, but there is more, for Kendall was a most remarkable man. Born in Vermont in 1809, he apprenticed with a Vermont printer and then worked for Horace Greeley in New York. Greeley was then a young printer and had not yet founded *The New York Tribune.* After a brief stint with the Mobile *Alabama Register*, he moved to New Orleans and co-founded the *Picayune*. There he became a successful newspaperman and a vocal proponent of the annexation of Texas. In 1841 he joined the ill-fated Texan expedition to Santa Fe and ended up imprisoned in a Mexican leper colony. He wrote more than twenty brave and fascinating letters from Mexico, and they were printed in the *Picayune*.

After Kendall's release from prison in 1842 he wrote a classic account of the expedition, then turned his interest toward advocacy of war with Mexico over the western territory. When the war began in 1846, Kendall signed up with Captain Benjamin McCulloch's company of Texas Rangers and reported from the front, gaining him accolades as the nation's first war correspondent. He reported on the Winfield Scott's invasion of Vera Cruz and was wounded in the battle for Chapultepec. After the war, he wrote a well-received history of the conflict.

With his nationwide reputation as a swashbuckling journalist secure, Wilkins left the day-to-day newspaper business, entering the Texas sheep industry in the early 1850s, but still writing to the *Picayune* about his experiences. He developed fine herds of Merino and Rambouillet sheep—first near New Braunfels, then on a ranch near Boerne—and promoted Texas and the Hill Country to all who read his columns. By the time he circulated the petition to form a new Texas county, he was one of the most prominent and admired citizens in the region.

Chapter Eight
Conflict

Two of the earliest German singing societies in Texas were outside the German Hill country: San Antonio established its *Maennergesang Verein* in 1847 and Austin founded its *Maennerchor* in 1852. New Braunfels' *Germania* sprouted in 1850; later it added the *Liedertafel* and the *Concordia* singing societies. Boerne's gesangverein dates back to the town's earliest days but was not formalized until 1860. Comfort didn't assemble its Liedertafel until 1870, but from 1855 to 1858 Ernst Altgelt, Fritz Goldbeck, Wilhelm Boerner and Fritz Holekamp sang as a quartet. In Sisterdale, Ottomar von Behr, Louis von Donop, Christian Rhodius and August Siemering formed a quartet in 1853 that sang together for five years. Fredericksburg organized its first singing society in 1858, when it hosted the Texas *Sangerfest*—a gathering of singers from New Braunfels, Pedernales, Austin, San Antonio and Grapetown.

The 1858 Sangerfest was actually the sixth in Texas. The first was during October 1853 in New Braunfels and marked the formation of Texas State *Sangerbund* (singers' league). That event followed a week of heavy rain that made it difficult to reach New Braunfels. The singers from Austin lost most of their baggage, including their music books, while crossing the Blanco River. Nonetheless, they made the event, as did groups from Sisterdale and San Antonio, in addition to the local New Braunfels singers. (Comfort did not yet exist; people in Boerne were still living in huts.)

The second Sangerfest was an altogether different event, and it heralded the Hill Country's eventual turn toward conflict and violence. The 1850s were a difficult time for Germans in the United States. There was a backlash against the flood of German and Irish immigrants, particularly those of the Roman Catholic faith. People whose families had lived on the continent for only a few generations became "nativists," asserting that only native-born white Americans should have the right to vote, and that the citizenship rights of new immigrants should be restricted. Secret anti-immigrant societies formed and backed political candidates sympathetic to their views, regardless of whether the candidate might be a Democrat, a Whig or a member of a splinter party. Then, coalescing and moving out of secrecy as the Whig Party disintegrated, these "Know-Nothings" became a potent political force on the national scene, calling themselves the American Party and standing for nativism, preservation of the Union and (particularly in its northern chapters) abolition of slavery.

In Texas, the Democratic Party stood adamantly opposed to the Know-Nothings, earning the gratitude of the German Texans. To the extent that German Texans participated in the political process, they tended to be Democrats and, later, Southern Democrats. But Hill Country Germans were not particularly involved in Texas politics. They were isolated by geography, language and choice. Their world revolved around their farms and local communities and, despite their love of abstract political theorizing and expostulating, they were not then prominent members of the Texas political mainstream.

These were the years when anguish over slavery moved to the forefront of national and state discourse. It is a fair generalization to say that Hill Country Germans were opposed to slavery and in favor of a strong Union, though, as we will see, the equation was not quite that simple. As national and state politics became increasingly polarized, some German leaders in the Hill Country felt that it was time to end their political isolation. In 1853, the Reverend Ervendberg advocated the formation of the *Democratischer Verein* in New Wied, near New Braunfels. What resulted was a social club called the *Geselliger Verein* that also served as a platform for political discourse. In the following year a *Politischer Verein* emerged in New Braunfels and the *Reform Verein* formed in Fredericksburg.

Looking back, the most influential political verein turned out to be a tiny conclave among the liberal intellectuals in Sisterdale, where Ernst Kapp, Ottomar von Behr and August Siemering formed the abolitionist *Freie Verein* during 1853. The emergence of this verein was tied to a nationwide German intellectual unrest that led to the formation of the national *Bund Freier Maenner* (League of Free Men) in Louisville, Kentucky, in that year. The bund meant to inspire German-Americans to greater political involvement and to coalesce their many voices into one. Under the banner of "liberty, prosperity and education for all," it also intended to further a liberal agenda that included elimination of slavery and recognition of women's rights.

Two months before the scheduled May 1854 Sangerfest in San Antonio, the intellectuals of Sisterdale's Freie Verein called for a German political convention in San Antonio at the same time as the Sangerfest. Joined by Adolf Douai, the editor of the new *San Antonio Zeitung*—"a Social-Democratic Newspaper for the Germans in West Texas"—they advocated social and political equality, based on the freethinkers' commitment to the natural brotherhood of mankind.

August Siemering of Sisterdale wrote a letter to the *Neu-Braunfelser Zeitung*, edited by botanist Ferdinand Lindheimer. Referring to the platform adopted by the Kentucky bund, he called for German Texans to organize to secure united action on important political events—most urgently, the upcoming presidential elections. Siemering did not mince his words, declaring that "our political opponents must be forced to recognize the justice of our demands, or else destroyed."

The platform that emerged from the San Antonio convention, written in German, was based on the Louisville Platform promulgated by the Bund Freier Maenner. It began with a provocative preamble: "Whereas, we are convinced that the people of the United States do not enjoy the liberties guaranteed to them by the Constitution… and whereas, we are satisfied that the existing parties have neither the will nor the power to improve the political, social and religious relations of the country in a manner to suit the wishes of a large number of American citizens; we have adopted a series of principles with a view of uniting with any party that will be newly formed and that will afford us the greatest guarantees for carrying out our aims," but, the preamble explained, "by doing so we disavow every intention to form a German party and declare that our association as Germans is induced by the consideration of language alone."

Some planks in the platform were not grandly controversial, calling for popular election of the President, senators and judges, favoring the Monroe Doctrine, a graduated income tax and a graduated inheritance tax, and opposing the grand jury system. Other planks exhibited a Sisterdale-style idealism: every actual settler should be given "a proper quantity of land, free of charge" and banks were to be restricted to the purpose of affording protection "to the poor against capital and to support commerce."

But what caught the eye of the Texas public was this clause: "Slavery is an evil, the abolition of which is absolutely necessary according to democratic principles. Since slavery concerns only the states, we demand that the federal government refrain from all interference in matters pertaining to slavery. However, if a state determines on the removal of this evil, it may call on the federal government for aid in the execution of its decision."

This amounted to chumming the waters for the Know-Nothings, whose American Party was gaining a foothold in Texas. Worse, its tone alienated the mainstream of the Democratic Party—dominated by the cotton interests in East Texas—which was ardently pro-slavery. And, finally, it offended a good many conservative German Texans who may have been opposed to slavery but were even more opposed to meddling in other people's business. The German isolationists who wanted to keep their heads down and go quietly about their lives were not pleased.

The state-rights aspect of asserting that slavery is a matter for each state to decide was lost in the absolute abolitionist tone of the language. And the vague wording of a state being able to "call on the federal government for aid in the execution of its decision" summoned images of army troops forcibly freeing slaves and imposing martial law on Texas. This first public political pronouncement by any sizeable group of Texas Germans fueled the suspicions and fears of the pro-slavery and anti-immigrant factions. It was an astoundingly impolitic position.

Lindheimer's *Neu-Braunfelser Zeitung* erupted in protest. Lindheimer—once a liberal firebrand, now an advocate of accommodating Texas sensitivities—denounced the convention's actions and advocated respect for regional customs and loyalties. A letter signed by 135 Germans complained that the delegates to the convention in no way represented the community's viewpoint. Alexander Rossy wrote a letter condemning the platform point-by-point and asserting that abolitionists at the national level were nativists as well. He complained that of the seven officers elected at the convention, six were not even United States citizens, nor were the delegate or the two alternates designated to represent Texas at an upcoming German political convention in St. Louis. Friedrich Ernst, the first German paterfamilias in Texas, wrote from Mill Creek in East Texas to assert that the convention's defiant stand was most unwise and might result in a denial of German political rights by slave owners and nativists. These expressions of opinion in the *Neu-Braunfelser Zeitung*, and subsequent exhortations by Lindheimer in his paper, heralded an emerging schism between the conservative Germans in East Texas and New Braunfels and their markedly more liberal and activist countrymen in Fredericksburg, Boerne, Comfort and Sisterdale. That distinction, however, was largely lost on the general population of the state; to some extent, all Germans in Texas were tarred with the same abolitionist brush. Newspaper editorials raised the specter of German secret societies operating within their singing clubs and political associations. Germans claimed that was nonsense; the New Braunfels Politischer Verein invited non-Germans to attend their meetings. But the damage was done. An anonymous critic in the *San Antonio Ledger and Texan* newspaper traced the roots of German abolitionism to the arrival of the Forty, ascribing to them liberal ideas that extended beyond free soil to free love. Ferdinand Herff angrily denounced the essay, but his reply brought only another onslaught of accusations against the Darmstadters.

Walter L. Buenger, an eminent scholar on Texas secession, argues that Texans resented the newly emerged Republican Party and its abolitionist notions as sectionalist, meddling and prone to stray from Constitutional rights. Buenger says that Texas Democrats "argued persistently that the Republicans' reliance upon some higher moral or divine code was a threat to the very nature of law because it could be interpreted capriciously with no regard for minority rights." Pro-slavery Texans saw the Republicans as divisive, revisionist and soft on the Constitution, the very antithesis of the national covenant. Texans wanted a union, but they demanded one that honored the premises that they believed were part of their original bargain.

Ironically, many Hill Country Germans would not have disagreed with pro-slavery Texans on this point. Most Germans were strict constructionists who believed that the question of slavery was one to be resolved within each state in a peaceful, democratic fashion. Germans believed the American promise that they could voice their opinions, but they also had faith that in the end the question of slavery would be resolved at the ballot box. The inartful language of the 1854 San Antonio convention managed to completely obscure this belief. Soon the Germans found themselves trying to explain that "calling on the federal government for aid" meant asking Washington for the money to fairly compensate slave owners. That may or may not have been the original intent of the language, but the explanation came too late and was drowned out by rhetorical clamor.

As the slavery question approached a boil, Texans found themselves with other reasons to resent the state of the Union. Texas's interest in being part of the United States had always been qualified. If Mexico had not threatened the fragile Republic, it might never have joined the Union. If the Republic were not bankrupt, it might never have given up its claim to eastern New Mexico in 1850. By the mid-1850s, just a decade after joining the Union, Texans were frustrated by the army's weak effort to defend Texas from Indians and Mexico, forcing the state to maintain a defensive force of rangers. When Texas attempted to bill the U.S. Congress for the expense of its defense, money was slow in coming. Leaving aside slavery (if that is possible), there was considerable resentment in Texas of a national relationship that it saw as riven by sectional interests, intrusive in its social policies and neglectful of its fundamental obligations.

This level of frustration made it even more difficult to explain and defend a typical German progressive opinion, because at the heart of that viewpoint (and the viewpoint of many conservative Germans) was a devout faith in the Union, to which new German citizens had only recently sworn allegiance. It is undeniable that there was no uniform political position among the progressive Germans—not to mention among the Hill Country Germans or the Texas Germans generally—but a popular position in Fredericksburg, Boerne, Sisterdale and Comfort was in favor of the right of Texas to continue slavery, opposed to the continuation of slavery, in favor of the right to secede and opposed to secession. These were nuances lost upon an agitated pro-slavery, secession-leaning majority. And they were good reasons for the Germans in the Hill Country to either revert to their prior low profile or to accept that advocacy of unpopular opinions has its consequences.

Statewide, though, Germans tended to remain loyal to the Democratic Party. In the governor's election of 1857 the pro-Union, anti-slavery Sam Houston ran as an independent with the support of the Know-Nothings. Reacting to Know-Nothingism, the Democratic Party, in Buenger's words, "became an effective defender of the Germans, and many Germans developed a long-lasting and persistent attachment to the party which defended their personal liberty and their right to a distinct culture." The Democrats mustered the support necessary to elect their candidate, Hardin Runnels, earning the gratitude of the German community. In 1859 Houston again ran against Runnels for governor. This time Houston tried to distance himself from the Know-Nothings, proclaiming himself an independent Democrat who stood for opposition to the African slave trade and preservation of the Union. Many Germans stuck with the mainstream Democrats and their candidate Runnels, which put them in alignment with secessionists. In New Braunfels, Lindheimer's *Neu-Braunfelser Zeitung* expressed dissatisfaction with southern extremists and opposed re-opening the slave trade, but pledged loyalty to the Texas Democrats and promised to support their nominee.

Given this general antebellum alignment of Texas Germans with the Democratic Party, it is possible that the storm that followed the San Antonio Sangerfest might have blown over, but influential progressive Germans made sure that it did not. While Ferdinand Lindheimer's *Neu-Braunfelser Zeitung* argued for respecting existing Texas institutions, objected to the Kansas-Nebraska Bill and praised the *Dred Scott* decision, Adolf Douai's *San Antonio Zeitung* stridently advocated abolition of slavery and adamantly opposed secession. Increasing the tension, Ferdinand Flake, editor of Galveston's *Die Union*, joined Douai's campaign and engaged in an editorial battle of words with Lindheimer. Sentiment against the abolitionist *San Antonio Zeitung* increased and readership declined, leading its owners to sell the publication to Douai, who raised funds for the purchase from fellow abolitionists that included Frederick Law Olmsted. In February 1855, Douai pushed the boundaries even further, calling for establishment of a separate free state in West Texas. With Douai becoming ever more radical, a June mass meeting of Germans in New Braunfels passed resolutions distancing themselves from his views and proclaiming their allegiance to the Constitution and the state. Jacob Waelder, who represented Bexar county in the legislature, was of a secessionist bent and loudly proclaimed that charges of German abolitionism were false and that Germans, as a group, were as loyal to the South as any other citizens of Texas. By 1856 Douai's *San Antonio Zeitung* became so controversial and the threats against Douai so intense that he sold out to Gustav Schleicher and fled for Boston.

What explains the differing public sentiment in conservative New Braunfels and liberal Fredericksburg, Sisterdale, Comfort and Boerne? New Braunfels was on the road between Austin and San Antonio. Were Fredericksburg and Boerne more liberal because they were more isolated from Texas political trends? If so, that does little to explain why outspoken San Antonio Germans tended to be liberal, even radical, and it does not explain why one of the state's most liberal German newspapers was in Galveston. Degrees of isolation did not match degrees of liberalism.

Some have searched for the source of the liberal-conservative split by analyzing when and why various Germans reached Texas. The first Germans to arrive in the Hill Country—the people who first settled New Braunfels—were mostly lower class workers looking for stability and a better life for their families. When the privileged, liberal and influential Forty from Darmstadt arrived in Texas, they went to Fredericksburg, then Sisterdale, Boerne, Comfort and San Antonio. Likewise, Forty-Eighters—a more educated and liberal group than the peasantry and proletariat that made up much of the first wave of colonists—tended to move into the new settlements beyond New Braunfels (and into San Antonio). Though only a few years separated their arrivals, the differences between the original "Gray" working-class Germans and the later-arriving "Green" educated Germans (as they divided themselves) was apparent from the beginning. The linguistic, cultural and physical isolation of the Green settlements beyond New Braunfels—perhaps combined with a rumored tendency of Germans to be stubborn and opinionated—might have left them out of (and insensitive to) mainstream Texas political thinking.

But the Gray-Green political split doesn't hold up under examination. By no means did all of the Forty or the Forty-Eighters prove to be Unionists. Ernst Altgelt—a merchant from the hotbed of freethinking at Comfort—wrote Texas Governor Edward Clark in the autumn of 1861 to volunteer his services should the governor call the militia to defend the state against invasion. He joined the Confederate Army and rose to the rank of captain. Gustav Schleicher, one of the leaders of the Forty, purchased the *San Antonio Zeitung* from Adolf Douai and maintained the paper's liberal tone for a time, but ultimately swung from Unionism to Confederate loyalty. Rejecting his liberal roots and the spirit of Bettina, he concluded that "crazy doctrines of communism… would destroy the individual, intelligent, free and untrammeled production… and substitute a government, moving and directing everything, in which all individual life would be merged."

Viktor Bracht came to Texas in 1845 with the Adelsverein, making him a putative Gray. He returned to Germany in 1848, wrote a book about his experiences in Texas, then sailed back to Texas in 1849. In 1860, he left Texas for New York and did not return until after Reconstruction—a pattern that more than one abolitionist German followed, and not what one might expect of a New Braunfels stalwart.

When Viktor Bracht sailed from Germany to Texas in 1849, he brought his brother Felix—who was thirteen years his senior—with him. Felix was a physician and was known for liberal tendencies. He left Germany with the Forty-Eighters, thus is a putative Green. But shortly after Texas seceded from the Union, Felix wrote Texas Governor Edward Clark to decline an official position in New Braunfels because he considered himself "somewhat unpopular among the union loving part of my fellow citizens of Comal." Instead, he asked to be made a Regimental Surgeon in San Antonio, because he wanted to purchase the *San Antonio Zeitung* from Gustav Schleicher, who had not yet turned far enough toward the Union to satisfy Bracht. "The San Antonio paper would in this manner be wrested forever out of the hands of the free soil clique there, which has done so much mischief to Western Texas, and which is, if we may credit the S. A. Ledger, still brooking treason."

Simple explanations of the division between liberal and conservative Germans are inadequate. It wasn't just a matter of class or arrival date or locus of settlement. There were tendencies within communities—Fredericksburg was liberal, New Braunfels was conservative—but it is difficult to spot the characteristics of the communities that caused that difference.

The source of the difference is most likely social. Community leadership and opinion-making mattered. Political discussions in local parlors or taverns sorted people into one category or another. In New Braunfels, the word of a respected and influential newspaper editor did much to sway public opinion; the German-language *Neu-Braunfelser Zeitung* was many citizens' only link to the English-speaking state.

It is possible to conclude that the principal source of German liberal, abolitionist thinking was the influential freethinkers in Sisterdale's Freie Verein. Von Behr, Degener, and Siemering were adamant and vocal in their beliefs. Edgar von Westphalen, the political and familial Marxist, was still among their number. It was they who conceived the idea of the 1854 convention, they who advertised its existence, they who rallied people to participate and they who guided the process of selecting the delegates. The Freie Verein, and the people they gathered about them, were more organized, more dedicated and more emotionally charged than the conservative German element. The event in San Antonio was not so much a convention as it was a demonstration, a political protest. It was an exercise in freethinking and intellectual freedom. It was meant to garner attention to a cause that its organizers must have known was unpopular, and it succeeded beyond their expectations. Where the members of the Freie Verein were influential, their commitment to their noble, humanistic cause spread and, reinforcing their message in isolated communities that offered no opposition, they increasingly radicalized Hill Country Germans.

In the end, it was German pro-Union sentiment that caused more problems for the Hill Country than did the anti-slavery movement. Because Unionism was less reliant upon the freethinking humanism that marked German opposition to slavery, and because it represented loyalty to the existing order, Unionism was more widespread in the Hill Country than was abolitionism. Remember that the Hill Country Germans had fled uncertain futures in an acrimonious nation torn by class strife, intellectual suppression and despotic government. Buenger says, "The Constitution, which Unionists almost always linked with the Union, gave Texans and all Americans a rational and knowable legal framework that regulated the place of individuals and communities within the larger society. For a people with a sense of mission and conditioned to abhor social discord as the greatest of political evils, the Union, before 1860, seemed the best vehicle to achieve their goals and prevent their fears from being realized." For many Germans in the Hill Country, the words "before 1860" were superfluous.

Buenger's take on Hill Country Germans as Constitutionalists makes for an ironic twist. When viewed through the lens of a search for national social and governmental stability (as opposed to a crusade for human rights), it is the Unionists who were the conservatives and the secessionists who were the radicals. German Unionists were not necessarily in favor of abolition of slavery; they were in favor of the status quo.

It becomes more confounding—and yet more revealing—to take that analysis a step further. The pro-Confederacy Germans of New Braunfels also sought to protect the status quo, which they saw as citizenship in, and loyalty to, Texas. Just as many Unionist Germans were not abolitionists, so were many secessionist Germans not pro-slavery, but they perceived the North and the Republicans as the constituencies that were trying to change the rules of the game. Texans in general wanted to belong to a union that respected their original bargain, and many Hill Country Germans sought to protect the status quo in the same way.

The strange mix of political alignments among the Hill Country Germans is easiest to understand by completely disregarding slavery, because that was not the issue in the forefront of the typical German political view. Germans on both sides of the equation were trying to protect the stability, security, property, communities and families for which they had fought since 1845. One group believed that they could best preserve the status quo by preserving the Union and its Constitution, protectors of their rights, and by letting the national political process fairly determine what those rights were. Another sought to maintain the status quo by rejecting sectionalist efforts to amend the Constitution, and by insisting that the terms of their original compact with the Union (or with a new union if necessary) remain unchanged—remain the at the status quo.

But just as the haze begins to clear, just as it appears that all Germans were protecting their status quo (however they might define it), we remember Adolf Douai, Ottomar von Behr, Ernest Kapp and the other strident abolitionists who would have gladly dashed the status quo, whatever it was, to advance their liberal social agenda. This element stands apart from the two groups that were protecting their very different statuses quo. It is not a simple equation.

Six years after the provocative convention in San Antonio, the candidates in the 1860 Presidential election were Abraham Lincoln of the Republican Party, Stephen Douglas of the Democratic Party, John Breckenridge of the National (Southern) Democratic Party and John Bell of the Constitutional Union Party (the haven for Whigs and American Party Know-Nothings who could not abide the other parties). Lincoln never even made it onto the Texas ballot. When the Texas votes were tallied, Douglas received 18 votes, Bell received 15,383 ballots, and Breckenridge carried the state with 47,454. In New Braunfels, Breckenridge overwhelmed Bell. In Fredericksburg, Bell received a slim majority. Voting was light in both towns. Were the results tampered with? Possibly, but the statewide results for Lincoln and Douglas suggest that tampering was either massive or completely unnecessary. In the Hill Country, the more likely causes for the outcome were that some German abolitionists were keeping their heads down, some were intimidated, and others—as Alexander Rossy complained—had not even undertaken to become citizens.

Sentiment for secession spread rapidly in Texas. Democrats, organized and motivated just as the Freie Verein had been in 1854, moved to dominate the process of deciding the relationship of Texas to the Union.

Pro-secession forces were vocal, aggressive and in places violent; their lawlessness was matched—and fueled—by minority abolitionists in North Texas who used arson to create unrest and apprehension. Vigilantes burned houses and tossed opposition printing presses into rivers. Responding to real and rumored abolitionist conspiracies, the pro-secession forces became even more outspoken and aggressive, forming vigilance committees prone to hanging suspicious characters on short notice.

The secessionists made sure that when the Texas Secession Convention met in January 1861, the delegates could be trusted to make the right decision. The convention passed a secession ordinance by a vote of 166 to 8 and scheduled a popular vote on secession for February. Troops under a Committee for Public Safety formed by the convention, augmented by the private militia of the pro-slavery secret society called the Knights of the Golden Circle, decided not to wait for what they saw as a foregone conclusion: before the vote was held, they began seizing federal property and negotiated the surrender of Brigadier General David Twiggs's federal troops in San Antonio.

The popular vote for secession was less lopsided than the Secession Convention results, but was still decisive: 46,129 for secession, 14,697 against. Comal County (site of conservative New Braunfels and radical Sisterdale) favored secession by an impressive 239 to 86. Fredericksburg's Gillespie County opposed secession by an overwhelming 398 to 16. Kerr County favored secession 76 to 57 (a high turnout in the lightly populated county), but Comfort's precinct voted against secession 53 to 34, meaning that Zanzenburg and Kerrville voted heavily the other way: 42 to 4 for secession. Bexar County favored secession 827 to 709, but Boerne's precinct voted 85 to 6 against (Kendall County had not yet been formed).

It is striking that for all the controversy over Hill Country Unionism, only Gillespie County and Boerne brought in impressive pro-Union percentages. The distinct split within Kerr County reflects more than the difference between Kerrville and Comfort; it presents some interesting facts that undermine any image of the Hill Country as monolithically anti-slavery and pro-Union. The community around Comfort and Cypress Creek has long been considered a haven for freethinking, opposition to slavery and advocacy of Unionism. But in 1860 Kerr County there were 49 slaves owned by 11 people among a total county white population of 672. It is not surprising that slaves were owned by less than two percent of the people in Kerr County (or perhaps it is surprising, considering that in conservative Comal county only one-half percent of the citizens were slaveholders), but it is unexpected that three-quarters of the slaves were owned by slave owners in the area of Comfort and nearby Zanzenburg (Center Point). The largest slaveholder in Kerr County was Zanzenburg's Dr. Charles de Ganahl, an Austrian physician who held twenty-four slaves. When it came time for Kerr County to elect a delegate to the Secession Convention, Dr. Ganahl was the choice. Forty percent of the voters in Comfort's precinct voted for secession, and that is probably a reasonable representation of the sentiment in the supposedly adamantly abolitionist community.

As secession turned to war, German Unionists had a naive belief that they could somehow remain removed from the fray. They seemed to think that as long as they remained loyal to Texas, they could express their preference for the Union—and even for abolition of slavery—as a matter of free speech and political expression. After all, before the Civil War erupted, people in every state openly debated the merits of these excruciating political differences. The ability to speak one's mind was a fundamental reason why many Germans had emigrated to Texas in the first place.

Some Hill Country Germans seem not to have appreciated that matters change when war is declared. Words that yesterday were controversial can today be treasonous. The civil and military leadership of Confederate Texas was deeply concerned about invasion. Unionists and abolitionists were potential spies and traitors who might threaten the safety of every legislator's or soldier's family. It simply was unacceptable to have a nest of Unionists anywhere in Texas. If a person could not declare loyalty to the Confederacy, he was expected to leave the state.

On June 8, 1861, Texas Governor Edward Clark issued a fiery proclamation that railed against the abuses of the Union and called for Texans to support the Confederacy. The decree demanded that all citizens of the United States, and any other enemies of the Confederacy, depart Texas immediately, setting the stage for officials to require Texas residents to execute loyalty oaths if there were some question of their sentiments.

Backing up Clark's demand of loyalty, on August 14, 1861, Jefferson Davis issued a proclamation: "I do hereby warn and require every male citizen of the United States of the age of fourteen years and upward now within the Confederate States and adhering to the Government of the United States and acknowledging the authority of the same, and not being a citizen of the Confederate States, to depart from the Confederate States within forty days from the date of this proclamation. And I do warn all persons above described who shall remain within the Confederate States after the expiration of said period of forty days that they will be treated as alien enemies."

For whatever reason, Hill Country Germans never accepted this reality, believing that they could maintain a sort of conscientious objector status, quietly sitting out the war on their Texas farms. Dr. Felix Bracht reported from New Braunfels to Governor Clark that the local company of Texas State Troops was having trouble filling its ranks. "Older persons, even such as used to be not overpatriotic before, are quite enraged and would like to see the laggards drafted." Bracht reassured the governor that "this is of very little consequence as there's a well organized military company of the K.G.C. [Knights of the Golden Circle], who will be ready upon your call at any time."

The Knights of the Golden Circle were not the only secret society organizing in the Hill Country. In June 1861 eighteen men in Gillespie County formed a Hill Country chapter of the Union Loyal League, a pro-Union organization that was popping up in Unionist circles around the state. After the war, Unionist John Sansom claimed that the purpose of the Hill Country chapter was "not to create or encourage strife between Unionists and Confederate sympathizers, but to take such action as might peaceably secure its members and their families from being disturbed and compelled to bear arms against the Union, and to protect their families against the hostile Indians." In other words, these men did not intend offensive action against the Confederacy, but meant to avoid service in the Confederate Army and to defend their families from Confederate depredations. They were on dangerous territory.

Near the end of 1861, the Texas legislature organized the Frontier Regiment, "a regiment of Rangers for the protection of the Northern and Western frontier of the State of Texas, to consist of ten companies." The Frontier Regiment (later designated the First Regiment, Texas State Troops) replaced a volunteer home-defense force of minute men and, later, a short-lived Confederacy-mustered First Regiment, Texas Mounted Riflemen. One of its companies was to be raised in Gillespie and Kerr Counties. (Nomenclature was mixed at the time: this company is also referred to as part of the 31st Brigade, Texas State Troops, and as the Texas Mounted Rifles.)

For a young man who did not want to fight for the Confederacy, perhaps a young German man of that disinclination, the Frontier Regiment offered the opportunity to serve Texas and the local community—and to forgo resisting military service—without an overt commitment to the secessionist states.

The Frontier Regiment got off to a slow start, in no small measure because Brigadier General Robert Bechem accepted his commission "provided that it would not be incumbent on me to visit the different Counties composing this District, as it would be utterly impossible for me to do so." Bechem was taken aback by the conditions at the edge of civilization: "In some of the frontier Counties the population is so very much scattered that even an organization into independent Companies [one for each county] seems to be almost impossible, and it would be rather hard on the people, who since the recent disastrous depredations of the barbarous indians scarcely dare to go out of sight of their own houses."

John Sansom, a former Texas Ranger and a Unionist, applied to become the enrolling officer for the Frontier Regiment's company raised in Gillespie and Kerr Counties. Confederate loyalist J. M. Patton wrote the Texas adjutant general in Austin, warning of Sansom's Unionist tendencies. According to Patton, Sansom had said that he "will be God damned if he would ever fight against the Federal Government (meaning the Lincoln government)," and had maligned Patton as "a damned old fool" who was "willing to fight for Southern men's negroes." But Patton's charges were refuted by several other local men who said that they had "no fears to risk him at the head of a Company," and "have no reason to believe him other than a good southern man." According to Sansom's supporters, Patton had long borne a grudge against Sansom.

Jacob Kuechler, another applicant for the job of enrolling officer, suffered no such controversy. Moreover, he had solicited and received the endorsement of the esteemed Samuel Maverick, who wrote Governor Lubbock, "I recommend Mr. Kuechler as the best Indian fighter in that section (viz Gillespie County). I have been out with him in dangerous places & I know him to be reliable. I also think he can raise a good company for frontier protection and that he will take only brave & good men."

A Fredericksburg resident and one of the Forty, Kuechler had become a United States citizen in 1853 and served a brief six-week stint in William R. Henry's Company of Texas Volunteers in 1854. Since 1858 he had been the Gillespie County surveyor. As it turned out, Kuechler was an active participant in the Union Loyal League and—like the other candidate, Sansom—was a dedicated Unionist. Maverick, a vigorous secessionist, must have been unaware of this one detail.

Unionist or not, being a good "Indian fighter" was arguably more important in Fredericksburg than having Confederate sympathies. Gillespie County Chief Justice William Wahrmund wrote Governor Lubbock from Fredericksburg in April 1862 to say that "the insecurity of property and even human life has become so great in the very heart of the more thickly settled portion of this County that I deem it my duty to make your Excellency acquainted with what has transpired during the last ten days…. The Indians have come upon us in larger numbers than ever heretofore. They no longer walk around in small bands in the dead of night to rob and run, but come in bodies of from ten to forty and kill and rob at midday."

There is no question but that the withdrawal of Union troops had emboldened the Comanches, and no question but that frontier defense was a pressing issue. But it is also true that complaining to the governor about local Indian difficulties improved the chances that local troops would be kept home, instead of pressed into the Confederate Army. This would work well for a company with Unionist tendencies.

In the end, Kuechler got the job over Sansom, and ran his enlistment process his own way. He refused to attend a meeting of Kerr County citizens who had come to Gillespie County, intent on enlisting. In February 1862 thirty-eight Kerr County citizens wrote Governor Lubbock, complaining that Kuechler enrolled only German Unionists in his company and that while he would reach beyond his jurisdiction into Blanco County to accept German enlistees, he wouldn't even open an enrollment office in Kerr County.

Kuechler's Kerr County opponents, led by D. H. Farr, complained that he was "borrowing German names to enable him to organize so as to ensure his election as captain and then to supply those places by substitution." In other words, Kuechler was enrolling Germans who did not actually serve and listing them as having voted him for captain. The charge may not have been hollow: Edgar von Westphalen, the brother-in-law of Karl Marx, was listed on a February 1862 muster roll as serving as a private in Kuechler's Fredericksburg company. A month later, he was reported to be a sergeant in a Kendall County company raised in Sisterdale.

After protesting Kuechler's phantom enlistees, Farr, who complained of "the dutch yoke of tyranny" in Hill Country government, leveled his most explosive charge: "I have understood that said enroling officer has been a violent union man and is thought to be a black republican."

Trouble was brewing.

Chapter Nine
Violence

In January 1862, while Jacob Kuechler was organizing his company for the Frontier Regiment, the Texas legislature created Kendall County, carving it out of Kerr, Blanco and Bexar counties. They appointed Adam Vogt, who owned the Tusculum site and had become a Boerne leader, commissioner to organize elections. The voters chose Boerne as county seat and elected John Sansom, fresh from his rejection as a Frontier Regiment enrolling officer, as the county's first sheriff.

In San Antonio, members from statewide chapters of the Union Loyal League met secretly in March to discuss formation of militias. Ernst Kramer, who had assembled a company of league militiamen in Comfort, attended on behalf of the Hill Country league members. The meeting only exposed the weakness of the militias; it was clear that without Union support no revolution could succeed. Kramer went home disillusioned.

San Antonio was the headquarters for the Confederate Rio Grande sub-military district, which included the German Hill Country. Former Texas Ranger and now Confederate Colonel Henry E. McCulloch was in command and became concerned in March 1862, writing the assistant adjutant-general of Texas that "I have discovered a pretty considerable undercurrent at work in this country against our cause." According to McCulloch, "men have been heard to say when we (the Confederates) lost a battle, that 'We' (the Union men) 'have gained a victory.' Others have sent up small balloons, while others have fired guns by way of rejoicing over these victories."

Three weeks later McCulloch warned that "many of the most notorious among the leaders of the opposition, or Union men, are leaving the country, principally in the direction of Mexico." McCulloch worried that these men were organizing in Mexico "to act in concert with men of like feelings about Austin, this place, Fredericksburg, and other points where they are still living among us." In his opinion, there was "a considerable element of this character in this section that will have, ultimately (if the war becomes any more disastrous to us), to be crushed out, even if it has to be done without due course of law." Those last few ominous words took on special meaning when he advised that "I have taken steps to prevent as far as possible the passage of these men out of the country into Mexico, by instructing the military under my command not to let any man go unless he is known to be our friend, and not then unless he can produce satisfactory evidence that he is not going to avoid the draft."

"I am," McCulloch continued, "fully aware of the responsibility of the step I have taken, and how much it perils my reputation as an officer." His men were clearly not expected to use gentle means to prevent Unionists from leaving the state for Mexico.

McCulloch's jangled nerves were not soothed when, a week later, he found a German-language notice posted in San Antonio urging resistance to the Confederacy. "Many Germans and some Americans are leaving here to avoid a participation in our struggle. I have directed the troops to permit none to go to Mexico, unless they have a pass from me, or can produce evidence that they are friends, and not leaving to avoid doing their duty to the country." Clearly agitated, McCulloch informed the Texas assistant adjutant-general that "I have indicated plainly on other occasions that I deemed it advisable to declare martial law here at some time, and I think the time has about arrived when it will have to be done."

McCulloch never got to satisfy his itch to declare martial law. He was transferred, and in April 1862 Brigadier General Hamilton P. Bee assumed command of the Hill Country. Despite the efforts of McCulloch and Bee, the flow of Texans to Mexico was not stanched. Leonard Pierce, Jr., the United States consul at Matamoros, reported in early May that "the crowds of refugees from Texas do not diminish in the least, although it is very difficult, owing to the strict watch kept upon their movements, for them to get out. Many are arrested; some are hung; others are taken and pressed into service." Pierce saw the exodus as a tragedy. "It is really painful for a consul to see men driven from home and the comforts of life, not even allowed to bring an article of clothing; the only cause of complaint in many cases that they were Northern men (had never killed anyone), and refused to fight against the United States." In his eyes, "no portion of the United States has been so badly oppressed as the Union men of Texas, and

I can learn nothing is yet done to relieve the refugees or avenge the oppressors. I have received reliable information that within one week six of those refugees have been hung on the frontier of Texas on trees and left hanging."

One force driving the exodus of Unionists in April 1862 was the Confederacy's enactment of a Conscript Act requiring military service of all non-exempt white men between 18 and 35 years of age. Texas argued that service in the Texas State Troops pre-empted the Conscript Act, but the message to the young men of Texas was clear: service in either the Confederate Army or the state forces was mandatory.

Soon the Confederate military—and militaristic Texas Governor Lubbock—had had enough of the Unionists in their midst. On May 28 General Bee declared martial law in San Antonio and Bexar County. On May 30, Brigadier General Paul O. Hebert, commanding officer for the Department of Texas, extended martial law to cover the entire state. He required all white males over sixteen years of age to register with the local provost-marshal and demanded that aliens in Texas execute oaths of loyalty to Texas and the Confederacy. Seeking to clear out lingering Unionists, he directed the provosts–marshal to "order out and remove from their respective districts all disloyal persons and all persons whose presence is injurious to the interests of the country."

James M. Duff was captain and commanding officer of a company of irregular volunteers known as Texas Partisan Rangers (or Dragoons). A Scotsman by birth, he had arrived in the United States in 1848 and had promptly enlisted in the army for a term that ended in 1854. When the Civil War began, he assembled a company of Texas volunteers that disarmed a company of Union troops during their expulsion from the state, despite protests from the federal troops that Duff was acting in contravention of the treaties reached between Texas authorities and Union General David Twiggs. Duff's volunteers morphed into Partisan Rangers and came under Confederate control.

On May 28, 1862, acting under orders from General Bee, Duff's Company left Camp Bee near San Antonio and marched toward Fredericksburg. Arriving on the thirtieth, Duff formalized Bee's and Hebert's declarations of martial law as applied to Gillespie County and a portion of Kerr County, giving citizens of those districts six days to report to the provost-marshal and take the Confederate oath of allegiance.

"I found the people shy and timid," reported Duff, but after visiting the various settlements and explaining the purpose of his mission, "they displayed much more confidence in us, and in a corresponding ratio more desire to serve the Government." Duff found that it was difficult to obtain feed for his company's horses. It seemed that Confederate sympathizers had already sold their grain to the military and that the only people who still had grain were those who refused to accept Confederate currency as payment. And so Duff "directed Lieutenant Lilly to wait on Mr. F. Lochte, a wealthy merchant of the place who had bought largely the produce of the country, and who would not sell for paper currency, and inform him that I required fifty bushels of corn. After some little hesitation he agreed to furnish it. After this I had no difficulty in getting forage and all other necessary supplies."

Duff's report seems understated. His lieutenant "waited on" Lochte and obtained the feed "after some little hesitation." To grasp the meaning of these phrases, it is helpful to know that General Hebert's proclamation imposing martial law specifically stated that "any attempt to depreciate the currency of the Confederate States is an act of hostility; will be treated as such, and visited with summary punishment." And it is helpful to know that one of Duff's own men described him as being "as cowardly, cold-blooded a murderer as I had ever met, even in the roaring days of the Kansas 'War.'"

On June 3, Duff's men went in search of Unionists in Medina County, resulting in the capture of about ten men, who were imprisoned in San Antonio. Returning to Fredericksburg after ten days or so, Duff "found beyond doubt that the few citizens of the place who were friendly to this Government did not possess moral courage enough to give information to the provost-marshal of the sayings and doings of those who are unfriendly." Desiring better intelligence, Duff summoned Confederate loyalists and procured affidavits from them about key Unionists in the county. The result was warrants for the arrest of Captain Jacob Kuechler of the Frontier Regiment, Gillespie County Sheriff Phillip Braubach (who also served as a Lieutenant in Kuechler's Company), Friedrich Doebbler (the merchant and innkeeper at Grapetown), and Friedrich Lochte, who had been reluctant to sell grain for Duff's horses. Duff's men rounded up Doebbler quickly, then chased down Sheriff Braubach in Austin and nabbed Lochte in Fredericksburg when he let his guard down. The three Unionists were imprisoned in San Antonio. Kuechler escaped. Duff suggested that "steps should be taken to arrest Captain Kuechler. He is a man of great influence; a German enthusiast in politics and a dangerous man in the community."

Ernst Kramer and his compatriots faced a difficult situation. "Then it was," he said, "that I began to really know people. Excepting a very few, all took the oath, and also betrayed their [Frontier Regiment] officers. All officers had to immediately flee for their lives." Kramer and his friends scattered for the hills.

Unwilling to sign a Confederate loyalty oath, and fully aware of Duff's harsh treatment of Unionists, some left their families behind; others took their families with them, establishing camps where they thought the Partisan Rangers could not find them. Duff pursued. August Siemering, a Sisterdale Unionist, said, "Several of them were caught and hanged or shot dead. There was hardly a day when one did not find an unfortunate German Union man hanged. Several of the prisoners whom Duff took along when he left Fredericksburg met their death near Boerne. They were hanged." According to a soldier in Duff's company, Duff "had given certain of his followers to understand that he wanted no prisoners brought into camp." The soldier soon noticed that neither he nor any of his compatriots who shared his concerns about Duff's methods were sent out to scout. "It was very suspicious, as presently many parties were detailed to scour the country who rarely, if ever, brought in any prisoners, and were very reticent about their doings."

Thomas Smith was a sergeant in the Confederate 32nd Texas Cavalry, and served in the Fredericksburg area in August 1862. He reported that "there is now a daily guard around Fredericksburg. The 'bushwhackers' or traitors are plentiful in this country but keep themselves hid, and they have selected a good country for the business." According to Smith, when a Unionist "chances to fall into the hands of the C. S. soldiers he is dealt pretty roughly with and generally makes his last speech with a rope around his neck. Hanging is getting to be as common as hunting."

On June 11 Duff moved his company to Blanco, where he found the "great majority of the people friendly, enthusiastically so," but still felt the need to root out "a small clique who are bitterly opposed to our cause." Identifying men named King, Prescott, Howell, Snow and Eaton as Unionists, he was nonetheless unable to capture them.

Local rumor indicated that the Unionists in Blanco, Kerr, Gillespie and the surrounding counties were gathering at Jack Hamilton's ranch in

Travis County, just across the Blanco County line. The mention of Andrew Jackson "Jack" Hamilton was sure to set off alarms. A prominent Texas politician and ardent Unionist, Hamilton had been driven from Austin and was feared as an insurrectionist. He eventually fled Texas for Mexico, and then the United States. In November Abraham Lincoln declared him a brigadier general of Texas volunteers and appointed him military governor of Texas in absentia. Months before Lincoln bestowed the honor upon him, Captain Duff was already referring to him as "General" Jack Hamilton.

A week after arriving in Blanco, Duff moved his camp to Boerne, where he went through his ritual of formally declaring martial law and demanding loyalty oaths. He took Julius Schlickum, a local merchant and captain of a Kendall County company of the Frontier Regiment, into custody on suspicion of forwarding information and communications for Unionists. For good measure, Duff imprisoned Mrs. Schlickum, too. Two days later Duff received orders to return to San Antonio and did so, leaving the Hill Country notably rattled by his visit.

The view of the Hill Country from San Antonio did not improve in July. General Bee convened a military tribunal in San Antonio to consider "all offenses accomplished or intended, which shall be injurious to the Confederate States of America, and beneficial to the United States of America." The defendants were to be the alleged Unionists rounded up by Duff and by other troops under General Bee. The first defendant was a man accused of "having personal interview with the U. S. consul at Matamoras, Mexico" and of attempting "to flee the country in order to escape Military Duty." The accused protested his innocence, the tribunal could find little evidence of his guilt, and he was acquitted.

The second defendant, D. A. Saltmarsh, was not so fortunate. Accused of having used seditious language against the Confederate States of America, he pled "not guilty" to having said "that the Confederate States had been whiped in several battles, & that the North was too strong for the South, and that he hoped the day would come that Texas wold be brought to her senses." Worse, it was asserted that he had said that "the fire eaters of the South, who had brought this war on would have to fight it out, and he hoped to God they would, that Texas had acted the fool & he hoped she would be brought to her senses & that he was a Union man and his sentiments were with the North, that he had always lived under the 'Stars and Stripes' and he wished always to do so." The tribunal found him guilty and sentenced him to twelve months in prison, followed by expulsion from the Confederate States.

Merchant and Captain Julius Schlickum of Boerne was tried in July. He protested that he was not a Unionist and had taken the requisite Confederate loyalty oath. The charge was that "in his general deportment he is calculated to create discontent and dissatisfaction with this Government and its currency." He was found guilty and sentenced to imprisonment until the war was over.

The incongruity of Schlickum—a captain of Texas State Troops—being convicted of Unionism was hardly unique. The next defendant on the docket—Gillespie County Sheriff Philip Braubach—was a lieutenant in Kuechler's company. The month before Schlickum's trial, Texas Brigadier General Robert Bechem was obliged to inform the Adjutant General that the prisoners in San Antonio included a major and a captain in his brigade—in addition to Lieutenant Braubach and Captain Schlickum—and that another captain was being pursued. "The indifference in the Counties displeases me very much," understated Bechem.

Most of the testimony against Sheriff and Lieutenant Braubach had to do with his affiliation with the now-infamous Kuechler. Friedrich Doebbler, himself under arrest, testified on Braubach's behalf. The formal charges were that he arrested some men only so that they could stay out of the Confederate Army, and that he disparaged the value of Confederate currency. The commission found him guilty, ordered him imprisoned for ninety days and assessed a $200 fine. But Brigadier General Bee was not satisfied with the sentence; it was revised to be imprisonment during the war and banishment from the Confederate States thereafter.

On July 25 Freidrich Doebbler, the Grapetown innkeeper, came before the tribunal. Friedrich Fresinius, a frequent accuser before the commission, called him disloyal and claimed that he wrote a disloyal article for the New York Democrat. A man named Krauskopff made the same unsubstantiated allegation, and Charles Nimitz of Fredericksburg repeated it, adding that Doebbler kept "Black Republican" newspapers in his inn. Other locals followed the trend in testimony. Doebbler was found guilty on July 28 and sentenced to imprisonment for the term of the war.

Things did not, however, work out as intended for Schlickum, Braubach and Doebbler. They escaped prison on the night of Sunday, August 2, and were never recaptured. By August 29 the tribunal worked its

Gillespie County Sheriff Philip Braubach, in New Orleans, wearing the uniform of the Union First Texas Cavalry. Photograph from UTSA Institute of Texan Cultures.

way around to Mrs. Schlickum, who had been arrested in Boerne more than two months earlier. It released her without trial.

A lot had happened in the Hill Country during the two months that Mrs. Schlickum had languished in jail. "In July," according to General Bee, "information was received establishing the fact that Jack Hamilton and other traitors were unquestionably in arms against the Government and had assembled in the [Hill Country] counties designated, their force being variously estimated at from 100 to 500. Numerous statements were also received that these banded traitors were moving their goods and families, with large supplies of provisions, into the mountain districts, and were carrying off the property in some instances of loyal citizens, and at last, to set beyond a doubt their objects and intentions, positive intelligence was received of their having waylaid and murdered one or two well-known secession or loyal citizens."

The assembly that General Bee was fretting about was a Union Loyal League rally The involvement of Jack Hamilton is far from clear, but it is certain that during July a group of league members met near Bear Creek in the hills between Fredericksburg and Comfort. They hoisted the Union flag, talked of revolution and formed a militia, designating carpenter and miller Fritz Tegener as a major commanding a Unionist battalion composed of three companies. The Gillespie County company was headed by fugitive Jacob Kuechler. The Kendall County company was led by Ernst Kramer, who had attended the Union Loyal League meeting in San Antonio. Henry Hartman led the Kerr County company.

The assembly named an advisory board that included Edward Degener. Degener's son Hugo was a lieutenant in the Kendall County company. Almost certainly also at the meeting was Hilmar Degener, Edward's other son. We have seen the Degeners before. Edward was a Forty-Eighter, the purchaser of Nicolaus Zink's farm at Sisterdale, a prominent member of the Latin Colony, a founder of Sisterdale's Freie Verein and one of the organizers of the 1854 political convention in San Antonio. We first saw Hugo and Hilmar Degener when their father told Frederick Law Olmsted that "if he could secure them here minds free from prejudice which would entirely disregard the conclusions of others in their own study of right and truth, and spirits which would sustain their individual conclusions without a thought of the consequences, he should be only thankful to the circumstances that exiled him [from Germany]." The Degeners' intellectual bent, and that of the other Hill Country freethinkers, ties directly to abolitionism and Unionism. It was their adamant intellectual independence that brought all three Degeners to Bear Creek.

Unknown to Tegener and the other Unionists, the meeting at Bear Creek had been infiltrated by a secessionist named Steward, an Englishman by birth. Steward went to the authorities and told them what he knew, which was not more than a few names, but the rumor of Hill Country resistance began to spread, and quickly reached the ears of General Bee. The league decided that Steward's betrayal merited death. They drew straws, and Ernst Beseler was saddled with the duty of execution. Steward was killed by a rifle shot as he drove cattle through a narrow ravine.

Reacting to the brewing insurrection, Bee appointed Captain James Duff, who had only recently returned from the Hill Country, as provost-marshal for the region and placed four companies of Texas Mounted Riflemen under his control. The goals were similar to those of Duff's previous foray: declare martial law and demand oaths of allegiance upon penalty of being "treated summarily as traitors in arms." That phrase—treated summarily as traitors in arms—was loaded with meaning for a man such as Duff.

Duff's four companies were also ordered to "send out scouting parties into the mountain districts with orders to find and break up any such encampments and depots as had been reported to exist there, and to send the families and provisions back to the settlements."

The reappearance of the dreaded Captain Duff took the wind out of Unionist sails. Scores of men who had been hiding in the hills and consorting with the Unionist militia returned to their homes, bit their tongues and took loyalty oaths. Freethinking Ernst Kapp, the scholarly proprietor of Sisterdale's Hydrotherapy Institute and a founding member of the Freie Verein, took the oath on July 4, 1862.

Even the hard core of the Union Loyal League's militia realized that they had gone too far. When Fritz Tegener heard of Duff's arrival in July, and learned of General Bee's determination to wipe out any Hill Country resistance, he convened a meeting of the league's advisory board. The board decided to disband the three militia companies in an effort to convince the Confederate authorities that armed conflict was not in the plan. For himself, Tegener was unwilling to swear allegiance to the Confederacy and he decided to flee for Mexico, letting it be known that any other militia members who felt likewise should meet him at the headwaters of Turtle Creek in Kerr County on August 1ˢᵗ.

On July 25, Edward Degener came to John Sansom's house on Curry's Creek for a talk. They discussed the Union Loyal League, and Degener filled Sansom in on the latest meetings and the decision by the advisory board to disband its militia. Hugo and Hilmar Degener would be riding with Fritz Tegener to Mexico, their father said, adding that he would be pleased if Sansom would join the group. Although he had been elected Kendall County sheriff just a few months earlier, Sansom was already making his own plans to head for the border. At Degener's suggestion he decided to join the league at its assembly point on Turtle Creek on the thirty-first.

According to Sansom, about eighty men gathered on Turtle Creek. After discussion, a few more than sixty departed for the Rio Grande on August 2 under Fritz Tegener's command. All but two—John Sansom and Pablo Diaz—were German. The men who did not join the expedition to Mexico returned to their families and homes, hoping for a better alternative, perhaps resigned to taking an oath in which they did not believe.

Even today, the headwaters of Turtle Creek are remote, lying in rugged hills southwest of Kerrville. In 1862, this was the frontier, and the chances of being observed or intercepted were low. But this is not to say that the Germans were entering uncharted territory. They headed west from Turtle Creek and met the South Fork of the Guadalupe River, then followed it upstream (southwest) on a course that led toward Camp Wood, a former U. S. Army post on the road to El Paso. Camp Wood was occupied by Confederate forces and would have to be avoided. Fritz Tegener was familiar with at least the first leg of their journey: his sawmill was beyond the Turtle Creek meeting point, on a stream that is now known as Tegener Creek.

Duff got wind of the Germans' plans. He dispatched a company of ninety-four men under the command of First Lieutenant Collin D. McRae of the Second Regiment, Texas Mounted Riflemen, to search for the band of Unionists said to be gathering. On August 3, a day after the Unionists broke camp at Turtle Creek, McRae's patrol departed their camp on the Pedernales River, southwest of Fredericksburg. They were searching for Tegener's Unionists, and they had information to aid them. How they came to have the information is unclear, though the name of one Baumann or Bergmann figures in most of the versions. Some have a Unionist going back toward Tegener's mill to catch a horse that had gotten away, and being intercepted by McRae's men. Another version says that Baumann was a spy in the midst of the Unionists. Yet another says that the Germans stole supplies from Bergmann, and he reported them to the authorities.

Sixty-plus horsemen, with extra horses along, leave an unmistakable trail when they move through the arid plains and hills of West Texas. It was not long before McRae's company was in hot pursuit. For four days they chased their quarry. Ignorant of the danger, the Germans took their time in the August heat, riding at a leisurely pace, making camp early, hunting for deer and turkey and singing and speech-making into the night. When they met four men on the trail—Tom Scott, W. B. Scott, Howard Henderson and William Hester—they invited the four strangers to join the trip to Mexico. The four decided to follow at least as far as the Nueces River.

On the evening of August 9 McRae's scouts spotted the Unionist party camped near the headwaters of the Western Fork of the Nueces River, on the inside of a horseshoe bend with bluffs opposite. McRae made camp in an arroyo more than two miles away, then accompanied scouts on reconnaissance. Returning to camp, he ordered his men to prepare for an attack at daybreak. After midnight, he moved his company to within three hundred yards of the Unionist camp. Splitting his men into two groups, he directed them to move toward the left and right flanks of the Unionists, within fifty yards of the sleeping men.

The Germans had posted sentries, more likely for Comanches than for soldiers. Around three in the morning Leopold Bauer and John Sansom took over the watch. Bauer entered a dense canebrake, with Sansom about twenty feet behind. Bauer stumbled into the enemy's lines. A shot rang out and he fell dead. Sansom returned fire. This is one of several points in the story (some preceding this moment) where versions diverge, but it appears that an exchange of gunfire ensued between the two camps. Fritz Tegener was wounded twice; Ernst Beseler—who had shot Steward from ambush for betraying the league—was killed; then all fell eerily silent for a half hour or more. Germans prepared for battle. Some slipped away into the brush. The Texas Mounted Riflemen waited for daylight. A second Unionist sentinel shouted an alarm, and was shot. Still McRae waited patiently for light.

John Sansom conferred with Hugo Degener, Hilmar Degener, Pablo Diaz and others. He recommended that the Unionists try to escape. Hugo Degener refused, and others—including about twenty men from Comfort who had joined Ernst Kramer's militia company—followed his lead. Sansom took his saddle and, joined by the Scotts, Henderson and Hester, went looking for a path of withdrawal.

When the firing commenced, it did not take long. The state troops advanced on foot slowly and steadily, firing as they advanced. Once within thirty paces of the Unionist camp, McRae ordered a charge. The Germans were routed and fled.

The numbers of dead and wounded vary from account to account. The tally was between ten and twenty Unionist dead, among them Hugo and Hilmar Degener and Pablo Diaz. Nine or more were wounded, including a Luckenbach. McRae's command gathered up eighty-three horses, thirty-three rifles, thirteen pistols and most of the Germans' provisions and equipment, abandoned in their flight. Accounts of dead and wounded on McRae's side vary widely; he reported eighteen wounded and two killed. McRae advised his superiors that "my officers and men all behaved with the greatest coolness and gallantry, seeming to vie with each other in deeds of daring chivalry." His commander, General Bee, reported that "Lieutenant McRae and his command behaved with admirable coolness and bravery, and did their work most effectually."

Some have questioned why it was necessary for McRae to pursue and engage Germans who were, after all, trying to flee the state for Mexico. The short answer was that the Governor and the Confederacy had ordered just that. And some have said that the Germans were planning to join the Union Army, thus were, or were about to be, armed enemies. The facts, however, don't bear that out; of the men who escaped the fighting at the Nueces, only a few ended up in Union service. Others waited out the war in Mexico or California. Several found their way back to the Hill Country and either hid from the authorities or submitted to the Confederate regime. Sansom claimed to have made repeated forays from Mexico into Texas, stirring up Union support. He said that nineteen were killed on the Nueces, nine more were killed when later caught by one of Duff's companies, eight were killed crossing the Rio Grande into Mexico in October, eleven joined the Union Army and the remainder—eighteen by his count—returned to the Hill Country, remained in Mexico or fled to California.

Whether or not the Unionists were planning on joining the Union Army, it is clear that they were not innocents fleeing Confederate abuse. They were provocateurs who knew full well the risks facing ardent Unionists in Texas. They knew that Unionists—even Unionists leaving the state—were to be treated summarily as traitors in arms.

Looking at all the facts, it would stretch credulity to claim that the Union Loyal League's militia meant to do anything but resist the Confederacy in some manner. If anything, their purpose may have been more than resistance: it is entirely possible to connect dots suggesting that the Union Loyal League was an insurgency meant to result in a free State of West Texas. The idea of an independent German colony dates back to Prince Solms. Advocacy of just such a result was one reason why Adolf Douai eventually fled Texas. The 1854 convention, the formation of militias, the cries of revolution, the refusal of pro-Union Germans to either leave Texas or compromise their beliefs—all these point to something more than simple political activism.

It is undeniable that the Union Loyal League was not nearly so benign as Sansom painted it, claiming that it meant only to "take such action as might peaceably secure its members and their families from being disturbed and compelled to bear arms against the union, and to protect their families against the hostile Indians." It is telling that when Lieutenant McRae's men fired the first shots in the morning darkness, Sansom and the four other Anglos saddled up and took flight, as did more than half of the Germans, but the remaining Germans under the command of Fritz Tegener chose to stand and fight even though the darkness provided perfect cover for withdrawal. John Sansom counseled Hugo Degener to flee, but he replied that "I would rather fight here until every man of us is killed than to go anywhere else." The core of the Union Loyal League—the Forty-Eighters from Sisterdale, Comfort and Fredericksburg—were Unionists, abolitionists and insurrectionists. They were, under the rules of engagement applicable across Texas, fair game.

Some people refer to the clash as the "Massacre on the Nueces," but the facts to this point in the episode hardly support any claim that predatory Confederate troops ambushed helpless pacifists. This was a battle on the Nueces. The massacre came next.

Some of McRae's men gathered up the wounded Germans and executed them. Then, rather than afford their opponents a decent burial, they piled their bodies on the plain and left them for the coyotes and vultures. McRae, who was wounded, probably did not participate in the executions and may not have known of them in advance. Even Sansom refers to him as "brave and fearless." McRae himself, in his report on the engagement, finessed the issue by saying that the Germans "offered the most determined resistance and fought with desperation, asking no quarter whatever; hence I have no prisoners to report." R. H. Williams, who was there with McRae's company, called it "cowardly murder." But in the world of General Hamilton Bee and Captain James Duff, in a world where troops were expected to seek out Unionists and were not expected to bring back prisoners, was it unexpected?

Edward Degener, a member of the Union Loyal League advisory committee whose two sons were killed on the Nueces, soon found himself facing General Bee's San Antonio military tribunal. Standing before the court on September 27, he knew that one of his sons was dead, but had no word on the fate of the other. He was charged with knowing about the militia that fled for Mexico but failing to inform the authorities. Charges included making "false seditious exaggerated and slanderous written statements" in August to "bring the Confederate Government into disrepute" and of corresponding with, assisting and aiding the men who fought McRae's company on the Nueces.

The evidence included a letter written by Degener, apparently taken from a German at the Nueces by Confederate Lieutenant Edwin F. Lilly, who served in McRae's outfit. Meant for delivery to a friend in Mexico, the letter described the hardships of life during the war and described Germans fleeing to the hills with Confederates in pursuit. "The troops from the South express openly the threat that they will not make any more prisoners; what this means, an American is only able to say. If the south is victorious, it may become necessary for the Germans to emigrate again. In what direction then?"

Confederate Private W. J. Edwards related a conversation he had with Degener, in which the German "said that he knew the men [at the Nueces] well, that they were the best shots in the country, that they would never have surrendered, we never would have whopped them if we had not had the advantage—He said that they were right, we were right,—they were fighting for their opinions & we for ours."

Degener was represented by capable counsel who summoned an impressive list of witnesses on his behalf. Ernst Kapp swore that Degener was neutral on the war and not opposed to slavery. According to him, Degener took the oath of loyalty. Ernst Altgelt said that he was present when Degener advised his sons to take the oath. He characterized Degener as believing that "the seven Cotton States would maintain their independence, though it might possibly be that the states west of the Mississippi might possibly be given up in the treaty."

Sisterdale's Christian Rhodius, who had married one of Degener's daughters, said that Degener tried to get his sons to take the oath but "they were strong-headed & set in their opinions & could not be controlled by their father." According to Rhodius, Degener had warned his sons not to participate in the insurrectionist meetings in the hills. But Rhodius said that "I do not regard him as a strong secessionist, meaning by that term a man who lays down his life or fights for the country—both of us became secessionists when the state seceded."

Gustav Schleicher—by now a Confederate supporter—allowed that Degener had participated in the 1854 San Antonio convention, but "he was disgusted with it, & in later years admitted it was folly, & I know that he scarcely went out of his house after in Election matters." Schleicher's support was, however, lukewarm, saying that Degener "staid at home & was fond of talking & making pointed remarks, but I do not believe he would do anything against the Govt., though he might talk—that is he would criticise the government, and say that the secession movement was wrong, but I don't think he would take any action against the Government. I don't know as a matter of fact whether he is a dangerous or seditious person."

Counsel for Degener made an impassioned speech, asserting that at most the evidence could be construed as proving Degener's neutrality. "But could the crime of *neutrality* be applied to an old man beyond the age of conscription, nearly 'three score years,' living upon the frontier in an Indian Country, with barely the means of support, who has fully complied with all of the laws and requirements of the Government, because forsooth he has not voluntarily shouldered his musket and gone forth to peril his life in the defense of his adopted Country?"

The tribunal was persuaded, barely. They found Degener guilty of two charges and not guilty of one; for his punishment he was required to post a five thousand dollar bond, conditioned upon conducting himself "during the war as a good and loyal citizen to the Confederate States." Degener was free.

The combined effects of Duff's raids, the battle on the Nueces and Bee's military tribunal broke the back of the Hill Country insurrection. Most of those young enough and rash enough to resist the Confederacy had fled. Those that remained, and those that sneaked back after the firefight on the Nueces, were at risk of being rounded up by Duff's patrols.

August Hoffman and eight friends made their way back to the Hill Country after the Nueces and hid out in the hills. One of their number got sick and saw a doctor, who reported his presence to the authorities. The patient was made prisoner and three of his companions were captured. According to Hoffman, the three were taken to the countryside, told to run for their lives, then shot in the back by Duff's men. Hoffman and his four remaining cohorts stayed on the run until April 1863, when "a man by the name of Hamilton interceded for us" and got them a job freighting for the Confederate Army.

Jacob Kuechler was one of those who made their ways back to the Hill Country. In October he headed back for Mexico in the company of ten companions. They were intercepted at the Rio Grande, and eight of their number were killed. Lucky more than twice, Kuechler escaped across the river.

In September Confederate President Jefferson Davis pronounced General Paul O. Hebert's declaration of martial law illegal. Only the executive, said Davis, could declare martial law. Hebert responded with a somewhat insubordinate letter, backed by written praise of martial law by Governor Lubbock, but dutifully lifted the sanctions.

As resistance in the Hill Country waned, the Confederate command's attention shifted to German communities to the east, in Colorado, Austin, Fayette, Caldwell and Bastrop counties. The Austin county enrolling officer complained of "a spirit of insubordination existing among the Germans in this region. I have it from the most reliable authority that they contemplate resistance to the conscript law as well as the contemplated draft." Major-General John B. Magruder replaced the chastened General Hebert and took a new approach, in December directing the enrolling officers to "cause all persons of foreign birth who exhibit opposition to the enforcement of the conscript law to be sent from this State and united with regiments in other departments before all other conscripts, and that where they are found most hostile to its operations they be sent first of all." Magruder ordered that "in doing this you will exercise much caution, causing it to be done quietly and without show if such a thing be practicable, in order that all odious distinctions between the good and loyal citizens of foreign birth and those who are refractory may be obviated, and that no difficulties from this cause also may arise between our native-born citizens and those of foreign birth."

But German resistance along the Colorado River intensified and Magruder was obliged to resort to more direct means. He ordered several companies of cavalry, backed by artillery, to LaGrange and directed that the ringleaders of the resistance be rounded up. The show of force—and not a little unofficial enforcement by Confederate loyalists, accompanied by unrestrained excesses of an Arizona brigade assisting in the exercise—proved enough. By late January 1863 the Confederate command reported to the Texas assistant adjutant-general that "the Germans and others who had been in rebellion have all quietly submitted to the draft and all have come to the different rendezvous and been enrolled as soldiers. Those who were not drafted and are at home profess to be loyal and promise to submit cheerfully to the laws of the State and Confederacy."

Chapter Ten
Illusions

In 1865 a group of Comfort citizens traveled to the site on the Nueces where their sons and neighbors had died. They collected the bleached bones, carried them back to Comfort and interred them under an obelisk inscribed *Treue der Union*. It is said to be the only monument to Unionist dead in a Confederate state. It has led to Comfort being seen as the center of Unionism in the Hill Country, even though Fredericksburg and Boerne were more inclined toward the cause and Sisterdale was the intellectual birthplace of resistance.

The Civil War was a rite of passage for the Hill Country Germans. It did not end their isolation or cause their sudden assimilation—the region remained largely German-speaking for generations after—but it brought home the reality that their communities were part of a larger construct, and that they existed within its strictures. Still, it would be a mistake to select those few years as the moment when Hill Country Germans were suddenly transformed into Texans or Americans.

What is remarkable is the change that came over the German communities in a span of less than twenty years, from arrival at Carlshaven to insurrection in Fredericksburg. Men and women who had huddled on the windswept coast, traded with Chief Ketemoczy, survived waves of yellow fever and cholera and trudged on foot into a wilderness of unknowns, now found themselves among feuding newspaper editors, firebrand politicians, nervous military commanders and rough vigilantes. Their frontier communities, once unified by a thirst for freedom and opportunity, were now divided over slavery and secession—issues entirely alien to their worlds, issues that threatened the very freedom and opportunity that they sought. It was as if another plague had been brought by outsiders.

The Civil War marks the conclusion of German settlement of the Texas Hill Country. The war extinguished the last grand, expansive, optimistic, idealistic movement among the Germans. During the Civil War the German Texans shed the last of their fantasies.

The Adelsverein tried to liberate the German underclasses, only to discover that it cost more money than expected, yielded less commerce than expected and did almost nothing to change the social dislocation in Germany. The Forty indulged their communal visions at Bettina and Tusculum and came away with a new understanding of how people really behave. The Forty-Eighters created their Latin colony and trumpeted their ideals at the San Antonio convention, only to have calumny heaped upon them, have large sectors of Germans in Texas disavow their beliefs and have their most ardent scribe flee the state.

The final blow to the Germans' idealistic view of their new home came when the old warhorses and young warriors of the Union Loyal League infiltrated the Frontier Regiment, formed secret militias, fomented revolution, then suffered brief but unrelenting Confederate military pressure that depleted their ranks, threw them into vile jails, hung them from trees, forced them into exile and killed them in cold blood at the Nueces.

It was the end of an era, the end of ideals that proved ill-suited to the realities of life in Texas. During Reconstruction there was no German celebration, no grand resurgence of liberal colloquy. The war was tragic and Reconstruction only a bit less so. It was a time for grieving, a time for reconsideration, a time to chart a new path. From that moment forward there were fewer illusions.

In 1869 John Meusebach moved from Fredericksburg to the small farming village of Loyal Valley (as in loyal to the Union) and spent his later years tending his roses and grapes. He died there and is buried in a family plot near Cherry Spring. Three creeks are named for him—a pittance. The most notable names in the Loyal Valley cemetery are those of Herman and Willie Lehmann, the brothers kidnapped by the Apaches.

Henry Fisher did not leave much of a mark after signing over his remaining interest in the Fisher-Miller colonization contract to the Adelsverein in 1845 for $5,000. He returned to Germany and died in Wiesbaden in 1867, leaving a widow and four children.

After moving from Fredericksburg to Sisterdale to Cypress Creek, Nicolas Zink eventually settled with his third wife, Agnes, at Spanish Pass, between Boerne and Comfort. He died there and is buried on a knoll at the base of the pass.

Bernard Monken and his father—the only survivors of their family's brutal trek from Carlshaven to New Braunfels—purchased a ranch near Van Raub, Texas, between Leon Springs and Boerne. For a time Bernard was a merchant and postmaster at Spring Branch. At his death in 1909, the ranch was divided among his three sons.

Fredericksburg leader and timid frontiersman Dr. Friedrich Schubert, who was actually Friedrich Armand Strubberg, returned to Germany and wrote more than fifty Wild West novels under the pen name Armand. The Adelsverein sued him in 1850 for malfeasance. The verein files containing his papers disappeared for a time (perhaps to protect his reputation), then mysteriously resurfaced in the 1960s and were purchased by Yale University. Strubberg died in 1889 in Germany.

In 1872 early verein cohort and staunch Democrat Ferdinand Lindheimer ended his work at the *Neu-Braunsfelser Zeitung* and resumed his career in botany. He is credited with discovering hundreds of plant species and subspecies, forty-eight of which bear his name. He and his wife Eleanor had two children and lived out their days in their house in New Braunfels. It is now a museum. Lindheimer died in 1879; he is buried in New Braunfels.

Emil Kriewitz, the noble who went native, lived out his days at Castell as a rancher, real estate speculator and postmaster. He is buried in the Llano County Cemetery.

Herman Spiess, the member of the Forty who represented the Adelsverein in its last active days, married the Mexican woman that was given to Ferdinand Herff. Her German name was Lena. In 1867 a doctor advised Spiess to move to a colder climate; he and Lena relocated to Warrensburg, Missouri, where he died.

Friedrich Doebbler remained in Grapetown and operated his inn. A stone school was built in Grapetown in 1880 (classes had originally been held in Doebbler's home), and is one of the few structures that remain, along with the town's legendary shooting club. Doebbler is buried in the Grapetown cemetery.

Jacob Luckenbach's son August was slain at the battle at the Nueces. In 1883, at age 66, Jacob sold his home along Grape Creek and moved to Boerne, to be near six children who lived there. When his wife Justina died in 1907, she was survived by eleven children, forty-two grandchildren and twenty-two great grandchildren. Jacob died precisely four years later in his small stone house that still stands on Boerne's Main Street.

Dr. Ferdinand Herff became one of the leading physicians and citizens of San Antonio, founding Santa Rosa Hospital and involving himself in many other worthy projects, including the construction of the San Antonio & Aransas Pass Railroad. He was a Boerne booster and spent a great deal of his time on his ranch there. Part of the ranch is now within the Cibolo Nature Center, founded by his great-great-great-granddaughter, Carolyn Chipman Evans.

Gustav Schleicher, the slippery member of the Forty who bought the *San Antonio Zeitung* from Adolph Douai, served San Antonio as a lawyer, then became a railroad construction engineer. He founded Cuero, Texas, as a railroad town and moved there. He was elected to Congress, where he flourished. He is buried in San Antonio's United States National Cemetery. Schleicher County bears his name.

Edward Degener relocated from Sisterdale to San Antonio after the Civil War and opened a grocery business. He was a member of the postbellum Texas Constitutional Conventions and was elected to Congress in 1870 as a Republican. For a time he served on the San Antonio City Council. He died in 1890 and is buried in the San Antonio city cemetery.

After mustering out of involuntary service in the Confederate Army, August Siemering immersed himself in the San Antonio newspaper business, founding the acclaimed German-language Republican paper *Freie Presse fur Texas*. He married Clara Schutze, the daughter of a pioneer Gillespie County teacher. She and their seven children survived his death in San Antonio in 1883.

During the Civil War Ernst Altgelt traveled from Comfort to Germany, returning in time to serve briefly in the Confederate Army. He moved to San Antonio in 1866, opened a law practice and invested in real estate. His house on King William Street may have been the first built there, and he may be the one who named the street after King Wilhelm I of Prussia. He died in 1878 on his ranch at Wassenberg.

After selling the *San Antonio Zeitung* to Gustav Schleicher in 1856 (and being run out of Texas), Adolph Douai moved to Boston, where he established a kindergarten that is said to be the first in the United States. His loudly proclaimed atheism annoyed the good people of Boston, and he left for Hoboken, New Jersey, and then New York City, where he founded several schools and continued his career as a teacher and journalist. He died in Brooklyn in 1888 and was cremated.

Jacob Kuechler made good his escape to Mexico and worked there as a surveyor during the Civil War. He was a delegate to the post-war Texas Constitutional Conventions and became a leading German Republican politician. He was commissioner of the Texas General Land Office for four years until 1874, then returned to private surveying positions for railroad companies. He died in Austin in 1893 and is buried in Oakwood Cemetery.

Edgar von Westphalen made his way to Mexico during the Civil War, possibly with the group that survived the affair at the Nueces (he was a member of Jacob Kuechler's Unionist Frontier Regiment company). He turned up in England in May 1865 and found lodging with Friedrich Engels in Manchester. Jenny Westphalen Marx reported that the London parks "reminded him of his prairies and his deserts of Texas." He left England for Germany after six weeks and moved in with the Marx family, ultimately becoming a minor civil servant in Berlin. He died there in 1890.

Ernst Kapp left his hydrotherapy institute and returned to Germany in 1865. While there he took ill; due to fragile health, he remained in Germany until his death in 1896 at Dusseldorf, but he left descendants in Sisterdale and Comfort. The spa at Badenthal has been restored and is in private ownership. His cabin door, studded with nails to repel arrows, is in a private museum in Comfort.

Surveyor and real estate speculator John James engaged in business and community affairs in San Antonio. Though he was opposed to secession, he managed to live out the Civil War there and enjoyed good relations with the Confederate officers. He died in 1877; there is a San Antonio park that bears his name.

After the Civil War, John Sansom resumed service as a Texas Ranger in the Hill Country, then retired to his ranch in Uvalde County. In his later years he moved to San Antonio. He is buried in Mission Burial Park, near the Mission San Jose.

George Wilkins Kendall continued raising sheep on his ranch outside Boerne, and is regarded as the father of the Texas sheep industry. He died in 1867; his descendants were prominent in San Antonio. Kendall County is named after him.

Ottomar von Behr lived in Sisterdale and made regular trips back to Germany to manage property he owned there. He died on one of those trips, leaving his widow in Texas. The Behr house at Sisterdale is still occupied by Behr's great-great-grandson, Charles Kohls.

These are the traces left by only a few of the people who participated in the German settlement of the Texas Hill Country. The original settlers left a convoluted, intermarried matrix of descendants, many of whom still live in the region. Because of the strong ties among Hill Country families, and because German remained the primary tongue until just a few decades ago, Hill Country towns were once considered closed societies where a newcomer was not afforded a hearty welcome. That has changed, and new arrivals make friends quickly. Still, there are strong, important legacies and traditions here, and the new arrival—or even the visitor—is well advised to keep a respectful ear tuned for German names that might have a great deal of history behind them. These were—and are—remarkable people.

Thoughts and Thanks

I research and write in a solitary manner, so I seldom have a long list of people to thank. But there are always a few that stick out in my memory.

I have never met Wolfram Von-Maszewski, but his translations of Solms's diary and his post-Texas writings are obviously a work of love and were an invaluable help to my work. Many of the Solms quotes during his travels came from Von-Maszewski's translations.

William Paul Burrier, Sr. of Leakey, Texas, is mildly obsessed with the battle on the Nueces and provided me some great documents and information that aren't widely known. I think someday he will produce the definitive book on that event.

Bjorn Freitag performed an immense amount of German translation for me while he completed his doctoral work at the University of Texas. He vanished shortly after leaving Austin; I hope he's doing well.

Charles Kohls of Sisterdale shared information about his great-great-grandfather, Ottomar von Behr. Georgeanna Dillon, who is a Stendebach and a Monken, graciously provided me with a couple of family history booklets and a fair amount of oral history. Ken Toepperwein is most generous with his family history, which is nothing short of remarkable. In a way, this book began with my interest in the Stendebachs, Toepperweins and Kohls: John Stendebach bought acreage outside Boerne in 1858 and homesteaded it; in 1880 he sold it to G. A. Toepperwein; in 1940, the Toepperweins sold it to Herbert Kohls (whose wife Lottie was a Sisterdale Behr); in 2002, the Kohls family sold it to me, complete with the original Stendebach cabin.

Local historian Ed Mergele has a comprehensive knowledge that inspires me and makes me want to absorb facts the way he does. Bettie

Edmonds is a Boerne historian and artist; she graciously provided access to the resources of the Boerne Area Historical Preservation Society.

As for authors who went before, Rudolph Biesele is the forefather of German Hill Country History. His book has been the gold standard for generations. It is only because so much new information has surfaced in the last seventy-five years that it was appropriate to look again at the subject that he covered so well for his 1928 doctoral dissertation.

In every Hill Country town, one or two local historians undertook the task of documenting the local stories, and my book relies on those efforts. These people—Garland Perry, Glen Lich, Oscar Haas, Guido Ransleben, Don Biggers and others—paved the way for me.

It is traditional for an author to thank their spouse. Most authors are gracious enough to do it at the beginning of their acknowledgments, instead of toward the end like this. I think it's okay, though—Jeanne is pretty secure about my love for her. I'm grateful that she tolerates me and my writing addiction, and I am most fortunate that she's a hell of an editor.

Finally, thanks to all the kind folks at the many libraries, agencies and institutions where I performed research: the Center for American History at the University of Texas at Austin; the Texas State Library and Archives; the Institute of Texan Cultures at the University of Texas at San Antonio; the San Antonio Public Library; the Boerne Public Library; the Comfort Public Library; the County Clerk's Offices of Bexar, Kendall, Gillespie and Comal Counties, and the Clerks of the District Courts of those counties; the Sophienburg Museum and Archives in New Braunfels; the Boerne Area Historic Preservation Society; and the Pioneer Museum in Fredericksburg and the archives of the Gillespie County Historical Society.

Bibliography

Adam, Kathryn L. "Foreign Visionaries in the Texas Hill Country: Early German Settlers in the Kendall County Area, 1847-1900." Master's thesis, Texas Woman's University, 1979.

Adams, Ephraim Douglass, comp. "Correspondence from the British Archives Concerning Texas, 1837-1846," *Southwestern Historical Quarterly*, 19:299 (1912).

Anonymous. "Die Lateinische Farm," *Deutsch-Texanische Monatshefte*, II:238 (1896).

Anonymous. *A Pioneer Family History, The Weitz Family in Texas 1852 – 1922; The First Stendebachs in Texas 1852 – 1961.* n.p., ?

Anonymous. *Diamond Jubilee Souvenir Book of Comfort, Texas, commemorating 75th Anniversary.* San Antonio: Standard Printing Co., 1929.

Barba, Preston Albert. *The Life and Works of Armand Strubberg.* Philadelphia: University of Pennsylvania, 1913.

Barr, Alwyn. "Records of the Confederate Military Commission in San Antonio, July 2 – October 10, 1862," *Southwestern Historical Quarterly* 70:93 and 289 (1966) and 623 (1967), 71:247 (1967), 73:83 and 243 (1969).

Bartlett, John Russell. *Personal Narrative of Explorations and Incidents in Texas, New Mexico, California, Sonora, and Chihuahua.* New York: D. Appleton & Co., 1854.

Baum, Dale. *The Shattering of Texas Unionism, Politics in the Lone Star State during the Civil War.* Baton Rouge: Louisiana State University Press, 1998.

Benjamin, Gilbert Giddings. *The Germans in Texas.* Austin: Jenkins Publishing Co., 1974.

Biesele, Rudolph L. "The Texas State Convention of Germans in 1854," *Southwestern Historical Quarterly* 33:252 (1930).

———. *The History of the German Settlements in Texas 1831-1861.* Austin: Von Boeckmann-Jones, 1930. Reprint, Austin, Eakin Press, 1987.
Biggers, Don H. *German Pioneers in Texas.* Fredericksburg: Fredericksburg Publishing Co., 1925.
Boerne Area Historical Preservation Society. *The Journey to Boerne, Finding and Making a New Home.* n.p., 1999.
Boerne Area Historical Preservation Society. Vertical Files and Records. Boerne, Texas.
Bracht, Viktor. *Texas in 1848.* Translated by Charles Frank Schmidt. Manchaca, TX: German-Texan Heritage Society, 1991.
Buenger, Walter L. "Secession and the Texas German Community: Editor Lindheimer versus Editor Flake," *Southwestern Historical Quarterly* 82:379 (1979).
———. "Texas and the Riddle of Secession," *Southwestern Historical Quarterly*, 37:151 (1983).
———. *Secession and the Union in Texas.* Austin: University of Texas Press, 1984.
Chipman, Donald E. *Spanish Texas 1519 – 1821.* Austin: University of Texas Press, 1992.
Clauss, C. Hugo. "Aus der Vergangenheit der Ansiedlung Boerne," *Deutsche-Texanische Monatshefte*, 7:308 (1902).
Clauss, C. Hugo. "Boerne und das Cibolo-Thal in Kendall County," *Jahrbuch fuer Texas*, 29 (1882).
Comal County Clerk. Records. New Braunfels, Texas.
Comal County District Clerk. Records. New Braunfels, Texas.
Comfort Public Library. Vertical files. Comfort, Texas.
Confederate States Army. *Proceedings of Confederate Military Commission convened at San Antonio, Texas, 1862.* Texas State Library and Archives Commission, Austin.
Copeland, Fayette. *Kendall of the Picayune.* Norman: University of Oklahoma Press, 1997.
Cramer, Ernest. Letter, "My Beloved Parents." October 30, 1862. Copy of translation courtesy of William Paul Burrier, Sr., Leakey, Texas.
De la Teja, Jesus. *San Antonio de Bexar, A Community on New Spain's Northern Frontier.* Albuquerque: University of New Mexico Press, 1995.

Dielmann, Henry B. "Dr. Ferdinand Herff, Pioneer Physician and Surgeon." *Southwestern Historical Quarterly* 57:268 (1954).

Dohmen, Frans J., trans. *Life and Memoirs of Emil Frederick Wurzbach, to which is appended some papers of John Meusebach.* (Yanaguana Society Publications III). San Antonio: Yanaguana Society, 1937.

Dresel Family Papers. San Antonio Public Library, San Antonio, Texas.

Elliott, Claude. "Union Sentiment in Texas, 1861-1865," *Southwestern Historical Quarterly*, 50:449 (1947).

Fey, Everett Anthony. *New Braunfels: The First Founders*. Austin: Eakin Press, 1994.

Fischer, Ernest G. *Marxists and Utopia in Texas*. Burnet: Eakin Press, 1980.

Flach, Vera. *A Yankee in German America*. San Antonio: Naylor Co., 1973.

Fremantle, Arthur James Lyon, Sir. *Three Months in the Southern States, April – June 1863*. Mobile: S. H. Goetzel, 1864.

Gallaway, B. P., ed. *Texas the Dark Corner of the Confederacy, Contemporary Accounts of the Lone Star State in the Civil War*. 3rd. ed. Lincoln: University of Nebraska Press, 1994.

Gammel, Hans Peter Marius, comp. *The Laws of Texas, 1822-1897.* 10 vols. Austin: Gammel Book Co., 1898.

Geiser, S. W. "Dr. Ernst Kapp, Early Geographer in Texas." *Field & Laboratory* 7:16 (1946).

Genealogical Society of Kendall County. Vertical files and records. Boerne, Texas.

Geue, Chester W. and Ethel H., eds. *A New Land Beckoned*. n.p., 1972.

Gillespie County Clerk. Records. Fredericksburg, Texas.

Gillespie County District Clerk. Records. Fredericksburg, Texas.

Glenn, Frankie Davis. *Capt'n John, Story of a Texas Ranger*. Austin: Nortex Press, 1991.

Goethe, Ottilie Fuchs. *Memoirs of a Texas Pioneer Grandmother*. Burnet: Eakin Press, 1982.

Goyne, Minetta Altgelt. *A Life among the Texas Flora: Ferdinand Lindheimer's Letters to George Engelmann*. College Station: Texas A&M University Press, 1991.

Goyne, Minetta Altgelt. *Lone Star and Double Eagle, Civil War Letters of a German-Texas Family*. Fort Worth: Texas Christian University Press, 1982.

Gray, Edith A., comp. *Recollections of Boerne and Kendall County.* Boerne: n.p., 1949.

Greer, James Kimmins. *Colonel Jack Hays, Texas Frontier Leader and California Builder.* New York: E. P. Dutton & Co., 1952.

Haas, Oscar. *History of New Braunfels and Comal County, Texas 1844-1946.* Austin: The Steck Company, 1968.

Herff, Ferdinand Peter. *The Doctors Herff: A Three-Generation Memoir.* Edited by Laura L. Barber. 2 vols. San Antonio: Trinity University Press, 1973.

Herff, Ferdinand. *The Regulated Emigration of the German Proletariat with Special Reference to Texas.* Translated by Arthur L. Finck. San Antonio: Trinity University Press, 1978.

Hoffman, August. Papers. Center for American History, University of Texas at Austin.

Inscoe, John C. and Kenzer, Robert C. *Enemies of the Country: New Perspectives on Unionists in the Civil War South.* Athens: University of Georgia Press (2001).

Ivey, James E. "The Comanche Spring Site." *Tierra* (Southern Texas Archaeological Association) vol. 6, no. 1.

Jacoby, Susan. *Freethinkers: a History of American Secularism.* New York: Henry Holt and Co., 2004.

Jordan, Terry G. and Marlis Anderson, ed. and trans. "Letters of a German Pioneer in Texas." *Southwestern Historical Quarterly,* 69:463 (1966).

Jordan, Terry G. *German Seed in Texas Soil, Immigrant Farmers in Nineteenth-Century Texas.* Austin: University of Texas Press, 1966.

Kaufmann, Wilhelm. *Die Deutschen im der amerikanischen Burgerkriege.* Munich: R. Oldenbourg, 1911.

Kendall County Clerk. Records. Boerne, Texas.

Kendall County District Clerk. Records. Boerne, Texas.

Kendall County Historical Commission. *A History of Kendall County, Texas.* Dallas: Taylor Publishing Co., 1984.

King, Irene Marschall. *John O. Meusebach, German Colonizer in Texas.* Austin: University of Texas Press, 1967.

Kleberg, Rosa. "Early Experiences in Texas II," *Southwestern Historical Quarterly*, 2:170 (1898).

Kuechler, Jacob. Papers. Center for American History, University of Texas at Austin.

La Vere, David. *The Texas Indians.* College Station: Texas A&M University Press, 2004.

Lehmann, Herman. *9 Years Among the Indians.* Edited by J. Marvin Hunter. 1927. Reprint, Albuquerque: University of New Mexico Press, 2004.

Lich, Glen E. *The German Texans.* San Antonio: University of Texas Institute of Texan Cultures, 1981.

Lohmann, F. H. *Comfort.* Translated by Inge Haley. Comfort: Comfort Heritage Foundation, 2004.

Malsch, Brownson. *Indianola, the Mother of Western Texas.* Abilene: State House Press, 1988.

Marten, James Alan. *Texas Divided: Loyalty and Dissent in the Lone Star State, 1856-1874.* Lexington: University Press of Kentucky (1990).

Marx, Paul. "Marx, Edgar von Westphalen, and Texas." *Southern Studies*, Winter 1983:386.

Mehring, Franz. *Karl Marx: The Story of His Life.* Translated by Edward Fitzgerald. 1935. Reprint, Ann Arbor: University of Michigan Press, 1962.

Meusebach, John O. "Answers to Interrogatories," *Mary C Paschal et al., v. Theodore Evans,* District Court of McCulloch County Texas, Nov. Term 1893. Austin: Pemberton Press, 1964.

Monken, Bernard. "Hardships of a German Family." *Frontier Times*, November 1965:36.

Olmsted, Frederick Law. *Journey Through Texas, A Saddle-Trip on the Southwestern Frontier.* Edited by James Howard. Austin: Von Boeckmann-Jones Press, 1962.

Penniger, Robert. *Fredericksburg, Texas: The First Fifty Years.* Translated by C. L. Wisseman. Fredericksburg: Fredericksburg Publishing Co., 1971.

Perry, Garland. *Historic Images of Boerne and Kendall County, Texas.* Boerne: Perry Publications, 1988.

Ransleben, Guido E. *A Hundred Years of Comfort In Texas, a Centennial History.* San Antonio: Naylor Co., 1974.

Reinhardt, Louis. "The Communistic Colony of Bettina." *Southwestern Historical Quarterly*, 3:33 (1899).

Richardson, James D. ed. and comp. *A Compilation of the Messages and Papers of the Confederacy including the diplomatic correspondence*

1861-1865. 10 volumes. Nashville: United States Publishing Co., 1902.

Roemer, Ferdinand. *Roemer's Texas 1845 to 1847.* Translated by Oswald Mueller. Austin: Eakin Press, 1995.

Sandbo, Anna Irene. "Beginnings of the Secession Movement in Texas." *Southwestern Historical Quarterly* 18:41 (1914).

Sandbo, Anna Irene. "The First Session of the Secession Convention of Texas." *Southwestern Historical Quarterly* 18:162 (1915).

Sansom, John W. *The Battle of the Nueces River in Kinney County, Texas, August 10th, 1862.* San Antonio: n.p., 1905.

———. Papers. Center for American History, University of Texas at Austin.

Schenck, Friedrich. "A Letter from Friedrich Schenck in Texas to His Mother in Germany, 1847." Translated by H. T. Edward Hertzberg, *Southwestern Historical Quarterly* 92:145 (July 1988).

Scott, Robert N., ed. *War of the Rebellion: A Compilation of the Official Records of the Union and Confederate Armies.* 128 volumes. Washington, D. C.: Government Printing Office, 1880-1909.

Seele, Hermann. *The Cypress and Other Writings of a German Pioneer in Texas.* Translated by Edward C. Beritenkamp. Austin: University of Texas Press, 1979.

———. *The Diary of Hermann Seele and Seele's Sketches from Texas.* Translated by Theodore Gish. Austin: German-Texan Heritage Society, 1995.

Shook, Robert W. "The Battle of the Nueces, August 10, 1862." *Southwestern Historical Quarterly* 66:31 (1963).

Siemering, August. "Sisterdale." *Dresel Family Papers*, San Antonio Public Library, San Antonio.

———. "Texas, Her Past, Her Present, Her Future." *Texas Vorwaerts*, Sept. 21, 1894.

Smith, Clinton L. *The Boy Captives.* n.p., 1927. Reprint, San Saba: n.p., 2003.

Smith, Thomas C. *Here's Yer Mule, The Diary of Thomas C. Smith, 3rd Regiment, Company "G", Wood's Regiment, 32nd Texas Cavalry, C.S.A.* Waco: Little Texan Press (1958).

Solms-Braunfels Archives. Center for American History, University of Texas at Austin.

Solms-Braunfels, Carl. *Texas, 1844-1845*. Houston: Anson Jones Press, 1936.
———. *Voyage to North America, 1844-1845*. Translated by Wolfram M. Von-Maszewski. Denton: University of North Texas Press, 2000.
Sophienburg Museum and Archives. Records and vertical files. New Braunfels, Texas.
Sörgel, Alwin H. *A Sojourn in Texas*. Translated by W. M. von Maszewski. San Marcos: German-Texan Heritage Society, 1992.
Tetzlaff, Otto W., trans. and ed. *The Emigrant to Texas, A Handbook and Guide*. Burnet: Eakin Publications, 1979.
Texas State Library and Archives Commission. *Departmental Correspondence, Texas Adjutant General's Department*. Boxes 401-382, 401-383 and 401-384.
———. *Records, Texas Governor Francis Richard Lubbock*. Boxes 301-35, 301-38, 301-39 and 301-40.
———. *Records, Texas Governor Edward Clark*. Boxes 301-35, 301-36, 301-37 and 301-38 and Executive Journal, microfilm reel 3476.
———. *Texas State Troops Records, Civil War Records, Texas Adjutant General's Department*. Box 401-828.
Tiling, Moritz. *History of the German Element in Texas from 1820 – 1850*. Houston: n.p., 1913.
Toepperwein, Emilie and Fritz A. *Charcoal and Charcoal Burners*. Boerne: Highland Press, 1985.
Toepperwein, Lucian Ferdinand. "History of the Family of Ferdinand Lucian Toepperwein." *Toepperwein*. Translated by Flora Wertheim. Boerne: Highland Press, 1984.
Underwood, Rodman L. *Death on the Nueces, German Texans Treue der Union*. Austin: Eakin Press, 2000.
Von Hinueber, Caroline. "Life of German Pioneers in Early Texas," *Southwestern Historical Quarterly*, 2:227 (1899).
Von Schweinitz, Helga. "Bettina, Communism's Failed Experiment on the Llano," *Old West*, Winter 1992:52.
Wade, Maria F. *The Native Americans of the Texas Edwards Plateau, 1582-1799*. Austin: University of Texas Press, 2003.
Wheen, Francis. *Karl Marx: A Life*. New York: W. W. Norton & Co., 2000.
Williams, R. H. *With the Border Ruffians: Memories of the Far West. 1852-1868*. London: J. Murray, 1908.

Wooster, Ralph A., ed. *Lone Star Blue and Gray, Essays on Texas in the Civil War.* Austin: Texas State Historical Association, 1995.

Index

Adelsverein
   appoints Meusebach commissioner general, 35
   Boos-Waldeck resigns, 11
   buys out Fisher, 28
   collapses, 85
   colonists. *See* Colonists
   financial troubles, 15, 31, 35, 41, 43, 55
   meets with Fisher, 18
   militia. *See* Colonists, militia
   origins, 7
   predecessor society, 8, 10–11
   promises to colonists, 15
   purposes, 7
   re independent German colony, 8
   sends additional funds to Meusebach, 44
   sues Schubert, 165
Agua Dulce
   colonist camp, 28
Altgelt, Ernst Hermann
   epilogue, 166
   re abolition and secession, 134
   re Degener at military tribunal, 160
   represents Vles, 121
Architecture
   Bettina, 81
   Comfort, 122
   Fachwerk, 49
   Fredericksburg, 64
   New Braunfels, 49
Armand. *See* Schubert, Freidrich Armand
Arnim, Bettina von
   namesake of Bettina, 81
Balcones Escarpment
   as Hill Country boundary, 9
   at La Fontana, 29
Bandera, Texas, 104
Baptiste (shepherd), 118
Bartlett, John
   re Behr, 91
   re settlements on Llano, 84
Battle on the Nueces, 155–59
Bauer, Leopold
   at Nueces battle, 156
Baumann, Mathias, 110
Bechem, General Robert. *See* Frontier Regiment
   organizes brigade, 141
   re Unionists in his brigade, 151
Becker, Mary Ann Schertz, 116–17
Bee, General Hamilton P.
   assumes command, 146
   convenes military tribunal, 150
   declares martial law, 147
   dispatches Duff, 147
   re Unionist insurrection, 153
Behr, Louise von, 89, 97
Behr, Ottomar von, 7
   at Sisterdale, 88, 91, 97
   background, 88

Bartlett visits, 91
　epilogue, 167
　Olmsted re, 91
Bene, Ludwig
　at Flores ranch, 50
　leads colonists to Fredericksburg, 56
　leads militia, 28
　San Saba expedition, 62, 68
　wagon road to Fredericksburg, 54
Bergmann, Anton, 112
Bergmann, Joseph, 110
Beseler, Ernst
　at Nueces battle, 156
　executes Steward, 154
Bettina, Texas, 80–82
Bexar County
　secession election, 138
Beyer, Anton, 121
Blum, Andreas, 111
Boerne, Ludwig von, 113
Boerne, Texas
　founding and life, 107–17
　liberal trend, 131
　name, 113
　secession election, 138
Boos-Waldeck, Count Joseph of
　at Nassau Farm, 8
　dispute over colonization, 10–11
Bourgeois d'Orvanne, Alexander
　agreement with Adelsverein, 9
　appointed director of colonization, 11
　at San Antonio, 17
　background, 9
　delivers documents to Anson Jones, 14
　dismissed by Adelsverein, 20
　friction with Solms, 17
　meetings at Washington on the Brazos, 14
　seeks contract extension, 10, 14
　threatens lawsuit against Adelsverein, 35

Bourgeois-Ducos Grant
　Adelsverein purchases interest, 9
　renewal, 14
　spurned by Solms, 18
　terms, 9
Bowie, Jim, 69
Bracht, Felix
　re abolition and secession, 135
　re troop recruitment, 140
Bracht, Viktor
　re abolition and secession, 134
　re Fisher-Miller land, 82
　re the Forty, 77
Braubach, Phillip
　arrested, 148
　at military tribunal, 151
Braunfels, Germany, 32
Breitenbauch, Louis von, 121
Bremen, Germany
　colonists joining there, 40
　Fisher as Texas consul to, 19
　Fisher meets with Adelsverein, 19
　Fisher recruits colonists there, 20
　Hill as Adelsverein agent there, 25
　Klaener letter to mayor, 44
　Rexroth's cigars, 111
　voyages from, 11
Brunko, Friedrich, 121
Buenger, Walter L., 131, 132, 136
Buffalo Hump, Chief
　meets Meusebach, 70
　Meusebach asks for council, 68
　Roemer re, 70
Bund Freier Maenner, 128
Burke, Johann, 110
Burkhart (merchant near Hochheim), 47
Burnet, David, 5
Cabet, Etienne
　philosophy, 76
Camino Real, Spanish, 21, 29
Cappes, Philip
　at New Braunfels, 60
　special agent for Castell, 56

INDEX

Carlshaven, Texas, 25, *See* Indianola, Texas, *See* Indian Point
  accommodations, 44
  conditions, 44–46
  Meusebach arrives, 36
  Monken family, 46
  second group of colonists arrives, 43
Carstanjen, Rudolph
  at Tusculum?, 109
Castell, Count Carl of
  appoints Spiess commissioner general, 77
  Castell, Texas, named after, 83
  demands reports from Meusebach, 55
  re Adelsverein finances, 35
  re Cappes and Schubert, 76
  re colonization, 8
  re the Forty, 77
Castell, Texas
  founded, 83
  Kriewitz and Kettner, 83
Castro, Henry, 16
Charcoal City, Texas, 104
Chocolate Creek
  colonist camp, 28
Christmas
  in Carlshaven, 25
  in Sisterdale, 97
Churches
  Comfort, 122
  Fredericksburg, 60
  New Braunfels, 49
Civil War
  Battle on the Nueces, 155–59
  Conscript Act, 147
  Frontier Regiment. *See* Frontier Regiment
  fugitives, 145, 146
  German Unionism, 139
  Indians emboldened, 142
  Knights of the Golden Circle, 138, 140
  loyalty oaths, 139, 147
  martial law, 146, 147
  martial law rescinded, 161
  military tribunal, 150–53, 159–60
  pursuit of Unionists, 149–50
  Union Loyal League, 140
Claren, Oscar von
  re New Braunfels, 40
Clark, Governor Edward
  re loyalty oaths, 139
Clauss, Hugo, 112
  re Dietert, 111
  re Staffel, 111
Cloudt (second at duel), 25
Coll, Jean von
  accounting, 42
  dispute with Fisher, 28
  duel with Koester, 25
  expenditures, 42
  Flores ranch, 50
  member of colonial council, 25
  Solms re, 38
Colonial council
  composition, 25
  meetings, 25, 26, 28, 30
  spending authority, 42
Colonists
  "grays", 134
  accounts with Adelsverein, 15, 44
  at Carlshaven, 25
  at Fredericksburg, 58
  at Lavaca, 24
  at New Braunfels, 30
  Comanche peace treaty, 70–72
  commerce at New Braunfels, 49
  conditions, 44–46, 47, 49–50
  confront Meusebach, 61
  diet, 50, 62, 85
  disease, 64, 85
  give letters to Solms, 38
  Indian pressure above Llano, 84
  journey to New Braunfels, 26
  letters from New Braunfels, 38–41
  militia, 17, 25, 28

planning for arrival, 20, 21
post-Adelsverein, 88
promises by Adelsverein, 15
San Saba expedition departs, 62
second group arrives, 43
second group travels to New Braunfels, 45
transship for Lavaca, 23
Colonization contracts. See Bourgeois-Ducos Grant, See Fisher-Miller Grant
during Houston presidency, 5, 9, 18
early schemes, 4, 5
Solms scorns, 18
Texas declares unconstitutional, 73, 74
versus land grants, n., 9
Colorado River
as Hill Country boundary, 9
contract boundary, 18
Colquhoun, Ludovic, 17
background, 107
purchases Boerne townsite, 107
Comal River
at La Fontana, 29
Comal Springs, 21
Comanche Indians. See Mope-tshoko-pe, Chief, See Buffalo Hump, Chief, See Santa Anna, Chief, See Ketemoczy, Chief, See Yellow Wolf, Chief
and Robert Neighbors, 65
at Sisterdale, 90, 97
Lehmann kidnapping, 119
meet with Meusebach, 66–68
negotiate peace with Meusebach, 70–72
pressure on Llano settlements, 84
Rozas kidnapping, 62
San Saba expedition, 64
Smith kidnapping, 120
Solms re, 21
treaty with Meusebach, 76

Union withdrawal emboldens, 142
woman promised to Herff, 81
Comanche Spring
Meusebach inn, 99
Meusebachs at, 99
Olmsted at, 100
Comfort, Texas
founding and life, 120–24
liberal trend, 131
name, 120
secession election, 139
Treue der Union monument, 163
Conference of Vienna, 1, 3
Coreth, Count Ernst von, 99
Coreth, Countess Agnes von
and Wuerttemberg, 92
marries Meusebach, 99
Cos, General Martin Perfecto, 69
Curry's Creek, Texas, 104
Cypress Creek, Texas
settled, 102
Cypressville, Texas. See Cypress Creek, Texas
Darmstadter Farm
acquired, 79
failure, 101
Darmstadters. See Forty, the
Davis, Jefferson
re loyalty oaths, 139
Decros Point, 24
Degener, Edward
at military tribunal, 159
buys farm from Zink, 89
epilogue, 166
Olmsted visits, 90
Union Loyal League, 153
Degener, Hilmar and Hugo
at Nueces battle, 157
death at Nueces, 157
Olmsted re, 90
Union Loyal League, 153
Delaware Indians
encounter colonists, 57
Democratic Party, 128, 130, 132

INDEX

DeMontel, Charles. *See* Scheidemontel, Carl
Deutz, Joseph, 114
Diaz, Pablo
   at Nueces battle, 157
   at Turtle Creek meeting, 155
   death at Nueces, 157
Dienger, Karl, 112
Dietert, Christian, 122
Dietert, Henry, 112
Dietert, William, 111, 112
Doebbler, Friedrich Wilhelm
   arrested, 148
   at Grapetown, 102
   at military tribunal, 151
   epilogue, 165
Donop, Louis, 119
Douai, Adolph
   at Sisterdale, 99
   editor, *San Antonio Zeitung*, 129
   epilogue, 166
   re abolition and secession, 133
   sells *Zeitung* and flees, 133
Dresel, Emil, Rudolph and Gustav, 98
Dresel, Julius
   at Sisterdale, 97
   re Comanche Spring, 99
Ducos, Armand, 9, 11
Duels, 59
   after Schubert trip to Llano, 59
   Coll and Koester, 25
   custom, 59
   Schubert and Gunst, 59
Duff, Captain James M. *See* Texas Partisan Rangers
Duff, Captain James M.
   appointed provost marshal, 154
   at Blanco, 149
   at Boerne, 150
   at Fredericksburg, 147
   background, 147
   character, 148
   issues arrest warrants, 148
   pursuit of Unionists, 149–50, 155
   re Fredericksburg resistance, 148
Edwards Plateau, 9
Edwards, Private W. J., 159
Elections
   1860 Presidential, 137
   secession, 138
Engel, Sophie
   names Luckenbach, Texas,, 103
Ernst, Johann Friedrich and Louise Weber
   meet Solms, 16
   re Adelsverein, 8
   re re abolition and secession, 130
Ervendberg, Louis Cachand
   advocates political verein, 128
   background, 16
   celebrates Carlshaven Christmas, 25
   church in New Braunfels, 49
   in New Braunfels, 32
   meets Solms, 16
   Solms re, 38
Fabra, Julius, 110
Fachwerk, 49, 122
Faltin, August, 122
Farr, D. H.
   re Kuechler, 142
Fechler (shepherd), 118
Ferdinand, brig, 23
Fietsam family, 46
First Regiment. *See* Frontier Regiment
Fisher, Henry
   associates with Adelsverein, 20
   dispute over authority, 28
   epilogue, 164
   expenditures, 42
   fails to obtain wagons, 24
   involvement in colonist uprising, 60, 61
   meets Solms at Galveston, 20
   meets with Adelsverein, 18
   named Texas consul to Bremen, 19
   obtains colonization contract, 9

recommends Schubert, 55
recruits colonists, 20
withdraws from colonial council, 28
Fisher-Miller Grant
character of land, 20, 69, 82
deadline, 73
deadline expires, 73
extension, 19
faulty boundaries, 18
plans to enter grant, 43
preparations for colonizing, 20
scale, 18
Solms obtains extension, 73
terms, 19
Flach, Christian
at Tusculum, 108
Flach, Vera
re Kapp cabin, 97
Flake, Ferdinand
editor of *Die Union*, 133
re abolition and secession, 133
Flores, family of Juan Jose de Abrego
ranch, 50
Fontana, La
access from coast, 23
acquired by Solms, 29
background, 21, 29
description of site, 29
ownership, 29
Solms arrives, 29
Solms selects for town, 21
Forty, the
at Bettina, 80–82
at New Braunfels, 78
at Tusculum, 108
background, 76
Bracht, Felix, 135
Flach, 108
Friedrich, 101, 108
guided by Kriewitz, 79
Hesse, 108
Kuechler, 141
meet Castell, 77

Schleicher, 134
Schultz, 101, 108
skills, 77
Speiss, 165
travel to Carlshaven, 78
utopian ideas, 76
Vogt, 101, 108
Zoeller, 108
Forty-Eighters, 164
"greens", 134
at Sisterdale, 89
emigrate from Germany, 88
Fourier, Charles
philosophy, 76
Frankfurt, Germany, 3
1833 putsch, 16
Boerne origins, 113
Lindheimer origins, 16
Fredericksburg, Texas
1860 presidential election, 137
conditions, 62, 85
Duff at, 147
established, 57–58
first settlers travel to, 56–57
initial survey, 54–55, 58
liberal trend, 131
Meusebach locates site, 53
route from New Braunfels, 56
secession election, 138
Freethinkers
at Comfort, 122
background, 89
re abolitionism, 129
French Revolution, 1, 2
Fresinius, Friedrich
re Doebbler at military tribunal, 151
Friedrich, Wilhelm
member of the Forty, 101, 108
purchases Tusculum site, 108
Frontier Regiment
Bechem organizes, 141
enrollment, 142
formed, 140

INDEX

Kuechler applies, 141
Kuechler leads, 142
Schlickum, 150
Unionist infiltrators, 151
Unionists, 142
Westphalen, 142
Galveston Bay and Texas Land Company, 5
Galveston, Texas
    Solms and Fisher meet, 20
    Unionism, 133
Ganahl, Dr. Charles de, 139
Garza, Raphael C.
    ownership of La Fontana, 29
German attitudes
    after Civil War, 163–64
    free land movement, 129
    political leanings, 128, 132, 129–37
    re abolition and secession, 128, 130, 132, 129–37
    San Antonio convention, 129–37
    Unionism, 133, 139
German Confederation, 1, 3
German culture
    "grays" and "greens", 134
    beer, 102, 111
    cigars, 50, 111
    intermarriage, 112
    shooting clubs (*schuetzenverein*), 102
    singing clubs (*gesangverein*), 102, 127, 129, 131
    singing competitions (*sangerfest*), 127
    social and political clubs, 128
Germania Society, 5
Germany
    economic and social pressure, 1–4, 14
    Frankfurt Putsch, 3, 16
    liberal movement, 3
    nationalism, 3, 31
Gillespie County
    secession election, 138
Goethe, Wolfgang von
    re Arnim, 81
Goldbeck, Fritz, 121
Goldbeck, Theodor, 122
Gonzales, Texas
    King boarding house, 41
    Solms and Meusebach meet, 41
Grants. *See* Colonization Contracts
Grapetown, Texas, 102
Groos, Johann Jacob
    background, 55
Grothaus, Friedrich, 121
Gunst, Captain (the "society's scamp")
    San Saba expedition, 59
Habermann, Henry
    at Comanche Spring, 100
Hamilton, Andrew Jackson "Jack"
    Unionist gathering, 149
Hartman, Henry
    commands militia company, 153
Hays, John C. "Jack"
    assists Solms, 17, 20
    at Walker's Creek, 16
    re Fisher-Miller land, 30
    Yellow Wolf, 16
Hebert, General Paul O.
    declares martial law, 147
Hecke, J. V., 4
Helligman (Indian encounter), 119
Hemphill, John
    at Grapetown, 102
Henderson, Governor Pinckney
    warns colonists, 58, 65
Henderson, Howard, 156
Herf, Julie
    at Bettina, 81
    joins the Forty, 77
Herff, Ferdinand
    at Boerne, 110
    epilogue, 166
    member of the Forty, 76
    re Indian pressure above Llano, 84

185

re lower classes, 95
re Spiess and Schleicher, 101
relations with Indians, 80
renounces utopianism, 96
treats Comanche for cataracts, 80
Herndon, John Hunter
  at Bandera, 104
Herrschel, brig, 23
Hesse, Christian
  member of the Forty, 108
  purchases Boerne townsite, 108
Hester, William, 156
Hill, B., 25
Hoffman, August
  as a fugitive, 161
Holekamp, Frederick and Wilhelmine
  at Sisterdale, 89
Holy Roman Empire, 1
Horne, Peter
  re New Braunfels, 38, 39
Houston, Sam, 5
  campaign for governor, 132
Houston, Texas
  Solms at, 12
Independent German colony or state
  Adelsverein plans, 8
  Douai advocates, 133
  Solms's plans, 26
  Union Loyal League, 158
Indian Point, 23, 24, 25, *See*
  Carlshaven, Texas, *See* Indianola,
  Texas
Indianola, Texas, 25, *See* Indian
  Point, *See* Carlshaven, Texas
Indians. *See* specific tribes or groups
  encounters, 116, 117, 118, 119
Industrial Revolution, 2
Industry, Texas, 16
James, John
  acquires Boerne townsite, 108, 109
  at Bandera, 104
  background, 17
  epilogue, 167
  meets Solms, 16

San Saba expedition, 62
Sisterdale land, 98
Johann Dethard, brig, 23
Jones, Anson
  Bourgeois seeks contract extension,
    10
  documents received from
    Bourgeois, 14
  meets Solms, 12
  valedictory speech, 75
Joseph, Magdalena, 120
Kaiser, Christian
  re New Braunfels, 40
Kapp, Ernst
  at Sisterdale, 92
  background, 91
  Badenthal spa, 92
  epilogue, 167
  re Degener at military tribunal,
    159
  takes loyalty oath, 154
Kendall County
  organized, 124, 145
Kendall, George Wilkins
  background and life, 125
  epilogue, 167
  Indian raid, 118
Kennedy, William, 8
Kerr County
  organized, 124
  secession election, 138
  slavery, 138
Kerrville, Texas, 103
Ketemoczy, Chief, 66, 67
Kettner, Franz
  at Castell, 83
Kheusser, Louise von
  divorce, 88
  Zink spouse, 26
Kickapoo Indians
  camp at Llano, 59
  San Saba expedition, 70
King, Henry, 118
King, John G.

Solms at boarding house, 41
Klaener, D. H.
    Adelsverein agent in Galveston, 42
    advances funds for Adelsverein, 44
    letter to mayor of Bremen, 44
Kleberg, Rosa
    re Solms, 12
Knights of the Golden Circle, 138, 140
Know-Nothings, 128, 130, 132
Koester, Theodore
    duel with Coll, 25
    expenditures, 42
    member of colonial council, 25
    Solms re, 38
Kramer, Ernst
    commands militia company, 153
    re loyalty oaths, 149
Kriewitz, Emil
    among the Comanches, 79
    epilogue, 165
    guides colonists to Castell, 83
    guides the Forty to Bettina, 79
    San Saba expedition, 79
Kuechler, Jacob
    arrest warrant issued, 148
    as a fugitive, 161
    at Tusculum?, 109
    commands militia company, 153
    epilogue, 167
    leads Frontier Regiment, 141
    member of the Forty, 141
Land Grants. *See* Colonization Contracts
Land scrip, 53
Latin Settlements
    background, 90
Lavaca. *See* Port Lavaca
Lavaca Bay, 21, 23
Lawhon, Jesse, 117
Lehmann, Willie and Herman
    kidnapped, 119
Leiningen, Prince Victor of, 8
    dispute over colonization, 10–11

Leiningen, Texas
    founded, 84
Lilly, Lieutenant Edwin F., 159
Lindheimer, Ferdinand Jacob
    at Carlshaven, 25
    at Sisterdale, 97
    background, 16
    editor, *Neu-Braunfelser Zeitung*, 129
    epilogue, 165
    homestead, 32
    meets Solms, 16
    re abolition and secession, 130, 133
    with Solms to San Antonio, 29
Lipans. *See* Apache Indians
Llano River
    contract boundary, 18
    Schubert balks at, 59
Lochte (eats bear's head), 58
Lochte, Friedrich
    arrested, 148
    encounters Duff's troops, 148
Lohmann, Ferdinand
    re Comfort, 122
Luckenbach, Albert
    Luckenbach, Texas, named after, 103
Luckenbach, Jacob
    epilogue, 165
Luckenbach, Texas, 102
    founded, 102
Luntzel (second at duel), 26
Lux, Johann Hubert
    re New Braunfels, 39
Magruder, General John B.
    supresses Unionists, 161
Mangold, Elizabeth
    divorces Zink, 88
    marries Zink, 88
    Zink mistress, 26
Marxism
    at Sisterdale, 96
Massacre on the Nueces, 155–59

Matagorda Bay, 21, 23
Maverick, Mary
   Solms meets, 24
Maverick, Samuel
   re Kuechler, 141
   Solms meets, 24
   Woll's raid, 107
McCoy's Creek
   colonist camp, 28
McCulloch, Colonel Henry E.
   re fugitives, 146
   re Unionists, 145
McRae, Lieutenant Collin D.. *See*
   Texas Mounted Riflemen
   pursues fleeing Unionists, 155
Meerholz, Texas
   founded, 84
Menger, John N. Simon
   soap factory, 110
Menger, William
   brewery, 111
Merz, Conrad
   kills panther, 57
Metternich, Klemens von
   background, 1
   impact on Europe, 1–4
Meusebach, John O.
   assumes leadership of colony, 41
   at Comanche Spring, 99
   at Loyal Valley, 100
   at Sisterdale, 92, 98, 99
   attempts to raise funds for colony, 44
   background, 35
   changes name, 38
   colonists confront, 61
   Comanche treaty inked, 76
   concerns about Adelsverein finances, 35
   creditors, 42, 43, 55
   deadline pressure, 73
   elected state senator, 99
   epilogue, 164
   faces Adelsverein financial troubles, 41
   legislative relief for colonists, 100
   locates site of Fredericksburg, 53
   marries Coreth, 99
   meets Comanches at San Saba River, 66–68
   meets Solms at Gonzales, 41
   named commissioner general, 35
   negotiates Comanche peace, 70–72
   obtains wagons from Torreys, 44
   re Schubert, 60
   resigns as commissioner general, 77
   returns to Germany, 99
   San Saba expedition, 64–65
   Sisterdale homestead, 99
   travels to Texas, 36
   writes Solms, 35
Miller, Burchard, 18, 24
Missions, Spanish
   Nuestra Señora de Guadalupe, 21
   Santa Cruz de San Saba, 10, 68
Monken, Bernard and family, 45–48
   epilogue, 165
Moore, John Henry, 69
Mope-tshoko-pe, Chief
   meets Meusebach, 70
   Meusebach asks for council, 68
   Roemer re, 70
Napoleon, 1
Nassau Farm
   Adelsverein sends colonists to, 10
   Meusebach attempts mortgage, 44
   Meusebach meets Schubert, 55
   named, 8
   Schubert retreats there, melee ensues, 77
   Solms and Meusebach visit, 41
   Solms re, 16
   Solms returns to, 20
Nassau, Duke Adolph of
   Coll as lieutenant in army, 42
   namesake of Nassau Farm, 8
   protector of Adelsverein, 7

Nativism, 128, 130
Navarro, Jose Antonio
    ranch, 29
Navarro, Jose Luciano, 29
Neighbors, Robert
    bears warning from Governor, 65
    delivers warning to Meusebach, 67
    San Saba expedition, 65
New Braunfels, Texas. *See* Fontana, La
    1860 presidential election, 137
    colonists' letters from, 38–41
    conditions, 38–41, 49–50
    conservative trend, 131
    description of site, 29
    early commerce, 49
    founded, 30
    re abolition and secession, 133
    route from Fredericksburg, 56
    secession election, 138
    Solms departs, 41
    Solms's departure date, 36
    Spiess visits, 76
Nimitz, Charles
    re Doebbler at military tribunal, 151
Old Owl, Chief. *See* Mope-tshoko-pe, Chief
Olmsted, Frederick Law
    funds Douai, 133
    re Comanche Spring, 100
    re Meusebach in Sisterdale, 99
    re Sisterdale, 90
Padillia, Juan Antonio, 69
Partisan Rangers
    Duff's company, 147
    pursuit of Unionists, 149–50
Pass Cavallo, 24
    ships grounded, 45
Patton, J. M.
    re Sansom, 141
Peneteka. *See* Comanche Indians
Pierce, Leonard Jr.
    Civil War fugitives, 146

Pink (dead dog), 119
Plewe (on San Saba expedition), 69
Port Lavaca, 40
Presidios, Spanish
    San Luis de las Amarillas, 10, 68, 69
Racknitz, Baron Johann von, 5
Rangers, Texas. *See* Texas Rangers
Ransleben, Guido, 120
Reinhardt (wood cutter), 118
Reinhardt, Louis
    re Kreiwitz, 79
Rhodius, Christian
    re Degener at military tribunal, 160
Ridley, J. Clark, 124
Riedel, Nicholas and Anton
    re New Braunfels, 39
Roemer, Ferdinand, 49
    at Fredericksburg, 62
    at New Braunfels, 48
    Flores ranch, 50
    re colonists, 50
    re Fisher-Miller grant land character, 69
    re frontier surveyors, 54
    re San Saba silver, 69
    San Saba expedition, 65
Roggenbuch (at Sisterdale), 92
Rossy, Alexander
    determines Vles ownership, 121
    re abolition and secession, 130
Round Top
    Nassau Farm, 8
    Soergel settles there, 15
Rozas, Lorenzo de, 67
    San Saba expedition, 62
Runnels, Hardin
    campaign for governor, 132
Russer, Alois
    re New Braunfels, 41
Salm-Salm, Princess Sophie of, 31, 36
Saltmarsh, D. A.
    at military tribunal, 150

San Antonio Zeitung, 129, 134
San Saba Colonization Company, 19
Saner, Patterson D., 110
Sansom, John
    at Nueces battle, 156
    at Turtle Creek meeting, 155
    epilogue, 167
    Frontier Regiment, 141
    Kendall County Sheriff, 124, 145
    re Nueces battle, 157
    re Union Loyal League, 140
    Texas Ranger, 120
Santa Anna, Chief
    meets Meusebach, 70
    Meuseback asks for council, 68
    Roemer re, 70
    visits Fredericksburg, 76
Schaefer, Heinrich
    re New Braunfels, 40
Scheidemontel, Carl
    at Bandera, 104
    with Castro, 104
Schenck, Friedrich
    member of the Forty, 78
    re Bettina, 80
    re Darmstadter Farm, 79
    re road to New Braunfels, 78
Schladoer, Heinrich, 120
Schleicher, Gustav
    epilogue, 166
    member of the Forty, 76
    re abolition and secession, 134
    re Bettina, 82
    re Degener at military tribunal, 160
Schlickum, Julius
    arrested, 150
    at military tribunal, 151
Schlosser (shepherd), 118
Schmidt, John
    kills bear, 57
Schubert, Freidrich Armand
    appointed to establish Fredericksburg, 55
    designs Fredericksburg church, 60
    discharged by Meusebach, 77
    epilogue, 165
    expedition to Llano River, 59
    manages Fredericksburg, 58
    Meusebach re, 60
    pseudonym, 55
Schultz, Leopold
    at Tusculum, 108
    member of the Forty, 101
Scott, Tom, 156
Scott, W. B., 156
Seele, Herman
    re Comfort, 123
    teaching, 32
Seguin, Texas
    Navarro ranch, 29
    Solms rendezvous there, 29
Shaw, Jim
    interpreter, 65
    San Saba Expedition, 71
Shawnee Indians, 59, 64
    guides, 59
    San Saba expedition, 70
    trading with colonists, 62
Shoenburg, Texas
    founded, 84
Siemering, August
    epilogue, 166
    political views, 129
    re Duff's Partisan Rangers, 149
Siluria, Texas, 45
Silver mine, Spanish, 68
Sisterdale, Texas
    Badenthal spa, 92
    Forty-Eighters drift away, 98
    founding and life, 88–100
    Freie Verein, 128, 129, 135
    intellectuals, 89
    liberal trend, 128, 131
    named, 98
    secession election, 138
    shepherd's funeral, 97
    Tiling re, 90

INDEX

Wuerttemberg visits, 92
Sloat, Benjamin
   Indian agent, 65
Smith, Clint and Jeff
   kidnapped, 120
Smith, John William
   death, 29
   re La Fontana, 21
Smith, Thomas
   re Unionists, 149
Soergel, Alwin H.
   re Adelsverein expenses, 15
   re travels, 56
Solms-Braunfels, Prince Carl of
   ancestral castle, 32
   appointed commissioner general, 11
   arranges Carlshaven Christmas, 25
   at Agua Dulce, 28
   at Matagorda and Lavaca Bays, 21
   at Nassau Farm, 16
   at Navarro ranch, 29
   background, 12
   colonial militia, 28
   creditors in Galveston, 41
   creditors in New Orleans, 41
   departs New Braunfels, 38, 41
   departs Texas, 41
   dispute over authority, 28
   financial records, 42
   friction with Bourgeois, 17
   German nationalism, 31
   inspects Bourgeois-Ducos grant, 17
   learns of Bourgeois's dismissal, 20
   learns of La Fontana, 21
   letters from Castell, 35
   letters from colonists, 38
   manner, 12, 14, 50
   meetings at Washington on the Brazos, 12
   meets Fisher at Galveston, 20
   meets Hays, 16
   meets Meusebach at Gonzales, 41
   meets Veramendi, 29
   member of colonial council, 25
   names Carlshaven, 25
   names New Braunfels, 30
   notified of Meusebach's apppointment, 35
   obtains contract extension, 73
   plans to avoid Texan towns, 26, 41, 46
   purchases La Fontana, 29
   re Americans, 26, 36
   re Coll and Koester, 38
   re Comanches, 20
   re Ervendberg, 38
   re Fisher, 24, 25, 42
   re Hill, 25
   re independent German colony, 8, 26, 158
   re Indians, 31
   re La Fontana, 29
   re Mavericks, 24
   re Somervell, 24
   re Zink, 28, 38
   rendezvous at Seguin, 29
   sails to Galveston to meet colonists, 23
   scorns colonization contracts, 18
   selects Indian Point landing site, 23
   Sophienburg, 31
   spurns Bourgeois-Ducos grant, 18
   travels to San Antonio, 16
   travels to Texas, 11–13
   writings inspire the Forty, 76
Somervell, Alexander
   Solms meets, 24
Sophienburg, 31
Spiess, Herman
   advance party for Forty, 77
   at New Braunfels, 76
   epilogue, 165
   member of the Forty, 76
Splittgerber, Julius
   re Fredericksburg conditions, 85

San Saba expedition, 59
Staffel, August, 111
Staffel, Heino and Adeline, 116
Steele, William H.
   and Colquhoun, 107
Stendebach, John
   Indian encounter, 119
Steward (Union Loyal League
   infiltrator), 154
Stieler, Herman, 119
Stockmann (at Sisterdale), 92
Strubberg, Freidrich Armand. *See*
   Schubert, Friedrich Armand
Surveyors and surveys
   as element of story, 54
   Crosky, 108
   Fisher-Miller Grant, 18, 19
   Fredericksburg, 54–55, 58
   frontier surveyors, 54
   Groos, 55
   Grothaus, 121
   Hays, 16
   James, 17, 98, 104, 108
   Kuechler, 141
   Russer, 41
   San Saba expedition, 62
   Staffel, 111
   Zink, 30, 48
Taverns
   Doebbler's inn, 102
   New Braunfels, 49
   Staffel's, 111, 112
Tegener, Fritz
   at Nueces battle, 156
   decides to flee to Mexico, 155
   leads Union Loyal League militia,
      153
Texas Mounted Riflemen, 140
   Battle on the Nueces, 159
   under Duff, 154
Texas Rangers
   Frontier Regiment. *See* Frontier
      Regiment
   Hays, 16
   Kendall, 125
   McCulloch, 145
   Partisan Rangers. *See* Partisan
      Rangers
   Sansom, 120, 141, 167
Texas State Troops. *See* Frontier
   Regiment
Theis, August, 118
Theissen, Gustav
   acquires Boerne townsite, 109
   background, 114
Tiling, Moritz
   re Kriewitz, 79
   re Sisterdale intellectuals, 90
   re Solms, 12
Toepperwein, Herman, 112
Toepperwein, Lucian, 112
Tonkawa Indians
   deer hunting camp, 51
Torrey, John and David
   army appropriates wagons, 45
   provide oxen to Monken group, 47
   provide wagons at Carlshaven, 44
Trails, cattle, 103
Trefflich, August, 110
Tremont House, 12, 20
Tusculum
   founding and life, 108–9
Twiggs, General David, 138
Union Loyal League
   as insurrection, 158
   Battle on the Nueces, 155–59
   Bear Creek meeting, 153
   chapter formed, 140
   decision to disband militia, 154
   flee for Mexico, 149–50
   independent German state, 158
   infiltrators, 154
   militia formed, 153
   San Antonio meeting, 145
   Tegener leads militia, 153
   Treue der Union monument, 163
   Turtle Creek meeting, 155
Utopians. *See* Forty, the

Cabet in Nauvoo, 77
Cabet in Texas, 76
Darmstadter Farm, 82
Herff renounces, 96
the Forty, 76
Vehlein, Joseph, 5
Veramendi, Juan Martin de (the younger)
  meets Solms, 29
Vereinsburg, 31
Victoria, Queen of England, 8, 36
Vles, John F., 121
Vogt, Adam
  at Tusculum, 108
  election commissioner, 145
  Kendall County Judge, 124
  member of the Forty, 101
Vogt, William, 111, 112
Waelder, Jacob
  re abolition and secession, 133
Wahrmund, William
  re Indian encounters, 142
Washington on the Brazos
  Solms visits, 12
Weber family, 46
Wedemeyer (second at duel), 26
Wendler, Fritz, 117
Wesser, brig, 20
Westphalen, Edgar von
  and Marxism, 96
  at Sisterdale, 96
  epilogue, 167
  in Frontier Regiment, 142
White, Samuel Addison
  as surveyor, 54
  sale of Indian Point, 24
Wiedenfeld, Franziska and Theodore, 120
Wilke (Herman?)
  San Saba expedition, 69

Wilke, Herman
  surveys Fredericksburg, 58
Williams, R. H.
  re Nueces battle, 159
Wrede, von (on San Saba expedition), 69
Wuerttemberg, Prince Paul of
  at Sisterdale, 92
Yellow Wolf, Chief
  battle at Walker"s Creek, 16
Zavala, Lorenzo de, 5
Zeuner (on San Saba expedition), 69
Zink, Nicholas
  at Cypress Creek, 102
  at Sisterdale, 88
  at Spanish Pass, 164
  background, 26
  builds *Zinkenburg*, 30
  construction at Fredericksburg, 30
  described, 26
  divorces Kheusser, 88
  epilogue, 164
  expenditures, 42
  leaves Sisterdale, 89
  member of colonial council, 25
  mistress, 88
  musters wagons for colonists, 26
  rendezvous at Seguin, 29
  Russer re, 41
  second at duel, 26
  sells land to Holekamp, 89
  Solms re, 28, 31, 38
  surveys New Braunfels, 48
  third marriage, 164
Zinkenburg, 30
Zoeller, Phillip
  at Tusculum, 108
  member of the Forty, 108